THE SPY WHO NEVER WAS
The Life and Loves of Mata Hari

The Spy Who Never Was

The Life and Loves of Mata Hari

JULIA KEAY

LARGE PRINT
MAINSTREAM SERIES
Oxford, England
Santa Barbara, California

Copyright © 1987 Julia Keay

First published in Great Britain 1987
by Michael Joseph Ltd, 27 Wrights Lane, London W8

First published in the U.S.A. 1987 by
Michael Joseph Ltd

Published in Large Print 1989 by
Clio Press, 55 St. Thomas Street, Oxford OX1 1JG,
by arrangement with Michael Joseph Ltd and
Harold Ober Associates

British Library Cataloguing in Publication Data
Keay, Julia
The spy who never was: the life and loves of Mata Hari
1. Wold War I. Espionage. Mata Hari, 1876–1917
I. Title
940.4'87'430924
ISBN 1-85089-291-1

Printed and bound by
Hartnolls Ltd, Bodmin, Cornwall
Cover designed by CGS Studios, Cheltenham

Contents

FOR JOHN

Acknowledgements

I am very grateful to the librarians, archivists and staff of the London Library, the Public Records Office, the British Museum Newspaper Archives, the Service Historique de l'Armée de Terre and the Musée Guimet for their efficient and invaluable assistance.

My thanks also to K. K. Singh for guiding me through the intricacies of Hindu mythology, to Charlie Gore for a wealth of information on the history of the MacLeods, and to Jennie Davies, Jenny Dereham and Vivien James for their support, encouragement and advice.

Above all, though, I want to thank John for allowing me to draw so deeply on his wisdom and his patience. To have so much of both at my disposal is more than any writer (or wife) deserves.

The author and publishers are grateful to the following for permission to reproduce copyright material.

Century Hutchinson Ltd, London Dial Press, New York	*The Real Isadora* Victor Seroff
Century Hutchinson Ltd, London	*Lonely But Not Alone* Queen Wilhelmina (Trans: J. Peere-boom)
Century Hutchinson Ltd, London Curtis Brown Associates Ltd, New York (literary agents)	*World War I* Hanson Baldwin

Constable & Co Ltd, London	*The Diaghilev Ballet* Serge Grigoriev (Trans: Vera Brown)
Grafton Books, London	*Secret Intelligence in the Twentieth Century* Constantine Fitzgibbon
Oxford University Press (East Asia) Harper & Row, New York	*Tropic Fever* L. Szekely (Trans: Marion Saunders)
Victor Gollancz Ltd, London Virago Press, London	*Testament of Youth* Vera Brittain

The extract from *Testament of Youth* by Vera Brittain published by Victor Gollancz Ltd is included with the permission of her literary executors and Victor Gollancz Ltd.

| Weidenfeld & Nicholson Ltd, London | *The Codebreakers* D. Khan |
| William Kimber & Co Ltd, London Hawthorn Books, New York | *Secret Service* Richard Rowan and Robert Deidorfer |

FLOWERS AND THORNS

WOMAN SPY SHOT

Mata Hari, the dancer, was shot this morning. She was arrested in Paris in February, and sentenced to death by Court Martial last July for espionage and giving information to the enemy. When war was declared she was moving in political, military and police circles in Berlin, and had her number on the rolls of the German espionage service. She was in the habit of meeting notorious German spy masters outside French territory, and she was proved to have communicated important information to them for which she had received several large sums of money since May 1916.

The Times. Tuesday, 16th October 1917

'LOVELY SPY' SHOT

Mata Hari Executed by the French at Vincennes

'Mata Hari', otherwise MIle. Marguerite Gertrude Zelle, the beautiful dancer spy, was shot at Vincennes at six o'clock this morning. She was driven from St. Lazare prison in a motor-car, accompanied by a doctor, a Protestant clergyman and two detectives. She fell dead at the first volley, and was buried in the prison precincts.

Daily Express. Tuesday, 16th October 1917

WOMAN DANCER SHOT BY FRENCH AS SPY

Mlle. Mata Hari Suffers Penalty for Betraying Secrets to Germans

Mata Hari, the dancer and adventuress who, two months ago was found guilty by a court-martial on the charge of espionage, was shot at dawn this morning. The condemned woman was taken in an automobile from St. Larare prison to the parade ground at Vincennes where the execution took place.

New York Times. Tuesday, 16th October 1917

EXECUTION DE L'ESPIONNE MATA HARI

La nommée Zelle, (Marguerite-Gertrude), dite Mata Hari, a été condamnée le 24 juillet 1917 par le Troisième Conseil de Guerre de Paris, à la peine de mort pour espionnage et intelligences avec l'enemie. La sentence capitale, qui fut prononcée a l'unanimité, a été exécuée ce matin. Mata Hari, qui a fait preuve jusqu'au bout de courage, a refusé de se laisser bander les yeux. Après l'exécution, le corps a été transporté au nouveau cimeliére de Vincennes, où a eu lieu l'inhumation.

Le Figaro. Mardi, 16 octobre 1917

The morning of Monday, 15th October had dawned cold and misty. In a clearing among the ancient oaks of the Bois de Vincennes, on the eastern outskirts of Paris, a group of twelve soldiers from a French artillery regiment stood at ease. None of the soldiers could have been much more than twenty years old, but the devastation of three and a half years of war had leached any hint of light or youth from their eyes.

Behind them slumbered the vast medieval Château de Vincennes, its dreams of past glory as the court of Louis XIV undisturbed by the tiny drama being played out beneath its walls. The magnificent forest that had once stretched from the château as far as the valley of the Marne, and had echoed to the sound of royal hunting horns as the Roi Soleil sported with his courtiers, had shrunk by now to a few thousand acres; and today's echoes were of a grimmer sound, for the Bois had been taken over by the army and now served as a parade ground, rifle range and practice field for military manoeuvres.

Suddenly an officer barked an order; the men snapped to attention and three cars drove slowly across the park, stopping in front of them. An old man stepped out of the middle car and held the door open for its other occupants: a plump, middle-aged woman, her black hair streaked with grey and drawn into a straggly bun; and her companion, an elderly nun. They were holding hands. The officer escorted the two women to a solitary, leafless tree where they stood for a moment, silhouetted black against the first grey light of the day. The women exchanged a few words; then the officer and the nun turned and walked back to the cars, leaving the other woman on her own by the tree.

Peering across the expanse of dew-drenched grass that

separated her from the soldiers, she tried to follow the formal steps of the macabre military ritual that would, in a few moments, extinguish her life. Shivering in the cold air she pulled her cloak closer round her shoulders and tucked a stray wisp of hair back under its pin. Her expression was puzzled, as if she really could not understand how she came to be there — facing a firing squad.

Maybe she was dreaming. Surely she had been given the wrong script for this final scene. Any moment now the curtain would fall; the spotlights would illuminate her graceful curtsy; and spontaneous applause would burst from an ecstatic audience. The group of men under the trees seemed to be moving in slow motion — a flicker of a smile crossed her face as she watched them. Soldiers: all her life she had loved soldiers. There was something irresistible about a man in uniform, and her audiences had always had a liberal sprinkling of gold braid and shiny buttons: she must not fail them now. Drawing herself up, she waited for the applause.

Since childhood Margarethe Zelle had been the supreme practitioner of the theory that if you ignored something for long enough it would go away. Reality was to be faced only if it promised pleasure or reward, truth adhered to only if it brought no pain. The war that had turned the faces of the young soldiers to stone and had left countless more dead in the mud had left few scars on her. If she had not quite managed to make it go away, she had certainly ignored it as resolutely as she knew how. Had it ever been suggested to her that she would be as much a victim of that war as the millions of others who were dying in its tortured path, she would have smiled pityingly at the very idea. That it might cost her her life would simply never have occurred to her.

The nun who attended the condemned woman would

interpret her little smile, her murmured words of comfort and the gift of her grey kid gloves to the officer commanding the firing squad, as signs of humility and the acceptance of the will of God. That, after all, is how she would have chosen to meet her own death.

But Margarethe Zelle had no faith in any God. The only remaining members of her family were far away and had offered no protest at her fate. No grieving circle of friends stood by to sustain her. It was not humility that enabled her to smile, to hold her head high and to present her executioner with the only possessions left to her in the world; it was pride — pride in a past strewn with the countless glittering sequins of stardom and the sweet memories of many, many loves.

If she could have glimpsed the aura of mystery and romance that would surround her story for years to come her smile would surely have been one of satisfaction. And if she heard the crack of the rifles it would surely have sounded like the first burst of that applause. For had she not been Mata Hari?

As the members of the firing squad shouldered their arms, Marechal du Logis Petay of the 23rd Regiment of Dragoons stepped forward to deliver the obligatory *coup de grâce*. He looked down at the crumpled figure slumped against the foot of the tree. It was hard to believe that, not so long ago, princes and generals, artists and poets had vied with each other for the favours of this woman, had composed odes in her honour and parted with large sums of money in return for a few hours of her company. The shapeless bundle at his feet bore no resemblance to the beautiful dancer who had been the toast of Paris. Could this really be the infamous Mata Hari?

*   *   *   *   *

Twenty years earlier, in 1897, another officer in another army had gazed at that same face and wondered. But the questions in his mind were about the future, not the past, and he marvelled not at her nondescript shapelessness but at her vivid beauty. Leaning on the deckrail of the *SS Prinses Amelia* bound for the East Indies, Captain Rudolph MacLeod of the Dutch Colonial Army was looking at his wife.

Even after eighteen months of marriage he still found it hard to believe that this lovely young girl really was his wife. Three years ago he had returned to Holland from the East Indies on sick leave. At the age of thirty-nine he had thought himself well into middle-age, worn out by seventeen long, hard years in the Colonial Service and heading for an invalid retirement. Yet here he was, on his way back to Java, not only restored to health but married to a girl young enough to be his daughter, and with a baby son of his own. He watched her as she settled the baby in a cradle under an awning. Now that they had reached the Mediterranean, the afternoon sun was getting stronger by the day, and Rudolph noticed how well its brightness suited her. In contrast to most of the other women aboard, who wilted in the unaccustomed heat, and shaded their pale Dutch skin from its burning rays, Margarethe seemed to blossom in its radiance.

He noticed, too, how the eyes of his fellow officers were drawn to her; how even the youngest and most bashful lieutenant seemed to grow in stature in her presence and not even the crustiest of generals was immune to her smile. It was an agreeable novelty to have something in your possession that was coveted by every man who set eyes on it, and he was well aware that his own rather dour reputation had been considerably enhanced, not only by his acquisition of so charming a bride, but by the unconventional manner of that acquisition.

Two of his fellow-officers, in an effort to tease their old friend out of his confirmed bachelorhood and cheer his lonely convalescence, had placed a notice in a newspaper in The Hague advertising for a suitable wife. It had seemed a harmless joke and, as such, he had gone along with it. The replies would inevitably come from disappointed spinsters with anxious expressions and could easily be ignored. He was therefore rather disconcerted when out of one of the envelopes fell a photograph of the writer. Here was no ageing spinster, no lonely old maid; on the contrary, the face that looked back at him was of a young and very beautiful girl with a cloud of dark curls, mischievous black eyes and a tantalising smile. The photograph was signed Margarethe Gertruida Zelle.

By responding to the advertisement Margarethe was committing the latest in a long line of shocking breaches of propriety. The heavy hand of parental rage should have dragged her off to the attic, there to be incarcerated with only a Bible for company until she had repented of her wickedness. But her father was in Amsterdam struggling to resurrect his business from bankruptcy and, since the death of her mother three years before, Margarethe had been living in The Hague in the somewhat perfunctory care of her uncle. An elderly bachelor was hardly the ideal guardian for a high-spirited fifteen-year-old. When above all else she needed wise guidance and a restraining hand, she received good-natured pats on the head and vague exhortations to 'be a good girl — now run along'. Left to her own devices,

Margarethe had put her own interpretation on those impre-
cise instructions and waltzed blithely into a series of
disreputable scrapes. The most serious of these had involved
the headmaster of the college where she had started to train
as a kindergarten teacher. The question of which one of them
was the predator and which the prey was never satisfacto-
rily answered, but word of their liaison got out and
Margarethe's nascent career had been brought to an abrupt
halt. Now, by answering this anonymous advertisement, it
looked as if she was launching into another equally scandal-
ous escapade.

But, to the amazement of Rudolph MacLeod's fellow
officers, the first meeting between the forty-year-old veteran
and his eighteen-year-old correspondent was followed,
within a week, by the news of their engagement. The attraction had been immediate and mutual. Rudolph, with his
twirling moustaches, gold-braided uniform and tales of oriental derring-do, was the very image of the dashing hero
Margarethe had always known would one day come and
sweep her off her feet. He, for his part, was so dazzled by her
youth and vivacity, and so delighted with his new role as a
hero figure, that he was happy to let her wind him round her
little finger. If he had any misgivings about their
unconventional courtship, or any doubts about the desirability of a man of his rank and ancestry marrying the daughter
of a bankrupt shopkeeper, they vanished in the glow of self-
esteem occasioned by the ribald envy of his contemporaries. They would marry as soon as they had her father's approval.

Adam Zelle (who would never have described himself as
a shopkeeper: he preferred 'Hatter', 'Milliner' or 'Purveyor
of Head-gear to Gentlemen') was delighted to approve the

match. Many years ago, when his elegant premises had graced the most fashionable street of Leeuwarden in the northern province of Friesland, he had been able to indulge his children — particularly Margarethe, the eldest and his only daughter — with every kind of luxury. He would then have subjected any prospective suitor to the most rigorous of cross-examinations. Now, recently remarried himself, with three sons to educate and his business falling apart, a cursory glance was enough. Enormously relieved that Margarethe had found herself such a distinguished husband, he gave them his blessing. On 11th July 1895, four months after their first meeting, they were married.

Marriage gave Margarethe just the independence she was looking for. After a honeymoon spent in Wiesbaden the newlyweds had returned to The Hague and Margarethe started spending Rudolph's money. It was essential that she should provide herself with a wardrobe not only befitting her new status as the Captain's wife, but also varied enough to do justice to the social whirl into which she fully intended to fling herself. Initially inclined to indulge her extravagance as a passing phase, Rudolph soon became seriously concerned about his finances. Fortunately the pressure on his pocket had been lifted by Margarethe's pregnancy which had curbed, for a while at least, her enthusiasm for parties.

Rudolph had been relieved when his posting back to Java had been confirmed. Not only was it much cheaper to live in the colony than in Holland, but there were fewer parties to attend and fewer dressmakers to patronise. But now, as the *SS Prinses Amelia* carried them ever closer to Java, it began to dawn on him that Margarethe might not be the only one forced to curb her self-indulgence. As a married man with a family, he would no longer be able to enjoy those little extra comforts that made Colonial Service in the East Indies bearable. He thought with a twinge of regret of long evenings spent drinking in the easy camaraderie of the Officers' Club, of his well-appointed bachelor quarters, and of the succession of demure brown-skinned beauties he had installed there to liven his lonely nights. He remembered, with increasing alarm, how he had pitied his fellow officers who were tied to their homes by bored, nagging wives and how they had envied him his freedom. Had he made a terrible mistake?

Looking again at Margarethe he told himself that for them it would be different. With such a wife who needed a mistress? She was as beautiful as any of his *nyays*, and certainly as passionate. Even before their marriage she had revealed a vibrant sexuality that had startled and delighted him. True, she was inclined to be headstrong, sometimes even wilful, but she had not given him any real cause to regret their marriage. On the contrary, she had fulfilled one of his dearest wishes by giving him a son.

Despite his name, Rudolph MacLeod was a Dutchman. He was the sixth generation of MacLeods to have served in the Dutch Army since Norman MacLeod of the Isle of Skye had joined the Dutch Scots Brigade at the end of the seventeenth century. During his service in the Netherlands Norman MacLeod had married a Dutch girl. Their son had risen to the rank of Colonel in the same regiment, but by then the Brigade had lost its Scottish nationality and was absorbed into the regular Dutch army. Successive generations of MacLeods had served with distinction in the Dutch armed forces and many had risen to high rank.

The present head of this branch of the family, Rudolph's

uncle Norman, currently held the rank of Vice-admiral in the Dutch navy and had been awarded a string of decorations in recognition of his services: Knight of the Order of the Oaken Crown; Knight of the Order of the Netherlands' Lion; Knight of the Second Class, with Star, of the Crown of Prussia; and Commander of the Order of Orange-Nassau to name but a few. Although the MacLeods now considered themselves as Dutch as any de Vries or van den Bosch, they remained fiercely proud of their Scottish ancestry. By naming his son Norman, Rudolph was saluting his forebears and aiming to continue the line. Looking at the curly-haired baby sleeping in the shade, he felt his doubts subside.

It was not unusual for a Dutch army officer to be taking his wife out to the Far East. The administration of the Dutch colonies in the East Indies had involved a great many people over a long period of time. Since the setting up of the United [Dutch] East India Company in 1602, through its disbandment and takeover by the Government in 1799, right up to the final independence of Indonesia in the 1940s, Dutchmen had headed east. Soldiers and civil servants, merchants and missionaries, politicians, planters and penniless adventurers had left home to make their fortunes in trade and speculation; to administer, police, protect and exploit this distant and disparate colony. Many of them took their wives and families along too.

But if they were following a well-trodden path, they were also stepping into the land of their childhood fairytales. One old Java hand, Augusta de Wit, recalled her early fascination for the fabled island. 'Time was when I never saw a globe — all spun about with the net of parallels and degrees, as with some vast spider's web — without a little shock of

11

surprise at finding Java hanging in the meshes. How could there be latitude and longitude to such a thing of dreams and fancies? An attempt at determining the acreage of a rainbow would hardly have seemed less absurd.'

The transition was in many ways easier for the men. They had careers to think of, professions to pursue, orders to obey and fortunes to make. But for the women it must have been a nerve-wracking experience. They were leaving behind comfortable, conventional domesticity, where there was a right way and a wrong way for everything and no shortage of relations to make sure you kept to the rules. Every detail of their lives in Holland had been in sharp focus, well-defined and familiar, whereas when they tried to envisage their future in Java, it became blurred and distorted, shimmering as if viewed through rippling water or the waves of rising heat. Everything would be different: the climate, landscape, people, religions, food, customs, etiquette and morals. Where there had been pale skies and brisk chill winds, now there would be the blazing tropical sun and drenching monsoon rains. Where there had been tall, red-faced men with bristling, blond moustaches and well-upholstered women with disapproving frowns, now there would be lithe, brown bodies, loosely draped in bright, fluttering colours. Where there had been quiet, formal Sundays with churchbells, and solid meals in heavily furnished dining-rooms, now there would be singing and laughter and the sound of bare feet pattering on cool stone floors. The contrasts between the austere, formal Holland that had been their home and the romance and beauty of Java that was now their destination must have filled them with apprehension.

Those passengers on the *SS Prinses Amelia* who were heading out on a second tour of duty would sprinkle their conversation with unfamiliar words — *Tuan, coolie, Hari Besar* — first making sure that the uninitiated were well within earshot. These listeners would be suitably impressed and, according to their nature, filled either with foreboding or with shivers of delighted excitement. Margarethe MacLeod shivered with the best of them.

Of all her youthful adventures this was surely the most exciting. At twenty years old, the doors leading from childhood into the grown-up world had not yet been closed behind her by the responsibilities of marriage and motherhood. Indeed, it probably had not occurred to Margarethe that there were any responsibilities involved in marriage. From being the cherished only daughter of an indulgent father she had, quite naturally, become the adored and cossetted wife of a successful soldier. She accepted her new status as she would have accepted a new toy or pretty dress and, like any gift, once received it was hers to do with as she pleased. The crest of every wave took her a little further from dull Holland and a little nearer to magical Java — the fabled land of the bedtime stories, 'the Island of Avalon; the Land of the Lotus Eaters; palm-shaded Bohemia by the sea; Merlin's melodious grave'. The rapture of her early days with Rudolph had by now subsided a little — there was certainly something reminiscent of the schoolmaster in his attitude towards her and she was learning to steer clear of his worst bouts of temper.

Other warning signs were there, too. In spite of his looks, his ancestry and his reputation, Rudolph, as Margarethe would soon discover, was a bore. Worse than that, he was arrogant and he was a bully. But it probably was not entirely his fault. The life of a Dutch colonial officer was guaranteed to develop to the full the slightest hint of these qualities in any man.

Java's plantation economy had been initiated by the United East India Company in the early 1700s. The Company demanded, and received, huge areas of land in return for assistance rendered in the numerous feuds between rival Indonesian states. As the spice trade diminished in value, this gave them the opportunity of introducing new and more profitable crops. In Java the first and most successful of these was coffee, soon to be followed by sugar, tea, indigo, tobacco and rubber. The United East India Company ceased trading in 1799 and was taken over by the Dutch Government. The East Indies became a fully fledged colony, and enormous profits continued to flow back into Holland. But the changes of the eighteenth and nineteenth centuries, both in administration and in agriculture, were of doubtful benefit to the people of the islands.

In 1830 Johannes van den Bosch was appointed Governor-General of the Indies with special responsibility for reorganising labour and agricultural production. Under his so-called Culture System the islanders, instead of paying to the Government a proportion of their crop, were required to give a portion of their land and their time towards the cultivation of these new cash crops. Those with no land to donate were put to work on Government-owned plantations. It was a thinly-disguised system of forced labour. Conditions for the labourers on the huge estates were appalling, and stand comparison with those of the slaves in the southern states of America.

The oppression was uncharacteristic of the Dutch who had a long-standing reputation for tolerance. But the Napoleonic occupation of Holland had left the country with a crippling public debt; the prospect of the enormous riches that would accrue from the development of the colony blinded them to the attendant injustice, and they became increasingly autocratic, demanding total subservience from all 'brownies' in return for 'the benefits of white civilisation'.

By 1897, when Rudolph returned to Java with Margarethe and Norman, attitudes in official Government circles in the Netherlands were changing. In a resurgence of traditional liberalism their declared policy became 'To take care of the people of the Indies and foster their interests'. But it would be another twenty years before the effects of this laudable ambition would reach those it was intended to benefit. Since neither Margarethe nor Rudolph were in the forefront of radical thinking, it is hardly surprising that, to start with, Margarethe was unaware of these problems. Adding the insouciance of youth to the blissfulness of ignorance she saw only the flowers.

The Dutch, it must be said, made every effort to keep the thorns out of sight. The town of Jakarta they renamed Batavia, the Roman name for the Netherlands, and, in the universal manner of expatriates, constructed a protective cocoon of Dutchness around themselves until Batavia resembled nothing so much as a suburb of The Hague. The only foreign influences that were permitted to filter through were those that would enhance the lifestyle of the people clustered within.

A contemporary of Margarethe's, Augusta de Wit, was one of the first Dutchwomen to take time off her social round to study Java and its peoples. But although she was both more articulate and more observant than Margarethe, her first impressions would have been very similar.

> The new-comer in Batavia Society is struck by a certain grace and easiness of manner that contrasts forcibly with the somewhat frigid reserve of the typical Hollander. Although home-life is essentially the same among Hollanders in Java as in their own country, yet there are differences in that here it has more physical comfort and less intellectual interest. Analogous contrasts meet one at every step. Life here has less dignity than it has in the mother country; but it has more grace.

While Augusta de Wit was bemoaning the lack of theatres, operas, concerts, lectures and good newspapers, Margarethe MacLeod, who had few intellectual interests, was glorying in the lack of dignity. And since physical comfort was high on her list of priorities she found it easy to settle in. Their first home in Java was at Semarang, a small but growing port on the north coast of the island. As soon as she set eyes on their house she loved it: the shady verandah was supported by graceful pillars; open doors led into airy rooms; simple mats were scattered on cool stone floors; and a faint breeze scattered the petals of the tanjong blossom, filling the air with fragrance.

The relatively modest income of an army captain went a good deal further here than at home, so they were able to employ servants to cook, clean, and run the house, and there was a *babu* or native nurse to look after little Norman. Margarethe need not lift a finger. In Holland there had always been boring duties to fulfil, pointless rules to obey and absurd conventions to observe. She had chafed at these restrictions — life was for parties, for fun and flirtation, for pleasure. Here, at last, was the luxury she deserved, and she slipped into the leisured life of a colonial wife with the greatest of ease.

Their stay at Semarang was a short one, for Rudolph was soon transferred to Tumpang near Malang in the East of Java. The move suited Margarethe, who had quickly realised that, though Semarang was delightful, the European community was small and her social life disappointingly limited. In Malang there would be shops and markets to explore, visits to make and receive, dinner parties and receptions to attend and, above all, opportunities to see and be seen. Rudolph, too, welcomed the change. He had noticed the first signs of restlessness in Margarethe but, back at work in earnest, was too busy to do much about it.

But even in Malang things were not entirely to Margarethe's liking. It did not take her long to discover that the much-vaunted informality within the Dutch community was only skin-deep; conventions may have been altered to suit the tropics, but they were still very much in force. Although it was considered quite acceptable for a lady to adopt the native costume of *kabaya* and *sarong* in the privacy of her home, after six in the evening she was expected once more to don full, formal European dress. The rules of protocol were still rigidly applied, as Augusta de Wit observed:

> There is the same eagerness for precedence, the same intimacy and tattle and neighbourly kindness, the same high living and plain thinking as in some rich, provincial town in Holland ... One would expect such an excess of bureaucratic etiquette to breed dullness and constraint unspeakable. It certainly somewhat galls the newcomer.

And, Margarethe realised with dismay, the slightest step

out of line was noted with frowns every bit as disapproving as those seen in The Hague or Amsterdam.

Although contacts between the Dutch and the native communities were kept to a minimum, Margarethe could observe, as did Augusta de Wit, the seemingly idyllic and carefree existence of the Javanese:

> They practically live out-of-doors. The women have a great love of flowers and are hardly ever seen without a rosebud twined into their hair, and the bare brown little bodies of the children are hung with tanjong wreaths. They take their bath in the river — the men leap into the stream and dive under; as they come up again their bare bodies shine like so many bronze statues. The women pause for an instant at the edge of the water, lifting both arms to twist their hair into a knot on the top of their heads. Half hidden in a clump of tall-leaved reeds by the margin, young girls disport themselves, making believe to bathe, as they empty little buckets made of a palm leaf over each other's head and shoulders, until their black hair shines, and the running water draws their garments into flowing clinging folds that mould their lithe figures from bosom to ankle, while their shapely shoulders are bare to the sun.

Within her small circle of peers there were few who could match Margarethe's exuberance or share her frustration at being barred from these simple pleasures. Those who had not already sunk into premature and matronly middle age seemed dreary and insipid beyond redemption. How could their blood not tingle at the vibrant beauty all around them? Why did they not long, as did she, to inhale the colours and scents, the heat and the sunshine to the point of intoxication? Rejoicing in the sheer sensuality of the tropics, she would wander through the garden, barefoot in the heavy scented twilight with her hair loose and tumbling about her shoulders. But she would much rather have joined the laughing throng by the river.

She saw little of Rudolph, for his military duties kept him fully occupied; when he did return to the bungalow he was drained of all energy after sweating through the heat of the day in his heavy European uniform. By now the novelty of being surrounded by those physical comforts so dear to her heart was wearing thin — Margarethe was bored. Surely there was more to life than having to be endlessly polite to Rudolph's superiors, or worse, their boring stuffy wives. Even during those rare evenings when they were entertained in the home of some native dignitary the conversation was stilted, their hosts polite but poker-faced and the inevitable performance of local theatre or dance groups so long, so incomprehensibly intricate and so formal as to preclude real enjoyment. Margarethe felt stifled. Other men's wives might be content to sit on their velvet chairs and bemoan the inefficiency of their servants or plan the seating arrangements for the next regimental dinner; she most certainly was not. There was a whole beautiful island out there, far away from their frowns and crying out to be enjoyed. Mutinously she tossed her head at their disapproval and went out to find it.

The gently rolling countryside round Tumpang more than lived up to her mental image. It was like a magical Garden of Eden, with brilliantly-coloured birds flashing through the treetops, grotesque fungi lurking in the damp shade of lacy ferns, and butterflies as big as bats swooping and fluttering through the dappled shade of the immense forest trees. Burying her face in the gloriously scented jasmine blossoms and decking herself in garlands of wild orchids and liana flowers she pirouetted euphorically after them. But emerging into the strong sunlight of a jungle clearing her scalp suddenly prickled as she came face to face with huge sculpted stones, half buried in the tangled undergrowth. Tracing the shapes with her trailing fingers, she could make out ornately carved figures, fantastical beasts, ferocious birds — the very fabric of fairytale and legend — unlike anything she had ever seen or imagined.

For Tumpang is surrounded by an astonishing profusion of ancient Hindu and Buddhist temples. Dating mainly from the eleventh, twelfth and thirteenth centuries, they range from small groups of statues, through isolated towers and solitary decorated gateways to elaborate, many-storied temple complexes, some intact and some in ruins. Some house exquisite statues of the Buddha; some are flanked by enormous stone guardians adorned with skulls and writhing snakes; while others are lavishly decorated with huge relief panels depicting scenes from the Hindu epics, the *Mahabharata* and the *Ramayana*.

Although Islam is now the central religion of Java, it is possible to apply to the Muslims of the island a variation on Napoleon's dictum concerning the Russians: scratch the Muslim and you will find the Hindu, scratch the Hindu and you will find the pagan. Each new religion that arrived — Buddhism around the beginning of the Christian era, Hinduism in the fifth century AD and Islam not until the fourteenth century — was adapted and to some extent diluted by old Indonesian beliefs and practices. Distinctions between Buddhism and Hinduism, always slender in Java, evolved into a form of Tantric Syncretism with strong overtones of magic. The temples around Malang and Tumpang date from the period of East Java's cultural supremacy between the tenth and the sixteenth centuries, and clearly illustrate the overlapping and eventual fusion of Sivaite and Buddhist cults in the region.

The largest and most impressive of these ruined temples, Candi Jago, lies little more than a mile from Tumpang and dates from the thirteenth century. Within the confines of its retaining walls, Buddhist sculptures and Krishna reliefs cohabit with the early *panakawan* carvings which are a distinctive Javanese addition to the Hindu epics. The small but exquisite Candi Kidal and the fiercely monumental Candi Singosari provide further evidence of the rich religious, cultural and architectural tradition of East Java, and both lie within easy reach of Malang.

Margarethe, however, knew nothing of either their history or the religions that were their inspiration. But as she tiptoed through the ruins with bated breath she found their atmosphere intoxicating. On one occasion she found herself confronted by the towering stone image of an awesome goddess. There was no mistaking the power of the massive six-armed deity as she stood with widespread legs on the back of a bull, holding a leering demon by the hair. But Margarethe was struck by the way her essential femininity was not the least diminished by her aggressive pose. This was no milk and water plaything, no shrinking violet — this was the personification of glorious, unrestrained womanhood. No narrow-minded pettiness could intimidate her; no disapproving frown make that proud head bow in submission. Margarethe returned to the bungalow deep in thought.

At every opportunity now she would slip away into the

forest. Sometimes she found nothing, but the suspense was sweet. Then her persistence was rewarded with the discovery of another forgotten and overgrown temple. She would enter through the gateway, trembling with anticipation, to find herself face to face with a tall, calm god mounted on the back of a ferocious steed, half man half bird, whose deepset eyes glittered with menace. There was something strangely compelling in the sightless gaze of the deity, a remote serenity that calmed the mind and slowed the heartbeat from its excited race. Shrinking from the venomous stare of the countless stone snakes that twined round the feet of this apparition, Margarethe was nevertheless moved to a feeling of almost religious awe by the encounter. Her subsequent preoccupation prompted Rudolph to enquire whether she was ill and, terrified lest her precious secret world be invaded, she stayed away from her treasures for a while to concentrate on her husband and son.

But the lure of the exotic was too great and soon she would be back, this time to gaze in breathless disbelief at an earthlier beauty. A succession of vast relief panels adorning the walls of yet another vine-festooned ruin replaced the religious awe with a more familiar sensation — the warm tingle of physical arousal. For here were dreamy, ethereal nymphs with naked breasts and flowing transparent lower garments treading the steps of an endless dance to silent music. Handsome young men whose muscular bodies were clad either in the briefest of loincloths or nothing at all enticed their shapely companions into unimagined pleasures amidst the luxuriant tropical foliage.

The carvings on one of the panels were obviously a story sequence: here the nymphs were being given orders by a chubby deity sitting on a flower; now they sat by a pool, dangling their feet in the water and arranging their hair in its reflection; then they seemed to be dancing, showing off to each other with laughing grace; and, in the final scene, they crowded round another seated deity shamelessly flaunting their nakedness before his serene gaze and slipping teasing fingers under his robes to tempt him from his piety.

Margarethe was transfixed. Although there is nothing as explicitly erotic in East Java as in, for example, the celebrated temples of Khajuraho in India, the seductive *joie de vivre*, the unashamed sensuality that shone out of these ancient works of art made her blood tingle. The freedom and lack of hypocrisy they proclaimed struck a chord in her receptive mind that would make the petty tyrannies of Netherlands-India even harder to bear. She was by no means the first to discover these hidden ruins. Indeed there were experts in Batavia who could have told her about the calm god, Vishnu, the vengeful goddess Durga, and recounted the story of the temptation of Arjuna by the shameless nymphs. But she had no desire to share her treasures nor to decipher them — that would be to destroy their magic. It was enough for her to know they were there.

Under the stimulating influence of her archaeological rambles, Margarethe's physical awareness blossomed. Female company was much in demand with the many unattached planters and soldiers who flocked to the town on short spells of leave, and Margarethe — always happy to be the centre of attention — responded warmly to their admiration. As in any small expatriate community, tongues wagged and rumours flourished. The Captain's health was wavering under the renewed onslaught of the tropics and, perhaps, under the increasingly vigorous demands of his wife. His temper, never the sweetest, deteriorated accordingly. Jealous of her admirers and painfully aware of the twenty-year age gap, he accused her of flirting with his subordinates and disgracing him in the eyes of his colleagues. Predictably, Margarethe poured scorn on his reproaches and charged him in return with caring more for his reputation than for his wife. Rudolph flew into a violent rage; Margarethe gave as good as she got, and the airy bungalow rocked with the fury of their rows. Marital harmony was temporarily restored by Margarethe's second pregnancy, which ensured, for a while, her compliance with Rudolph's demands that she spend less time on frivolity and more time with her family. A daughter, Jeanne-Louise, was born to them in May 1898.

Although Norman was his favourite, Rudolph adored both his children. He constantly fretted over their health and drove the servants to distraction with his continual fussing over diet and hygiene. His concern was justified in such a notoriously unhealthy climate, but Margarethe interpreted it as a slur on her own ability to look after them. She took refuge from his obsession amongst her beloved ruins, sometimes spending whole days drifting through their splendour. The more he reproached her for her unwillingness to conform to his ideal, the more she would retaliate — she made him late for official functions that demanded their prompt attendance, refused to defer to the wives of superior officers and neglected to invite newcomers to visit. Although this behaviour caused Rudolph acute embarrassment, it seems otherwise to have passed almost unnoticed — there was charm and sweetness enough in her smile to earn her the instant forgiveness of anyone but Rudolph. Harmony tottered again, and then came the move that would result in its final collapse: Rudolph was posted to Sumatra.

It was a welcome promotion, and Rudolph's immediate departure (while Margarethe stayed to pack up their possessions and follow on in a few months) gave them both a much-needed breathing space. But Sumatra was quite a different proposition from Java. The inhabitants of this neighbouring island were fanatically Muslim and, here as elsewhere, the followers of Islam had never readily accepted the colonial yoke. Here, too, were few of the creature comforts and social elegances so carefully nurtured in Java. Every ounce of Dutch energy was channelled into the transformation of raw jungle into trim plantation. The efficiency with which this vast undertaking was effected was staggering — over a period of twenty years nearly two and a half million acres of dense tropical forest were cleared and given over to the production of tobacco and rubber. In those pre-ecology-conscious days it was a feat that would earn for the Dutch the admiration of every other colonial power with possessions in the tropics. By any standards it was an extraordinary achievement and spoke volumes for their organisational abilities. But the cost of such a colossal assault on the land, in human suffering as well as in damage to the ecosystem, was never calculated.

Sumatran tobacco was proving so popular in America that even this impossible rate of jungle clearance was not enough to satisfy the Dutch. The workforce had to be increased — it didn't matter how, so long as there was an endless supply of labourers to slash, cut, burn and destroy the huge forest to make way for more tobacco — and bring in more money.

... the Dutchmen sent for Chinese coolies from Singapore and Penang and the fierce struggle between

25

the human will and the desperately resisting virgin forest began. Men died like flies in autumn. The forest exhaled germs of disease. It breathed upon the intruders and, poisoned by its breath, the coolies died in shoals. The fit ones cleared away the dead and continued the life-and-death struggle.

A young Hungarian, Laszlo Szekely, who spent twenty years as a planter in Sumatra, could, by virtue of his nationality, take a more detached and objective view of conditions on the plantations than was possible for a Dutchman. He described the arrival on the island of a new batch of coolies, mostly very young and some still almost children, who had been recruited in remote Javan villages: 'Clever recruiting officers would go from one hidden *kampong* to the other and entice the credulous, good-natured Javan land workers with fine stories, with silver coins and promises'. When the innocent boy had pressed his thumbprint onto the proffered contract, he found himself 'taken in custody by the Coolie Importing Company and transported to Sumatra, Borneo or other islands where labour was insufficient.'

To all intents and purposes he now belonged to the planter, bound for a minimum of three years (which was usually extended indefinitely by trickery beyond his comprehension) to a life of unremitting hardship.

He may not run away for that is forbidden by his contract. He is doing forced labour — he is a slave. He slogs from morning to night toiling and stooping; he has to stand up to the neck in stinking marshland while greedy leeches suck his thin blood and malaria mosquitos poison his sickly body. But he cannot run away: for the contract binds him. The *tjentengs*, the watchmen of the firm, who have the strength of giants and are bestially cruel, track down the fugitive. When they catch him they give him a terrible hiding and lock him up, for the contract binds him.

To a lesser degree the life of the Dutch planter in Sumatra during this time was also harsh. The climate and the jungle were cruel to the European constitution; living conditions on the remote, newly-created plantations were primitive; and the work, even of an overseer, was cripplingly hard. For weeks at a time he would live deep in the forest, isolated from all other Europeans, surrounded by and in charge of several hundred Malays, Javans and Chinese, on whose goodwill he could certainly not depend. He was in turns exhausted, frightened, ill, lonely and exhausted again. Every month he would be allowed a few days leave. He would head straight for Medan, the main port and capital town of northern Sumatra, and immediately set about drinking himself into oblivion.

Rudolph MacLeod's promotion had been to the post of Garrison Commander in Medan; a role in which he personified the oppression so hated and feared by the indentured labourers. And it was here that Margarethe and the children joined him in May of 1899. It was not the ideal place to bring a young family but Rudolph's finances had been seriously depleted by Margarethe's extravagance and he could not afford to maintain two households. In a rare letter he wrote to warn Margarethe of the domestic dangers, but characteristically omitted to discuss any of the wider issues with her.

You will have to be more watchful than ever when you

come here — and it is doubly important to make sure everything is constantly cleaned. If one is not continuously busy with sweeping, especially around and under the flower pots, all kinds of vermin crawl around. Last night I saw the largest scorpion I have ever set eyes on. Although its bite would not be immediately fatal, it does cause a high fever and is particularly dangerous to small children. You will have to be sure to inspect the rooms every day yourself, clean the children's beds and always be fully aware of your heavy responsibility for the children.

For the first time Margarethe found herself forced to confront the thorns. Now, when she ventured out to visit the wife of one of Rudolph's fellow officers or to explore the bazaar to see what little luxuries had arrived from Holland on the latest boat, instead of being greeted with a courteous kiss of the hand from a blushing admirer, she was jostled and leered at by perspiring, red-faced youths who staggered when they walked. There was also something threatening, just short of insolence, in the way the natives would step out of her way on the pavement — a glitter in their eyes that was certainly not affection. The brooding menace that hung over the island stifled her and made her long for the tranquillity of the bungalow in Tumpang; the neighbours whom she had dismissed as being unbearably insipid appeared, with hindsight, to have been comfortingly serene; there was no question here of being able to stroll unchallenged and unobserved among the forgotten treasures of the past.

Frightened by the tangible tension, Margarethe clung to Rudolph for comfort. But he was in no mood to oblige. His position as Garrison Commander was an onerous one. For the past thirty years the Dutch had been involved in a sporadic guerrilla war with the Aceh and Batak peoples of northern Sumatra. The livelihood of these previously successful traders had been badly affected by Dutch colonial rule and, under the guidance of their mullahs, they were pledged to a *jehad* against the infidels. By increasing their military presence and adopting a policy of 'ceaseless pursuit', the Dutch had recently succeeded in subduing the guerrillas. But only by remaining ceaselessly vigilant were they able to maintain their dominance. The strain of his responsibilities was beginning to tell on Rudolph. The illness which had taken him back to Holland in 1895 threatened to recur, and, like most of his contemporaries, he was drinking heavily in an effort to convince himself he could cope. He had no time to listen to Margarethe's complaints and fears; all he asked of her was that she fulfil her role as his wife by entertaining his visitors and caring for his children. She should stop imagining things and leave him to get on with his work — an attitude which left Margarethe sobbing with vexation and as apprehensive as ever.

Then, in a cruel justification both of her fears for the family's safety and of his obsession with the health of the children, tragedy struck. On the evening of 25th June 1899, without warning, both Norman and Jeanne-Louise were seized by violent attacks of vomiting. The garrison doctor was summoned. Throughout the night Rudolph and Margarethe kept a desperate vigil, watching the small, pale bodies of their children being wracked and twisted by convulsive retching.

By sunrise the crisis was past for the baby girl, and by noon she was sleeping, exhausted but safe. But as the hours passed and the day wore on there was no respite for two-year-old Norman. His strength faded with every spasm. Dehydration, the dreaded sequel to every tropical disease, turned his skin a flaky grey. There was nothing the doctor could do and in the early hours of 27th June the little boy died. The diagnosis was poison.

The poisoner is said to have been the lover of the child's nurse, but whether he killed the child, as was rumoured, because Macleod had casually seduced the nurse or because he himself had been savagely beaten by MacLeod for some misdemeanour is irrelevant. What is certain is that such a brutal revenge would never have been exacted had it not been for the depth of racial, cultural and social tension that permeated the very air of Sumatra. Norman's death was an indictment, as well as a direct result, of the arrogantly insensitive Dutch attitude towards the people they governed.

The mortality rate amongst Europeans in the East had always been shockingly high. 'Two monsoons was said to be the average life-expectancy of the British in India, and among the Dutch in the East Indies a consistent rate of fifty per cent mortality during the first year was maintained well into the nineteenth century. By the end of the century, with improvements in medical science, this rate had dropped to below twenty per cent, but children in particular were still at terrible risk from malaria, typhoid, dysentery, cholera and rabies, not to mention heatstroke, insect and snake bites. Sudden death was part of life in Netherlands–India; few families escaped intact and the numerous tiny graves in every churchyard bore poignant witness to the recurring tragedy.

But the pain was no easier to bear for being anticipated, and for Rudolph and Margarethe it was exacerbated by the manner of Norman's death. How infinitely cruel that they had managed to bring the child safely through the most dangerous early months of his life only to see him snatched from them by a cold-blooded murderer. The servant thought to be responsible had, not surprisingly, vanished without trace and in their grief and rage the stricken parents turned on each other. Rudolph castigated Margarethe bitterly for ignoring his warnings: if she had taken proper care of the children it would never have happened. She shrieked back at him that he should never have brought them to this god-forsaken place to start with — they had all been perfectly safe in Java.

For the rest of his life Rudolph would publicly mourn the loss of his son, and even twenty years later the mere mention of Norman's name could still reduce him to tears. But Margarethe reacted differently; she could not confront her anguish. Like a white-hot branding iron or a rabid dog, it was something to be kept at a safe distance, to be locked up far away where it would have no more power to hurt. The impenetrable wall she constructed around it would house, in later years, many another stark reality and unpalatable truth; even in the hour of her death she would keep her mind firmly closed to the horrors within.

Devastated by the disaster, Rudolph was in no state to withstand the next blow: he was posted back to Java without the expected promotion to Lieutenant-Colonel that should have followed his appointment in Medan. His career, twenty-four long years of it, had come so far but would go no further. He slid into a state of morbid depression punctuated by bouts of ungovernable rage in which he blamed Margarethe not only for Norman's death but also for his failure to win promotion. He drank relentlessly and became so violent that Margarethe feared for her safety. Stronger

31

marriages would have foundered under such circumstances — this one did not stand a chance.

Their return to Java brought no solace as Rudolph's next posting was to a remote garrison far from the diversions of Batavia or Malang. Margarethe now felt as if she had been condemned to a slow, lingering death by suffocation. Here she was, still only twenty-three years old, isolated in the back of beyond with a man who terrorised her, whom she was coming to loathe and in whose oppressive company she seemed destined to waste what was left of her precious youth. For nearly two years the miserable pair were imprisoned in each other's company. His work tied them to Java and Java tied them together, for it was just not practicable, financially or conventionally, for Margarethe to live there on her own.

Finally Rudolph decided to retire from the army — it was the only possible solution to an intolerable situation. In March 1902 they returned to Holland. For Margarethe it was the end of five years of life in a kaleidoscope; five years in which passion, boredom, exhilaration, fear, subservience, frustration and grief had tumbled over each other in bewildering succession. In the aftermath of this whirlwind she was left with only one clear idea — to escape from the man who had exposed her to the tumult yet had prevented her from reaping any joy from it, and to lead her life on her own terms, whatever they might prove to be.

METAMORPHOSIS

Margarethe's plans, however, took her no further than the Amsterdam quayside. As she picked her way miserably through the puddles on the grey dockside, shielding her face from the icy prickle of spindrift from the sea, the future suddenly seemed as bleak as her surroundings. The prospect of being free of Rudolph had occupied her mind to the exclusion of all else and she had given no thought to the alternatives. Independent living required independent means; but Margarethe had no money. Her father, Adam Zelle, had effectively washed his hands of her on her marriage and no longer considered her to be his responsibility; even had he been willing to help, he was financially no better off than he had been five years before and would not welcome the return of a prodigal daughter. Although Margarethe's resolve faltered somewhat as she began to appreciate her predicament, she refused to be daunted. It was a husband's duty, surely, to provide for his family, therefore Rudolph must provide for her and Jeanne-Louise. If he would find a house for them and give them enough money to live on, she would bother him no further.

She should have known better. Far from wanting to help her, Rudolph seemed determined to make her life even more of a misery than it had been in Java. When she approached him with her suggestion his only response was to hurl abuse. Was she not content with having ruined his career and caused the death of his son? Did she now intend to bankrupt him as well? He was going to rent an apartment in Amsterdam for himself and Jeanne-Louise and as far as he was concerned she could go to hell. Margarethe was stunned — it had never occurred to her that he would try and keep Jeanne-Louise. But he held the whiphand; he had money, position, friends, relations and she had nothing, not a single weapon to use against his determination.

Taking full advantage of his power to make her suffer, Rudolph allowed Margarethe to move into the flat with them and then proceeded to humiliate her at every turn. He bullied her unmercifully, treating her like the lowliest of servants; between bouts of drinking he shouted at her, threatened her and even beat her. He lost no opportunity to thrust her helplessness down her throat and then sat back and watched her grovel. Margarethe took it all. She had nowhere else to go and she would not leave Jeanne-Louise. Eventually, Rudolph grew bored by her lack of resistance; one day, after they had been back in Amsterdam for about two months, he waited until Margarethe was out of the flat on an errand, then packed up his belongings, tucked Jeanne-Louise under his arm and left.

His intention had been to destroy her, but this time it was his turn to misjudge the situation. While Margarethe had been with Jeanne-Louise she had still had something to lose. With the child gone that was no longer the case — on the contrary, she now had everything to gain and her rage at Rudolph's iniquity acted as a catalyst. The abject waif was transformed overnight into a lioness. It took her two days to track Rudolph down to Arnhem, where he was staying with a cousin, two more to apply to the courts for a legal separation and custody of her daughter, and only a week for the courts to decide in her favour, with the added condition that Rudolph pay 100 guilders a month in maintenance for Jeanne-Louise.

Jeanne-Louise was destined, like so many other children in similar situations, to become a weapon in the hands of each of her parents for use against the other. Both Rudolph and Margarethe loved their daughter, but the determination of each one to keep her was strengthened by an equal determination that the other should not. It was an unequal struggle: as Margarethe had known in her heart from the beginning. Refusing to pay her a penny in maintenance, Rudolph brought all the weight of his reputation, rank, ancestry and family into the battle. He spread the word amongst his many acquaintances that Margarethe was a disgrace to his distinguished name. He published announcements in all the leading newspapers warning tradesmen not to supply her with goods or cash, saying he would not be responsible for her debts. When Margarethe, in desperation, took Jeanne-Louise to stay with her father, Rudolph threatened to demolish the few remaining shreds of his business if he continued to shelter them under his roof, and Margarethe was forced to leave. She sought protection with her absent-minded uncle in The Hague who had given her a home before her marriage, but he was approaching senility and Rudolph had no trouble in convincing him that it was a mistake to take pity on a fallen woman who had broken every one of her marriage vows. As a last resort Margarethe begged Rudolph's sister, who had always been kind to her, to let them stay with her. Rudolph came to visit them, feigned remorse, then slipped out of the house with Jeanne-

Louise when Margarethe's guard was down. She never saw her daughter again.

By now Margarethe was mentally, emotionally and physically exhausted by this prolonged battle. Rudolph had successfully deprived her of everything: she had no home, no money, no hope of any sympathy from family or friends and, worst of all, no children. This time he had very nearly succeeded in destroying her.

But not quite. Norman's death, three years before, had shown her a far greater horror than anything she was facing now. On future occasions her ability to isolate and obliterate any reality too harsh for her own comfort would land her in appalling trouble. But this time it saved her sanity. To have dwelt on her wretchedness, particularly over the loss of Jeanne-Louise, would have been to succumb to it. It too must be banished if she was going to survive.

In the midst of the turmoil she had learnt another valuable lesson; even at the top of the social tree the law of the jungle prevailed - the strong survived at the expense of the weak. Success was the key to survival and power was granted only to the rich and the well- connected. If she were ever to get the better of Rudolph she would have to arm herself with these weapons — his weapons — before she could rejoin the battle. But for now it was time to concentrate on the only thing she had left — herself.

She was twenty-six years old, she was alone and there was nothing and nobody in the whole of Holland who cared what happened to her. The possibilities dawned slowly — she could stop banging her head against the brick wall of disapproval that Rudolph had so carefully constructed around her; she could thumb her nose at the haughty frowning matrons, abandon her mistakes and failures, and slip out of the treacly grasp of respectability and convention. She did not have to stay in Holland at all — she could go to Paris.

*   *   *   *   *

If Java was the Garden of Eden, Paris was an Aladdin's cave. It was the spiritual home of artists, poets and musicians, the fountain at which the leisured aristocracy refreshed their jaded palates, and the end of the rainbow to every pleasure seeker, fortune hunter and social climber of Europe. It was sophisticated, cosmopolitan and libertarian. It was everything that Amsterdam and The Hague were not and — best of all — it had never heard of Rudolph MacLeod. Margarethe's decision to go to Paris, as opposed to Rome, Berlin or Vienna, was probably influenced by the fact that she had learned to speak French at school, but the only explanation she was ever heard to give for her choice was the tart comment 'I thought that all abandoned women ended up in Paris'. The French capital was certainly the one place where she could be sure of being able to put the horrors of the last few years behind her. In such a dizzy, dazzling city she might even find something of the success and influence she would need to get back at Rudolph. She arrived in Paris in the spring of 1903.

By the autumn she was back in Amsterdam — broke, exhausted and deep in thought. Her stay in Paris had been short, uncomfortable and financially and socially disastrous, but it had not been wasted. Fame and fortune had not dropped into her lap, but they were there for the taking if you went about it the right way. She had taken a tiny room in a *pension* and accepted the first work she was offered. But even in the *Ville Lumière*, a city that claimed such masters as Henri de Toulouse-Lautrec and Camille Pissarro among its children and where Auguste Rodin and Paul Cézanne were exhibiting their greatest works, artist's models were paid the merest pittance. Margarethe had been forced to fall back on the model's traditional alternative in order to survive, and had privately admitted to herself that prostitution was a far more amusing way of earning a living. For a while she had even ridden horses in a circus — there was no possible route to the top that she was not prepared to try. But it had soon become apparent that, even in Paris, it was the same old story; with no strings to pull there was no shortcut out of poverty.

Yet Margarethe had kept her eyes and ears wide open: from her humble vantage point she had seen how the glittering social whirl of Paris revolved round the private salons where the rich and the famous vied with each other to provide the most lavish entertainment; where money and champagne flowed in equal quantities; where the latest scandals were avidly discussed, jewels and dresses compared and artistic protégés introduced and discarded at whim. Writing years later, one of the most dazzling of its stars, Liane de Pougy, would recall how her life consisted of 'nothing but joy, pleasures, parties and feasting. Every night there was a party, always at least seventy people and always the most amusing and the most famous, all having a lovely time watching, flattering, gossiping, tippling. And what jewels — at one reception Marthe Besnut was wearing three millions' worth'. It was a heartless, self-absorbed world constantly in pursuit of whatever novelty would keep boredom at bay, but it contained everything Margarethe was looking for.

It was also exclusive. Careful study of those who were

permitted entry to this hallowed company had shown her that the ladies at least fell into two distinct groups. If you belonged to the beau monde you were either married or widowed (or eminently marriageable), probably titled and certainly extremely rich. Your name was ancient, your lineage (or your husband's) irreproachable and you jealously guarded your reputation as an indefatigable charity fund-raiser, patroness of the arts and proud employer of the best chef in Paris. Since Margarethe had burned her boats as far as attracting an eligible husband was concerned, and her experiences of marriage had in any case left her with no desire to repeat the experiment, that group had to be ruled out. She was well aware, too, of the double standards that prevailed even in this liberated world, forcing a wife to observe the niceties, to accept the polite compliments of her husband in the full knowledge that he was on his way to a rendezvous with a member of the second group, the *demi-monde*. This looked far more promising. The *demi-monde* held no horrors for her as she had no reputation to safeguard or virtuous relations to deceive. It would be a blessed relief, too, to be able to drop the genteel facade she had adopted when she had married Rudolph. What a delicious prospect: to live in a charming apartment paid for by her handsome lover, her days a delightful round of couturiers and jewellers, beauty salons and furriers, and her nights sparkling with candlelight and kisses.

So the decision was made; the next problem was how to attract a rich lover. It obviously was not enough just to be beautiful — Paris was full of beautiful women — you had to be special, to stand out from the crowd and to make a name for yourself. Margarethe withdrew to Amsterdam where she sat down to consider her assets.

Who were the most celebrated courtesans in Paris? And where had they come from? Many had been actresses; Margarethe considered this possibility but she knew nothing about acting or the theatre, and the prospect of having to learn lines made her shudder. Some had made their names as singers; but that was out of the question as she had never been able to sing. Then there were dancers — this was an idea worth exploring. Although it took years of training to become a classical dancer, there must be less technical and more appropriate styles of dancing. She had heard talk of the extraordinary American girl, lsadora Duncan, who had startled Paris with her highly individual performances. She had had no formal training yet she had created a sensation with her free interpretations of everything from Chopin waltzes and Liszt's *Rakoczy March*, to scenes from fifteenth-century Italian paintings and stories from the Greek myths.

lsadora had been in Paris at the time of Margarethe's arrival and the artistic fraternity had proclaimed her as heralding 'a more liberal and enlightened attitude toward, not merely the dance, but life in general'. Her performances intrigued that small and arrogant group of socialites who thought of themselves as *tout Paris* and into whose company Margarethe longed to be admitted. But lsadora had wanted more. She wanted her audiences to respect her, not to treat her as some sort of titillating novelty; she dreamed of filling theatres, of influencing the public's entire perception of dance as an art form, and of founding dance schools to teach her theories and methods to future generations. Disgusted at Paris's refusal to take her seriously she left for Munich where she already had a loyal and passionate following. Margarethe never saw her perform, but had been much taken by pictures she had seen of the strange wafting creature with the dreamy expression and floating, diaphanous costumes.

Paris had also been full of talk about the *Exposition Universelle* of three years ago which had given rise to a tremendous vogue for all things oriental. She had pricked up her ears at mention of the eastern pavilions at the *Exposition* in which palaces and temples had been reconstructed in the Champs de Mars; where a whole Javanese village had been faithfully reproduced in the Esplanade des Invalides; and where a troupe of Bedaya dancers had performed to the accompaniment of a native *gamelan* orchestra. Such talk had filled her with nostalgia for her rambles among the forgotten ruins of Java, and now it presented her with the answer.

Always ready to admit that she had few qualifications of any sort and none at all of an academic nature, Margarethe was nonetheless aware that there could be few people in Paris with a more thorough knowledge of things Javan than herself. Her acquaintance with the dances of the island had not, moreover, been limited to happy hours poring over ancient carvings and statues. She had sat through countless performances of the formal *serimpi* court dances, bewildered by their complexity but entranced by the exquisite costumes and headdresses of the dancers. More to her taste, she had frequently stopped to watch the troupes of popular entertainers who toured the villages and towns, staging informal shows in the markets or on the local *maidan*. The pulsing rhythms of their music and the infectious atmosphere generated by their performances had been spellbinding in their intensity. And if the motivation behind her study of books and manuals devoted to Indonesian

41

dance had been more to satisfy her prurience than to further her artistic understanding, some of the latter had inevitably been absorbed in the process.

Superficial familiarity with these different styles of dancing allowed her to believe, as a more serious student could never have done, that there really was not a great deal to it. A convincing atmosphere and sufficiently exotic costumes would surely hide a multitude of technical inaccuracies and shortcomings, and although she had never had a formal dancing lesson, she knew that a great part of her beauty lay in her supple, graceful body. It was worth a try; after all, she really did have nothing to lose.

* * * * *

On 4th February 1905 Frances Keyzer, Paris correspondent of the London magazine *The King*, wrote one of a series of articles on 'The Parisians of Paris'. This one was subtitled 'A Dancer from the East' and concerned a select evening party, attended by the author, at which 'a Lady MacLeod would try the effects of her talent and beauty on the spoilt Parisians'.

Vague rumours had reached Keyzer of 'a woman from the Far East, a native of Java, wife of an officer, who had come to Europe, laden with perfumes and jewels, to introduce some of the richness of Oriental colour and life into the satiated society of European cities'. The carefully chosen audience were agog with curiosity; the hum of excited speculation died away as the door opened.

A tall dark figure glided in. Her arms were folded upon her breast beneath a mass of flowers. For a few seconds she stood motionless, her eyes fixed on a statue of Siva at the end of the room. Her olive skin blended with the curious jewels in their dead gold setting. A casque of worked gold was set upon her dark hair and a breastplate of similar workmanship beneath her arms, she wore a transparent white robe and a quaint clasp held a scarf around her hips. She was enshrouded in various veils of delicate hues, symbolising beauty, youth, love, chastity, voluptuousness and passion.

Little suspecting that the 'lady' under all the jewels and veils was shaking with nerves, the audience watched spell-bound as:

> ... with slow, undulating, tiger-like movements, she appealed to the Spirit of Evil to help her avenge a wrong. The movements became more and more intense, more feverish, more eager. She first threw the flowers, and then divested herself one by one of the veils, implying that, as a sacrifice, she gave beauty, youth, love, and finally, worked to a state of frenzy, she unclasped her belt and fell in a swoon at Siva's feet.

It had required every ounce of her courage to present this moving tableau. But Margarethe had hit the jackpot. For the first, and possibly the last, time in her life her judgement was faultless. Her performance was an amazing cocktail of styles, religions and costumes and contained elements of the stately *serimpi* as well as of the erotic Hindu temple dances, but it probably resembled the popular *ronggeng* street-dances of Java more than either of these.

According to Sir Stamford Raffles, Governor-General of

the East Indies during the brief period of British rule in the nineteenth century, the *ronggengs*:

> … do not generally descend to the performance of those disgusting and disgraceful postures and motions which are stated to be so frequent on the continent of India, but they are not free from the charge of impropriety in this respect. Their dress is coarse, but in other respects resembles that of the more select dancers. Their hair is dressed after a peculiar fashion, abundantly oiled and ornamented with flowers. Their action is usually distorted, their greatest excellence seeming to consist in bending the arms and hands back in an unnatural manner and giving one or two of their fingers a tremulous motion.

Margarethe had no intention of limiting her gestures to tremulous motions of one or two, or even all, her fingers. She resolutely ignored both the strict taboo on 'sinuous undulations of the body' and the golden rule that required dancing girls to be 'demure and restrained'. She dodged the charges of impropriety and precluded the epithets 'disgusting and disgraceful' by labelling her act 'sacred oriental art', and then proceeded to weave it round some of the more sensuous themes from her beloved Hindu and Buddhist temple wall-carvings. Her costume, too, owed more to her imagination than to any of the traditional styles and she had added the stage name 'Lady MacLeod' as a sop to the snobs.

However incongruous it would have seemed to anyone with a measure of oriental scholarship, the end product was a very astute combination that showed Margarethe to be fully aware of the hypocrisy of the 'spoilt Parisians'; they wanted to be entertained, certainly, but they had their standards. However spectacular the entertainment, it must be wrapped in a suitably highbrow cloak, have some element of culture, some redeeming aura of style before Paris could possibly accept it. By presenting herself as an aristocrat, and her performance as an interpretation of sacred dances of the highest cultural integrity, she was pandering to their intellectual pretensions and legitimising their gleeful appreciation of her overt sexuality. The salons were entranced.

As Keyzer reported:

> ... words may give an idea of the beauty and poetry of the dances, but nothing inanimate will render the emotion conveyed by the performer, nor the colour or harmony of the Eastern figure. It was a tropical plant in all its richness, transplanted to a northern soil. Curious and interesting comparisons were made between Lady MacLeod and Miss Duncan, who delighted Paris with her classical dances, until the heavy German atmosphere left its imprint upon her after her stay in Berlin. It is impossible to see two manifestations of art so totally different. Miss Duncan is the Vestal, Lady MacLeod is Venus.

There were certainly oriental experts in Paris who, if consulted, could have dismissed her dances as bearing no resemblance at all to any recognised oriental dance form. But the salons had no wish to consult the experts. Indeed, had they been asked to sit through a full performance of the formal and infinitely decorous *serimpi* dances of Java, or the intricate, stylised and physically and mentally exhausting *kathakali* of Southern India they would have been yawning before the first interval. Lady MacLeod's presentations were much more their style and it would have been sheer idiocy to invite some high-minded intellectual to burst their pretty new balloon.

The rapture of her reception took Margarethe completely by surprise; Paris had swallowed her exotic pantomime down to the last bangle, and now was joining in the game of make-believe. But she cottoned on quickly. When rumours spread that the ravishing Lady MacLeod was the daughter of some oriental potentate she immediately realised the value of such publicity. When questioned about her past, she demurely confessed that she had, in fact, been born in the holy city of Jaffnapatam on the Malabar coast of India. Her father had been a high caste Brahmin and her mother a temple dancer who had died in childbirth at the age of fourteen. Her childhood had been spent in the care of the priests of the temple who had trained her to follow in her mother's footsteps as a temple dancer. Paris clapped its hands with glee and begged for more. Margarethe flung herself wholeheartedly into the fantasy.

> From the time I first took my uncertain steps I was shut up in the great temple of Siva, where I was to be trained in my mother's footsteps through the holy rites of the dance. Of these early years my mind retains only vague recollections of a monotonous existence in which, during the long morning hours, I was taught to imitate the movements of the *bayaderes*, and in the afternoons I was allowed to walk in the gardens while weaving garlands of jasmine for decorating the altars. When I reached the threshold of womanhood my guardians

decided to consecrate me to Siva and I was initiated into the holy mysteries of love and worship.

Her appearance lent credibility to the masquerade. Certainly she bore little resemblance to the popular image of the Dutchgirl as a flaxen-haired milkmaid. But this image is misleading: the population of Holland is as complex as that of any country in Europe. When the Dutch finally threw off the yoke of Spanish domination in the late sixteenth-century, the Netherlands became a haven for the oppressed and persecuted, for freethinkers and outcasts from all parts of Europe in search of asylum and freedom. The wide range of differing racial types who descended on Holland have blended over the centuries with the native population to create this complexity. It has been suggested that Margarethe's ancestors may have belonged to the dark-haired, dark-skinned Woudker tribe of Friesland, and to contemporary eyes there is certainly more of the gypsy than the oriental in her appearance. But there were few among her audience in Paris with more than the haziest notion of what an Indian temple dancer would look like. Once more it was enough for them to know that she was different. Marcel Lami of the *Courrier Français* tried to explain the effect she had on her audience.

Strong, brown, hot-blooded, her swarthy complexion, full lips and liquid eyes speak of distant lands, burning sun and tropical rain. She sways under the veils that cover and reveal her at the same time. And it is like nothing we have ever seen before. Her breast swells languorously, her eyes glitter. Her hands rise and fall like slivers of passionate sunlight. Facing her is a golden

idol, an ancient sculpted image that has been worship-
ped by hands that are not like our hands, prayed to by
betel-stained mouths that are not like our mouths: her
profane dance is a prayer, her passion is a prayer. We do
not understand what it is she seeks. The mystery in the
dancer's trembling hands is mirrored by the mystery in
the idol's staring eyes. It is an eternal desire for we-
know-not-what offered to we-know-not-whom. The
lovely body bends in supplication, coils and recoils; it
is like desire dissolving in desire.

Her spontaneous creation of so exotic a childhood, triumphantly snatched up by her audience, threatened to soar
out of her control. She had to sustain her new role and bring
the story up to date without either stretching credibility to
breaking point or losing their interest. It would be a delicate
balancing act and the realisation of how much was at stake
was a terrible strain on her nerves and on her imagination.

Playing for time to perfect the next instalment, Margarethe feigned reticence and Paris had to be content with a few
juicy crumbs: she had been rescued from the temple and
swept off to Java by a dashing young Scottish officer who
had fallen madly in love with her; after their marriage he had
revealed himself to be a savage monster who had cruelly
maltreated her, even, it was whispered, biting off one of her
nipples in a frenzy of jealous rage. Paris gasped. She had
borne two children (or was it just one — the story seemed
to vary, but Paris put the inconsistency down to its own ten-
dency to exaggerate) who had met tragic deaths at the hands
of a drink-crazed servant. Demented by grief, their heart-
broken mother had taken a knife and plunged it with her
own hands into the murderer's heart.

The fairytale was getting out of hand, gathering its own momentum and spawning all manner of absurdities. For every detail Margarethe let slip, six more would grow out of nowhere. When this last little gem got back to her she nearly panicked — surely there was a limit even to Paris's gullibility. But in the best tradition of fairytales, just at the point where the abyss of disbelief was opening at her feet, in stepped Emile Guimet, the first in a succession of fairy godfathers who would miraculously materialise whenever Margarethe was facing a crisis.

A shrewd and successful industrialist from Lyons, Guimet had made a fortune from the manufacture of washing-blue and then had invested it in the accumulation of a fine collection of oriental art treasures. In the process he had also acquired a wide knowledge and appreciation of the paintings, sculpture, jewellery, fabrics and artefacts of China, Japan, South-East Asia and India. His collection had eventually reached sufficient proportions to warrant permanent and public display and so, in 1885, he had founded his own museum to house the treasures and exhibit them to the world. The Musée Guimet opened to a fanfare of praise; fashionable Paris flocked to his doors and Guimet donned the gratifying mantle of cultural mentor to the beau monde. The *Exposition Universelle* of 1900 had increased public interest in his collection, now he bad to sustain that interest if he was not to see his pride and joy sliding quietly into oblivion as just another feature of the Paris landscape.

At the beginning of March 1905 Guimet saw Margarethe dancing at a private party given by the Baronne Kiréevsky. As one of the leading orientalists of his day, Guimet was in an ideal position to expose her as an imposter. But under the aesthetic exterior beat the calculating heart of a businessman. He was pragmatic enough to realise that by denouncing her as a fraud he stood to gain only in self-righteousness and certainly would not endear himself to those whose patronage he so earnestly sought.

On the contrary, if he could adopt her as his protégé and persuade her to perform in his museum, her audience would come too. And since Guimet was as human as the next man, and no more impervious to Margarethe's considerable charm, he certainly had no wish to be the cause of her disgrace — better by far that they should help each other. He approached her with the suggestion, would she agree to dance for him? Margarethe could hardly believe her good fortune. The patronage of such a distinguished authority would establish her credentials beyond any question.

In the event Guimet provided even more. He was prepared to take a gamble in the interests of attracting public attention, but he was not prepared to risk his reputation. The performance must be meticulously planned and lavishly presented. She could take her pick from his collection of oriental jewellery and silks to create a truly authentic costume; he himself would design a suitably exotic setting and furnish it with appropriate items from his priceless display. Dancers would be engaged to act as her attendants, the best musicians would accompany her, and invitations would be sent to anybody who was anybody. Paris would be dazzled. There was just one small matter that troubled him, one discordant note in his oriental symphony — her name. How could she possibly expect to succeed as an authentic oriental dancer if she insisted on calling herself Lady MacLeod?

Margarethe pondered. She could see his point. Lady MacLeod might sound aristocratic, but it did not sound in the least bit romantic and it certainly was not oriental. Neither did it match the developing style of her dancing which, with the encouragement and evident approval of her audiences, was becoming increasingly suggestive and provocative with every performance. MacLeod was a constant reminder of the past, of Rudolph, of Holland and of everything she wanted to forget. All of a sudden it seemed obvious. A new name would be a means of distancing herself from this unsatisfactory past and of completing her transformation from nonentity to celebrity.

It would be a crucial decision. Her new name must be evocative but accessible, oriental without being obscure and must contribute both to the glamour and the mystery of her image. There has been any amount of speculation about how she made the final choice. The most frequently mentioned possibility is that it was taken directly from the composite Malay word for 'the sun', *matahari*; *mata* meaning 'eye' and *hari* meaning 'day'. Had Margarethe alone been responsible for choosing her name, there would be a certain logic in her choice. But she was being advised by Guimet; he would never have allowed her to perform a dance dedicated to the Hindu god Siva unless the name was somehow appropriate. While Margarethe was rummaging through her memory for any Malay she could remember, Guimet was concentrating on the Hindu pantheon.

He was spoiled for choice: most of the Hindu gods and goddesses have more than one name and the major deities have several, one for each aspect of their personality and power. Thus Siva, the most complex and most powerful of the gods, has more than a hundred names. Margarethe had decided to dedicate her performance to Siva because, as both creator and destroyer, he had seemed to offer a wide range of wonderfully dramatic themes for her interpretation. But her choice had been unwittingly apposite for, as Guimet would have known, amongst his other names, Subramanya, Bhola Mahadeo, Hari and Shankar, to mention just a few, the god is also known as Siva Nataraja, Lord of the Dance.

In an effort to sustain such an appropriate theme, Guimet would naturally have gone on to consider any female connections. Research would have told him, had he not already known, that Siva's consort, Parvati, personifies the female energy of Siva as well as being a goddess in her own right. She similarly has a multiplicity of names. Some, like Shakti, represent the mild, beneficent side of her character, while others including the better-known Durga and Kali, depict her fierce and fearsome aspects. When Guimet found the name Mata among those belonging to the least demure aspects of the goddess he must have been triumphant - he had found the connection he was looking for. Mata Hari, the wife, or consort, of the god Siva. It was perfect.

A BIZARRE GODDESS

The invitations went out. Monsieur or Madame was invited to attend a presentation of Brahminical Dances to be performed by Madame Mata Hari in the library of the Musée Guimet on the evening of 13th March. Guimet's decision to set her performance in the rotunda which housed the library was inspired. Although one of the smallest rooms in the museum, it lent itself perfectly to the transformation into a Hindu temple. The books, ranged on shelves round the outer walls, were well out of the way, and a colonnade of pillars formed an inner ring round the open space where she could dance. An image of Siva stood on an improvised altar in front of a richly embroidered wall-hanging. Strange statues were displayed on plinths draped with exotic fabrics, and garlands of white flowers were twined round the pillars. Sticks of burning incense filled the air with the heavy fragrance of jasmine and sandalwood; the floor was scattered with flower petals; and candles concealed behind tinted glass screens suffused the tableau with an intimate red glow.

Inspired by this sumptuous setting, Margarethe danced as she had never danced before. Although no audience had ever quibbled about the details of her costume or her dancing, she herself had never been quite satisfied; the niggling doubts about what she was trying to achieve had made her nervous and uncertainty had cramped her style. Now, with Guimet's expertise and encouragement to support her, all these anxieties vanished and her confidence soared. Her interpretation of the 'Poem of the Princess and the Magic Flower' was more poignant, the 'War Dance of Subramanya' more majestic and her 'Invocation of Siva' more sensuous than ever before.

Although she described herself as a dancer and no one ever thought to question the appellation, what she did on stage was not strictly speaking dance. Certainly in her interpretation of stories from the Hindu myths she moved rhythmically to the accompaniment of suitable music, but the performance consisted more of a succession of dramatic poses strung together by what were variously described at the time as 'graceful gestures', 'supple undulations', 'passionate writhings' or 'serpentine gyrations'. It was an intentionally fluid format which would allow her to adapt the style of each performance to suit the audience of the moment. There were no definable dance-steps, no formal structure, it was dancing only because it was obviously not anything else, and the fact that she was able to construct a credible performance out of so little speaks volumes for her physical grace, her vivid imagination, and the sheer force of her personality.

The balancing of decorum with daring, simplicity with sensuality, and restraint with audacity required fine judgement; eventually she would become highly skilled in the art but in the early days of her career it was not always easy to hit exactly the right note. Luckily, at the Musée Guimet, her elation was infectious and the watching guests, stimulated by the heady atmosphere, found themselves being drawn into the drama. Their excited applause encouraged her to more daring poses, their gasps of delight led her into more provocative gestures until the performance was in danger of plunging into shameful excess. It was only rescued from disaster by the touchingly happy smile, almost a grin, which, despite herself, Margarethe could not prevent from creeping onto her face. It relieved the tension and endeared her to an audience that could easily have turned against a display of such passion. As it was they loved her.

Since his object in presenting her had been to publicise his museum, Emile Guimet had made sure that the press were there in force. The only English journal to carry a report of the performance was, rather incongruously, a magazine called *The Gentlewoman*, and its correspondent was obviously concerned to protect the sensibilities of his readers.

All Paris is talking of the beautiful woman known as Mata Kari [sic] whose real name is Lady MacLeod. Mata Kari arrived here but a short month ago from Java where she was born of European parents and married Sir George MacLeod, a Scotchman, a colonel in the Dutch Colonial army. For reasons which do not concern us Lady MacLeod decided to come to Paris and initiate the Parisians into the classical dances of her adopted country. Having danced at one or two private receptions she came under the notice of M. Guimet who offered her the celebrated museum near the Trocadéro as a frame for her interesting performances. On two consecutive nights the halls and staircases leading to the circular library were filled with all that Paris contains of the artistic, scientific and literary world.

M. Guimet had issued over 600 invitations and to judge by the crush on the second night there were few who had not accepted.

The Paris press were less restrained. *Le Matin* spoke in tones of hushed awe of the 'mysterious and sacred dances of India', the 'seance set to harmonious and savage music' and the 'supple and lascivious gestures of the oriental dancer'. *La Presse* went to town.

From Java, on the burning soil of which island she grew up, she brings an unbelievable suppleness and magic charm. No one before has dared to remain like this with trembling ecstasy and without any veils in front of the god — and with such beautiful gestures, at the same time daring and chaste. She is indeed Absaras, sister of the Nymphs and the Naiads, created by Sundra for the perdition of men and sages. Mata Hari does not only dance with her feet, her arms, eyes, mouth and crimson fingernails. Mata Hari, unhampered by any clothes, dances with her whole body. Erect in her glorious nudity, she offered to the gods the passion that burned in her, and then, without any feeling of shame, rose gracefully, wrapped one of her veils around her and, thanking both Siva and the Parisians, walked off amidst thunderous applause.

Margarethe was jubilant. She was also very relieved; the press were in an understandable muddle about where both she and her dances came from, but no one seemed to care very much and no one had bothered to check. They had welcomed her performance as a heaven-sent opportunity to practise their purple prose and had never thought to ascertain from which heaven it came. Emile Guimet's reputation had removed their doubts as it had hers; if he approved then who were they to question?

Her eyes must have widened a bit as she read of her 'glorious nudity'. Even she had not dared to go that far. The nudity, as with everything else, had been implied rather than manifest. In fact she had gone to a great deal of trouble to procure an all-concealing, flesh-coloured body stocking that reached from her jewelled brassiere (or 'breast-plate' as it was rather uncomfortably described by one bashful journalist), to her golden anklet. It was possible, if a little unlikely, that the dim lights of the library had fooled the audience into believing her to be completely naked. But it was one more instance of the gathering momentum of her reputation that the story spread, abetted no doubt by those who had been favoured with an invitation glamorizing the event for the benefit of their less fortunate acquaintances. It really did seem, Margarethe mused, that you could get away with anything in Paris.

Within a week of her triumph at the Musée Guimet Margarethe found herself inundated with invitations to appear at soirées, receptions, fund-raising balls and intimate social gatherings of every description. To each invitation she modestly murmured that, as a professional, she would of course have to charge a fee. 'Why yes, but certainly my dear, whatever you say' came the reply from breathless hostesses desperate to keep one step ahead of their rivals. Margarethe could, and did, name her price. Her original patroness, Baronne Kiréevsky, hosted a charity ball in aid of the Russian Red Cross to raise money for the victims of the war with Japan. Entertainment was provided by Madame Mata Hari and her fee was one thousand francs in gold. For a similar sum she danced at a literary reunion dinner; the academics pronounced themselves 'vastly entertained' and the queues at her door grew ever longer.

Her spectacular success catapulted her right to the heart of the world that had seemed so inaccessible just a few months before. In May she was invited to perform at a party given by Cecile Sorel. From lowly beginnings Sorel had reached the heights to which Margarethe now aspired by way of the stage. Glittering star of the *Folies Bergère*, she was now also one of Paris's most successful hostesses. Even her arch rival, Liane de Pougy, had to admit that she had made a great success of her life. 'She is absolutely tiny, as is the fashion, and her blond ringlets frame the innocent smile of a child. Her only desire is to charm everyone, and she appears so sincere that it always works.'

The famous smile, which Liane de Pougy suspected was still in place when *la superbe Sorel* was fast asleep, was bestowed with equal charm on countess or kitchen-maid. Its sweetness removed any nervous pangs Margarethe might have felt about performing in such exalted circles and gave her the courage to stop dissimulating; since rumour still insisted that she danced naked, she might as well do so. When her last veil fluttered to the floor of the salon the audience, which included Gaston Menier, the 'chocolate king', realised that the body-stocking had been discarded and society's darling posed before them clad only in her ornate brassière and a tiny jewelled *cache-sexe*. This was nudity indeed.

Eighty years on it is easy to be dismissive of the sensation created by Margarethe's state of undress. But in that same year, 1905, Isadora Duncan's career nearly foundered in the face of Kaiserin Auguste Victoria's shocked reaction to seeing her pupils, children aged between four and eight years old, appearing on stage with *bare limbs*. Lady bathers on English beaches still made sure they were covered from shoulder to knee in the most elaborate and modest of bathing dresses before coyly emerging from their changing rooms. The New York press had disapprovingly likened Isadora Duncan's diaphanous and more or less revealing costume to 'a species of surgical bandage of gauze and satin of the hue of raspberry ice' which 'threatened to fall off during her entire show'. But the Parisians had never been subjected to the moral tyranny of a Queen Victoria; they would have poured scorn on the Kaiserin's insistence that the sole duties of a woman were 'Kinder, Kirche, Küche'; and they had been able to appreciate Isadora's 'surgical bandages' as 'artistic draperies which revealed an admirable knee'. Yet for all their tolerance the majority of Parisians were as moral and virtuous as their German or British counterparts. That capricious and arrogant elite, the beau monde, on the other hand, believed that their wealth, talent, birth or sheer social brilliance transcended convention. To be prudish was to be bourgeois; morality was for the masses and their own appetites existed only in order that they might be indulged. In the privacy of their own homes there was little they would not dare.

Margarethe's audacity, however, took them completely by surprise. Although it was a little galling to find their frontiers of propriety being extended by a newcomer, to have been shocked would have been to break their own rules. They had their reputation to protect, they would show the world that Paris was ready for anything.

It was hard for Margarethe to decide which delighted her

more: the success, the money, or the independence. Indeed the pleasure she derived from all three was sufficient to put all thoughts of Rudolph, if not of Jeanne-Louise, right out of her head. She gloried in her success, spent her money and underlined her independence by renting a stylish apartment in the fashionable rue Balzac. She bought herself a horse and could be seen every morning riding in the Bois de Boulogne with a posse of admirers in tow. Her original plan to attract a wealthy lover to set her up in style now seemed to have its limitations. How much more satisfactory to set yourself up in style. And why commit yourself to just one lover when you were surrounded by a throng of eligible candidates from whom to choose? The gentlemen of the beau monde now competed for the favours of the sensational Mata Hari in much the same way as their wives vied with each other for the services of the most fashionable couturier.

Mrs Clarke, an English lady living in Paris at the time, was astounded at the power and influence of the most fashionable couturiers and horrified by their arrogance.

> The Raphael of his trade gave himself the airs of a distinguished artist; he received his clients with vulgar condescension, and they, no matter what their rank, submitted to his insolence in the hope that he would enable them to outshine their rivals. Ambassadors' wives and grand ladies would go to take tea with the fellow and dispute the honour of filling his cup or putting sugar in it. When there was going to be a ball, ladies would go down on their knees to him to make them beautiful. Queens and Empresses are not such favourite clients with him as the wives of millionaires or popular

actresses, and his prices are as uniformly high as his manners are superior.

The most successful courtesans, like the most successful couturiers, could charge what they liked in the certain knowledge that cupidity would triumph over common sense. But it would never have occurred to Margarethe to be either condescending or insolent to the succession of gallants who came knocking on the door of number 3 rue Balzac, flowers in hand and trinkets in pocket. Instead she had a talent for making each man who called feel that he was the one person in the world she wanted to see. Those who visited her out of curiosity or because it was the fashionable thing to do soon found themselves returning a second and a third time for the sheer pleasure of her company. Certainly she knew how to flatter and fascinate a man but she also knew how to entertain him, how to make him laugh, and how to make even her most tongue-tied admirer feel like a king. The general consensus of opinion among the young bloods of Paris was that 'on s'amuse vachement bien chez Mata Hari'. Those who were not granted the ultimate prize seemed content just to worship at her feet.

But her instant stardom, however much appreciated by her male admirers, did nothing to endear Margarethe to those it threatened to eclipse. Liane de Pougy, approaching the end of her reign as queen of the *demi-monde* but still mistress of the barbed compliment and the veiled insult, did not bother to disguise her feelings towards Mata Hari, dismissing her as 'coarse, inelegant, very aggressive and certainly no friend of mine. Her eyes may be beautiful, but they have a mean and shifty look in them and her expression is altogether hard and vulgar. Her voice is too loud, she dresses badly and when she walks she strides out in a most unfeminine way'.

Colette, the novelist and journalist whose outrageous exploits, both in private and in public, would themselves scandalise fashionable Paris in years to come, was for once not so outspoken. But she made it very clear that she was not impressed by Margarethe's style.

> She didn't really dance at all, but she knew how to un-dress, she had a long, dark, slender body and she moved in a very effective way.

She recalled how, at a garden party given by some friends, she had been confronted by:

> ... a tall, awkward looking woman dressed in a tailored outfit of large black and white checks, yellow shoes, a white veil with a loud pattern and most unfortunate hat. Luckily she told me her name, for I wouldn't have re-cognised this apparition as the pseudo-hindu.

Her rivals' collective dislike of Margarethe had nothing to do with her being a foreigner — three of the greatest cour-tesans of the Belle Epoque, Caroline Otero, Lina Cavalieri and Cléo de Mérode, were respectively Spanish, Italian and Belgian. Rather it was her reluctance to join their club, play the game by their rules and take her place in their pecking order that turned them against her. But if they sought to humiliate her by labelling her coarse and vulgar, they sadly underestimated her allure. Her dress-sense, or lack of it, might well have had the exquisitely elegant Cléo clasping her hand over her eyes in horror, and her beauty might not have matched that of 'La Belle Otero' for classical perfection, but her sultry looks and slow, sensual smiles were potent enough to bring men flocking to her side. Besides, she was enjoying herself too much to pay any attention to their remarks. Even as a child she had never joined in the whispered giggling of her contemporaries — she had never had any close female friends and did not miss their friendship now.

While the disgruntled *demi-mondaines* muttered amongst themselves about the newcomer, the society hostesses found themselves in something of a cleft stick. Although they had no one to blame but themselves for having introduced the glamorous oriental dancer into Paris society, it had been none of their design that she should then move in on their husbands. But to snub her openly would be to admit to undignified doubts about their husbands' fidelity and invite the smug commiserations of their more confident fellows. Their husbands, too, would be slow to forgive any attempt to deprive them of their new plaything. All they could do was put a brave face on it and trust that Mata Hari would prove to be one of the more fleeting of Paris fashions. In the meantime the charade had to continue and invitations to perform still flooded in to the rue Balzac.

But Margarethe had no intention of being a fleeting fashion. In the course of 1905 she accepted more than thirty-five public engagements in addition to her countless private performances. She appeared on the stage of the Olympia Theatre music-hall to her widest audience yet for the startling sum of 10,000 francs. She danced at the Trocadéro Theatre and at the *Folies Bergère*, in the private theatre of the Comtesse de Tredern, in the home of the Princess Murat and several times at the invitation of Henri de Rothschild.

As she reached and passed each step in her ladder of ambition, her ultimate goal was similarly advanced. She had dreamed of a rich lover; she now had many, therefore she could afford to be selective. Henceforth she need only favour the richest, the most aristocratic, the most good-looking or, best of all, those with the highest military rank and the most dazzling uniform. She had dreamed of riches; her purse was overflowing, therefore she could spend as much as she liked in the comfortable knowledge that there would always be more where the last lot came from. Her extravagant tastes, which had so infuriated Rudolph, could now be indulged to the full. She spent money like water, on dresses, hats, shoes (she is reported at one time to have owned more than five hundred pairs), jewels, furs, furniture and ornaments. She ran up colossal bills with dressmakers and tradesmen, assuring them airily that they would be paid soon enough. She had sought fame and achieved notoriety.

From having been a means to an end Margarethe's dancing now seemed to be an end in itself and she had great plans for her future career. When reviewers admitted to 'never having seen such dancing before' she took this to mean not that her interpretations were extraordinary but that they were sublime. Maybe it was time to explore the possibilities of cities other than Paris. She had heard wonderful things about Berlin, Vienna and Rome although she thought on the whole it would be best to avoid Amsterdam.

But if Margarethe's thoughts were on the future, she took good care to keep one eye at least firmly on the present. It was time for a few more fantasies to keep Paris talking about her. In September she demurely revealed to a gossip-hungry journalist that she was about to give up her career as a dancer, that she was engaged to marry one Prince

Troubetskoi and they would leave soon after the wedding for Tibet where they would go into retreat in a lamasery. The bombshell had exactly the desired effect. To her admirers' earnest entreaties for the honour of a few hours in her company were now added their impassioned pleas for her not to desert them — without her presence Paris would be a mere shell.

Margarethe had learned from her experience with Emile Guimet that, when planning a new venture, it paid to have the advice and support of an expert. If she was on the threshold of an international dancing career, she would need not just an agent, but the very best agent. Hovering on the fringes of her adoring entourage was a gentle, unassuming lawyer by the name of Edouard Clunet. Although he did not aspire to the select company of her lovers, Clunet would prove himself to be her most faithful friend in times to come. Margarethe was touched by his devotion and found his undemanding company a refreshing change from that of her more assertive swains. When she mentioned to him her idea of finding an agent to handle her affairs Clunet advised her to go straight to the top. On his recommendation she therefore approached the man who was acknowledged to be the premier impresario and theatrical agent of pre-war Europe.

Gabriel Astruc, a close friend of Marcel Proust, had arranged the Parisian concert debuts of the Polish pianist and harpsichordist Wanda Landowska in 1903 and the young Artur Rubinstein in 1904 and would later be responsible for similarly introducing the incomparable operatic bass Feodor Chaliapin as well as Diaghilev's Ballet Russe. Together with Sergei Diaghilev he would be instrumental in converting Paris to an appreciation of classical ballet, an art form that had never been taken seriously by the French.

Since he was aware of this incomprehension he rightly judged that the French were not yet ready for the complexities of an Isadora Duncan, and had therefore declined to represent the American. But Mata Hari made no such intellectual demands on her audiences and had already proved that she could bring in the crowds; since Astruc was in the business of filling theatres he was happy to accept her as a client. He would remain her agent and long-suffering counsellor for the next ten years.

Astruc agreed that there was no reason why she should not achieve as great a success abroad as she had in France. He may even have been aware, as she undoubtedly was not, that her days as the toast of Paris were almost certainly numbered. But he had contacts throughout Europe and in January 1906 he signed her up for a two-week engagement at the Central Kursaal in Madrid. Professionally this first venture outside France was an anticlimax. As a gesture towards her new image as a serious dancer Margarethe decided to resurrect her body-stocking, much to the disappointment of her Spanish audience. Where was the 'glorious nudity' they had heard so much about? Her reception was enthusiastic but far from rapturous. Of far more significance, although she did not realise it at the time, was an introduction given to her by her devoted Edouard Clunet. Anxious that the object of his worship should not be lonely in a strange city he had suggested that she make herself known to his good friend Jules Cambon, the French Ambassador to Madrid. Unlike Clunet, Cambon not only aspired to, but achieved membership of that select but growing circle of lovers. But, like Clunet, Cambon, a diplomat of rare vision and integrity, would also prove a valuable and patient friend.

His company certainly did much to lessen the blow dealt to Margarethe's pride by her disappointing reception, but she did not have time to dwell on either. Astruc sent news of her next engagement. Here was vindication indeed of her aspirations — she was to dance at the Monte Carlo Opéra in none other than the ballet scene of Massenet's opera *Le Roi de Lahore*. Gulping a little at the prospect of appearing for the first time before an audience of cultured music-lovers, who were bound to be more critical than the sensation-lovers of the salons and music-halls, Margarethe headed for Monte Carlo.

Her performance in the ballet scene was an unqualified success. Jules Massenet himself was in the audience, and professed himself entranced. The crueller gossips might cast aspersions on the nature of Mata Hari's effect on such a celebrated libertine, but his approval could only enhance her reputation.

Though she could not help enjoying his admiration, this new success made Margarethe feel distinctly and unexpectedly uncomfortable. From the moment she had first stepped nervously into the public eye, before her debut at the Musée Guimet, she had been haunted by the constant fear that one day her bluff would be called, her fantasies exposed and her myth exploded. She had got away with it so far because she had always managed to stay one step ahead of her critics and remain firmly in control of her career. She had understood her audiences and they had understood her; the unspoken agreement between them that no questions would be asked and no great demands made on either side had been a comfortable conspiracy designed to massage the self-esteem of all those involved. But the world of classical ballet and grand opera took itself very seriously. The cultural elite would be even less willing to tolerate an imposter than would the social elite, and the only reward on offer seemed to be an opportunity to work yourself into the ground. She had put every ounce of her energy into the preparation of her Monte Carlo debut and this time she had survived. But how long would it be before they saw through her? And was she really prepared to make the enormous effort and commitment necessary to maintain her foothold on this exalted but precarious tightrope?

The answer to this last crucial question was 'no'. As soon as the last performance of *Le Roi de Lahore* was over, she turned tail and fled, cursing the ambition that had driven her to seek greater things. But pride would not allow her to return directly to Paris. Word of her triumph in Monte Carlo would have preceded her and she would have no answers for those who wondered at her premature return. In the knowledge that she had to get away while her reputation was intact, and on the pretext that she was exploring new avenues for her talents, Margarethe left France abruptly and arrived in Berlin in February 1906.

It did not take her long to discover that, under the influence of the Kaiserin, Berlin was still very much on its best behaviour. Brave the artist who stepped over the bounds of propriety as laid down by Her Imperial Highness and socially suicidal the hostess who dared patronise a performer of doubtful morals, however talented, as Isadora Duncan had lately discovered to her cost. The prominent members of Berlin society who formed the committee of the 'Association for the Support of the Dance School of Isadora Duncan' had been forced to withdraw that support when rumours had reached them of Isadora's 'improper relationship' with the stage designer and director, Gordon Craig.

lsadora had been prepared to compromise for the sake of her beloved school to the extent that she appointed her sister Elizabeth as Principal in her place, thus restoring the school's respectability in the eyes of society. But she had not been prepared to give up Gordon Craig. Instead, according to the pianist Victor Seroff, she preferred to argue her case publicly. During a lecture on 'dance as an art of liberation', given in the Berlin Philharmonic Hall:

> ... she became so carried away by her enthusiasm and the eloquence of her delivery that she ventured into her theories about the rights of a woman to love and bear children as she pleased. Her declaration ... provoked a scandal rather than an appreciative reaction. Some of the audience hissed, others threw onto the stage whatever they could lay their hands on in the theatre, and half of those present left the hall.

By the time Margarethe arrived, lsadora had left Berlin and, ironically, was living in a little village on the coast of Holland awaiting the birth of her child by Gordon Craig. So once again Margarethe found herself unwittingly shadowing the footsteps of the dancer whose example had prompted her own choice of career. But if Isadora's example had paved the way to Margarethe's success in Paris, in Berlin it had quite the opposite effect. In fact the prospects were so unfavourable that she seriously considered packing her bags and moving on. Then a chance meeting changed her mind.

The first thing that caught her eye was, inevitably, the uniform: broad epaulettes with heavy dangling fringes, rows of shiny buttons and a positively Ruritanian profusion of gold braid. A second look showed her that the man inside all this was tall, blond and very nearly as handsome as his attire. Like a philatelist unexpectedly spotting a Penny Black or a trophy hunter coming face to face with a Marco Polo sheep, Margarethe's reaction to this apparition was spontaneous and predictable. This one would be the pride of her collection — it must not be allowed to get away.

It was easy to arrange an introduction. With a stiff bow and an exemplary clicking of the heels, Lieutenant Alfred Kiepert of the Westphalian Hussars professed himself delighted to make the acquaintance of the beautiful Mata Hari. As it happened Kiepert was more than happy to be caught. The eldest son of a wealthy landowner from Wuppertal, possessed of a large private fortune and married to a renowned beauty who was also a considerable bore, the handsome Lieutenant was finding life with no problems just a little dull. Margarethe, at her most seductive, promised to provide him with all the excitement he could want. Judging the situation with a practised eye, she led him a skilful and tantalising dance before agreeing to become his mistress. By the end of February Kiepert had installed her in a sumptuous apartment in the Nachodstrasse.

The arrangement suited them both perfectly. Kiepert proved to be a generous if somewhat aggressive lover, and Margarethe brought him just the spice and excitement he was looking for. Since his wife and family were living in the country not far from Berlin, Kiepert had other calls on his time, but this only served to enhance their relationship. He was never around long enough for the excitement to lose its edge and she was in no danger of being suffocated by his demands. Happy to revert for a while to her original plan of living in luxury at someone else's expense, Margarethe could enjoy a measure of independence without the constant pressure of a career to sustain. She perfected her German, continued to indulge her passion for spending money and tantalised her other admirers with reminiscences of her performances and glimpses into her mysterious past. There might come a time when Berlin would be ready for her to dance for them, so there was no harm in whetting their appetites.

Then, unexpectedly, her real background caught up with her. A letter arrived from Rudolph's lawyers in Holland stating that their client wanted a divorce. The shock was so sudden that it crashed right through Margarethe's carefully constructed defences. For the first time in three years she was forced to confront all the misery and grief that she thought she had buried beyond recall. It was harrowing to discover that even seven years after Norman's death and three years after her separation from Jeanne-Louise, the pain of thinking about her children could still bring her sobbing to her knees.

But the same strength that had taken her to Paris in the first place lifted her to her feet again now. She was still hoping that one day she would be in a position to fight Rudolph for custody of Jeanne-Louise, and had no intention of meekly surrendering her claim to the child. Aware of the requirement under Dutch law that both parties give their consent to a divorce, she wrote immediately to the lawyers announcing her refusal to co-operate.

But Rudolph had a card, or rather a photograph, up his sleeve. He had somehow got hold of a picture of Margarethe posing in the nude, taken during one of her private performances in Paris; now he threatened to produce it in court as evidence of how unfit she was to be a mother. Jeanne-

Louise was by now nearly eight years old — quite old enough to be aware of and affected by the scandal that would inevitably ensue should the case be made public.

To Margarethe's way of thinking, compassion and self-denial were as dangerous as deep emotion — all three had too much power to hurt her. On only two occasions in her life would she voluntarily expose herself to their treacherous sting. This was one such occasion. She was determined not to expose Jeanne-Louise to that scandal. There was little comfort in the knowledge that Rudolph, for all his faults, would always protect and cherish his daughter; there was no comfort at all in the bitter reflection that Jeanne-Louise would never even know of her agony. She agreed to Rudolph's request without further protest. The divorce was granted in Amsterdam in April 1906 and Rudolph was given custody of the child.

This unceremonious jerk out of an agreeable present into the tortured past left Margarethe drained. She became so withdrawn and pensive that Kiepert found himself starting to question his investment. But his doubts acted like salt on the raw wound of her pride and when she forced herself out of her melancholy reverie it was as much to prove to herself that she was still a dazzling success as it was to keep him by her side. Determinedly masking her misery she launched into feverish activity. Not a party was thrown but she was there on Kiepert's arm, not an exhibition was mounted, lecture delivered or show staged without the beautiful Mata Hari in attendance. She even insisted on accompanying Kiepert on a trip to view the military manoeuvres in Silesia, blissfully unaware of the attention that would one day be focussed on what to her was just another social event. But though her spirits seemed to recover, there was an elusive difference in her manner: her famous smile was now rarely seen and the sparkle in her eyes had turned into something more like a glitter. She seemed to have lost the capacity for joy that had contributed so much to her success and, try as she might, she never really managed to recapture it.

Margarethe stayed in Berlin until September. When a letter arrived from Astruc with news of an engagement to dance in Vienna, in a performance of her own choosing, *not* a ballet or a grand opera, she was ready to move on. She explained to Kiepert that in her passion for him she had been neglecting her career and that she could not keep her adoring public waiting any longer. Kissing him a fond farewell and promising to return as soon as they would let her go, she left for Vienna.

The capital of the Austro-Hungarian Empire was at the height of its glory, as cosmopolitan and glittering as Paris and just as hedonistic. Mata Hari was assured of a rapturous welcome. Whether as a ploy to keep them talking or just because she no longer cared very much one way or the other, she danced without the famous body-stocking at the Salle d'Art and then with it at the Apollo Theatre. The heated arguments among the young bloods of the city as to which was the more erotic were taken up by the press. The Viennese newspapers vied with each other to print the juiciest stories about the dancer and, like their French counterparts before them, got into a terrible muddle about her origins. They described her variously as Dutch, Javanese, Balinese and Indian; she was 'slender and tall with the flexible grace of a wild animal', 'a striking beauty with the tender face of a young girl', 'a bizarre goddess, dark as the night', and, a rumour that she would one day have cause to regret most bitterly not having denied, she counted no less a personage than the German Crown Prince among her lovers.

But the press were not wholly, or even mainly, to blame for the extraordinary tales that circulated about her. December 1906 saw the publication in Amsterdam of a book entitled *The Life of Mata Hari — the Biography of my Daughter* by Adam Zelle. Margarethe herself never believed that it was really written by her father. She was probably right when she said: 'Two writers went to visit my father because I was famous. He was short of money and they offered him a large sum to put his name to the book and provide them with some photographs of me, and then they went away and wrote this horrible book'. Certainly, if it had been written by Adam, it would have revealed in him an ability to fantasise that would have done credit to Margarethe herself, for its pages were peppered with more titled ancestors and more romantic nonsense than even she had been able to concoct. But more than anything else it was the fact that the book portrayed her as seven years older than she really was that made her describe it as 'horrible'. Infuriated, she wrote to a prominent lawyer in Amsterdam asking if she should sue the publishers. 'He told me it would do no good to sue them. He said I should do nothing about it as I would only make more trouble for myself.' But if she was enraged by the slight on her age, she must have appreciated the extra publicity and even been able to laugh at the way its nonsensical contents added to the general confusion surrounding the mysterious Mata Hari.

All this while Margarethe was still playing to packed houses in Vienna. But in spite of the bright lights and adoring crowds she was restless and unhappy. In January 1907 she wrote to Astruc that she was tired and in need of a complete break. She was going on a trip to Egypt to find some peace of mind amongst the oriental treasures of the past. There was nothing for her in Egypt; no lovers, no fame — even the treasures were a disappointment. The only thing she discovered during her two-month trip was how much she hated being on her own and she scurried thankfully back to her lover in Berlin. But Kiepert's passion for his moody and extravagant mistress had been cooling even before she left and she was not so blind as to misinterpret the lack of warmth in his welcome nor so abject as to wish to stay where she so obviously was not wanted.

Resolutely squaring her shoulders she comforted herself with the thought that she still had her looks, her figure and her youth (after all the Viennese papers had said she looked like a young girl, even if she was thirty-one years old). She had only ever intended Berlin to be an interlude; now it was time to resume her career. When she came to think of it, why on earth had her success in Monte Carlo made her so nervous? Had not Jules Massenet himself described her as a 'charming artiste'? Well now she believed him. And here was the perfect opportunity for her to prove it. It had just been announced that Gabriel Astruc was to stage the first performance of Richard Strauss's new opera. If ever a part had been designed with her in mind it was the 'Dream Dance' in *Salome*. Suddenly she could not wait to get back to Paris. She tossed off a quick note to Astruc telling him she was on her way, would he please contact Strauss directly suggesting her for the role, and hugging herself with glee at the thought of the welcome awaiting her, she took the next train back to the city she now thought of as home.

Margarethe installed herself in style at the Hotel Meurice and announced that she had prepared several new and spectacular dances during her absence which she was now ready to present to the public. But she had been away for nearly eighteen months and Paris had not waited for her. New names and new faces had taken over: Colette was revealing all (or at least more than Margarethe had ever dared to reveal) on the stage of the Trocadéro Theatre; the exotic Moroccan dances of Sulamith Raha were pulling in the crowds at the Olympia Music Hall; Mata Hari was yesterday's news. Astruc was able to secure occasional engagements for her but they were less prestigious than she had come to expect and certainly not remunerative enough to keep her in her chosen style. The biggest blow was that Richard Strauss had not even bothered to respond to Astruc's suggestion that she might dance in his *Salome*.

But if invitations to dance were hard to come by, the same was not true of lovers. By 1908 the Belle Epoque was in its death throes. A new generation of artists, inspired by Braque and Picasso, were reacting against the naturalistic impressionism of Monet, Degas, Pissarro, and Renoir by developing the stark, almost geometrical style that would be derisively labelled Cubism. The musical Impressionists too, Debussy, Ravel, Massenet and Fauré, would soon find their lyrical romanticism challenged by the innovatory styles of Stravinsky, Schoenberg, Milhaud and Poulenc. The glorious era which had produced such a proliferation of talent and had kept Paris in a fever of social, artistic and musical excitement since the 1880s was in swift decline, and would finally end, as so much else would end, in the abyss of 1914. Its last few years were tinged with a hysteria that suggested it had been given a glimpse of the horrors to come. The high-priests of the social world, those privileged members of the *classe des loisirs* to whose jaded appetites Margarethe owed her fame, were desperately sucking the few remaining drops of pleasure from a barrel that was almost dry. As the last generation of that truly leisured elite who had no need to work for a living, they were a species on the point of extinction. They dined and danced and squandered fortunes at gaming tables; their high-pitched, brittle laughter tinkled around their elegant yachts on the Côte d'Azur; they bought racehorses and watched them run at Longchamps and Auteuil, and the more adventurous bought cars and roared through the streets of Paris terrorising pedestrians and horses alike. They were echoing Margarethe's own long-held credo that 'life was for parties, for fun and flirtation and pleasure' and for the duration of what she regarded as a pause in her career she was happy to join them.

Margarethe had come a long way in the three years since her debut at the Musée Guimet. The 'unfortunate hats' had long since been discarded in favour of chic creations in impeccable taste, the 'masculine stride' had become the most feminine of glides and the ardour of her admirers was heightened by the startling contrast between this model of fashionable elegance and very sexy lady they knew to be lurking inside. There seemed no limit to what they were prepared to pay for her favours and none was ever heard to complain that she did not give them good value for their money.

Wealth and independence soon restored Margarethe's morale, but it would have been a sturdy soul indeed who could remain impervious to so much flattery and adoration. She had stubbornly refused to let Strauss's rebuff upset her and persisted in her claim that she was just 'resting' from her career. It was the only line she could take - the alternative was to admit that she had failed, not only as a mother but also as a dancer, and that was to admit defeat. So she listened to the honeyed words that were whispered in her ear by a hundred different voices on a hundred different nights; she was adorable, bewitching, an unparalleled beauty, and the world was at her feet. When Astruc approached her in January 1910 with the offer of another engagement at the Monte Carlo Opera she knew that they had spoken the truth.

She was to dance the role of Cleopatra in *Antar*, a play by the Algerian poet Chekri-Gavem, set to the music of Rimsky-Korsakov, under the direction of Monsieur Antoine. The production was a triumphant success; the audience greeted Mata Hari 's return to the stage with delight, and even the sternest of critics could find nothing more damning to say than that the famous dancer had put on a bit of weight since her last appearance in Monte Carlo. Everyone agreed that her dancing was as beguiling and graceful as ever. Everyone, that is, except Monsieur Antoine.

To understand the impact of Mata Hari's performances it is necessary to understand also the contemporary attitudes to dance. A distinguished music critic, commenting on a performance given by Isadora Duncan, summed them up neatly: 'Until she appeared and gave the dance a new form and life, helping us to realise that the dance can be an art, it had no validity other than as a mere diversion. No one who considered himself an intellectual gave the dance as it was serious consideration. It either appeared in the guise of social dancing and, therefore, could not be pronounced an art, or it represented ballet dancing — a diversion for the less intelligent-minded and for old gentlemen known as balletomanes.' And while there are those who consider it blasphemy to mention lsadora Duncan and Mata Hari in the same breath, certainly, to judge by contemporary accounts, the performances of the two dancers had much in common, particularly in terms of style. One critic, writing of Isadora, described how:

> … she does not undertake the terpsichorean art in the ordinary way, but illustrates poems or poetic ideals to music with what seem to be perfectly artless and natural dance movements … Not a single routine step is taken and the whole dance seems to be like something that might have happened in ancient Greece … She has been analysing and memorizing the steps and attitudes of the classic nymphs of antique art.

Isadora had drawn on the myths and legends of Greek mythology for her inspiration just as Margarethe had drawn on those of the Hindus: exchange Greece for India, or sometimes Java, and the critic could just as well have been writing about Mata Hari.

To the modern eye, photographs of the 'Isadorables' (as Miss Duncan called her students) prancing through the undergrowth in costumes taken from the Greek myths are ridiculous to the point of embarrassment. Equally, were Mata Hari to present her 'demonstration of Eastern dances' to a modern audience she would most probably be booed off the stage. With the benefit of hindsight it is easy to differentiate between the two dancers and to know which has had the greater influence on the subsequent development of their art. But that is not to denigrate the judgement of those who acclaimed Mata Hari as 'the uncontested Queen of the dances of yore'. What she lacked in talent she more than made up for in presentation; where Isadora believed her dancing 'more appropriate for an audience of artists and intellectuals than for the general public' and had 'no desire to draw the audience's attention to her personality', Mata Hari went to great lengths to woo the general public and draw the maximum possible attention to herself. It is hardly surprising therefore, in view of what the public could only interpret as lsadora's arrogance, that while she did win the acclaim of artists and intellectuals, Mata Hari enjoyed the greater popular success.

As an artist and, if not an intellectual, at least a professional, Monsieur Antoine was not impressed by Mata Hari 's performance in *Antar*. During one of the rehearsals he threw his script to the floor and exclaimed, within her hearing, 'that girl dances like a clodhopper'. Making no allowances for what might well have been temperamental hyperbole, Margarethe took immediate umbrage. From that moment on she made his life a misery: she was late for rehearsals, argued with his every instruction and antagonised everyone involved in the production.

But Monsieur Antoine had the last laugh. When *Antar* finished its run in Monte Carlo he took the production to Paris where it would play in his own theatre on the boulevard Strasbourg. On no account would he take Mata Hari. She waved her contract at him; he turned his back. She threatened to sue him for damages and breach of contract; he told her to go ahead. The press gleefully took up the story and the whole affair became the subject of heated public debate with her admirers up in arms to defend her against Antoine's charges and her critics sagely affirming that the director had only stated what they had always known. But where once upon a time Margarethe might have shrugged the whole thing off on the basis that any publicity is good publicity, this time she had been touched on the raw. Leaving instructions with her lawyers that they were to take the matter to court, she crept away to lick her wounds.

The six months she had spent with Kiepert in Berlin had been her longest commitment to any relationship since her marriage. As long as her career was going smoothly she preferred her independence; in Paris it had suited her to distribute her favours more or less evenly among her various lovers rather than concentrate on just one or two. But now her confidence was threatened and she desperately needed reassurance. For once money and fame were not enough — she needed a friend.

Felix Rousseau was, needless to say, very rich. A banker in his early forties and the most persistent of all her Parisian admirers, he had stood out from the crowd on two counts — he was one of the few who actually worked, very successfully, for his own living, and he had been pleading with Margarethe for months to accept his exclusive patronage. He must have been very much in love with her for when she suddenly agreed to this suggestion he accepted her change of heart without question although he must have been aware of the reasons behind it. He even consented, at vast expense and no small personal inconvenience, to find her a house in the country where she could get right away from Paris, Monte Carlo, theatres, indeed anything that could remind her of the *Antar* affair. In fact he went one better and installed her in the delightful little Chateau de la Dorée in the village of Esvres near Tours.

THE END OF AN ERA

Margarethe's urban admirers would scarcely have recognised the solitary woman strolling in the formal gardens that lay like a lace collar round the château. They would have found it hard to reconcile the slightly dishevelled figure, sunbonnet in hand, who stooped over the rosemary bushes to inhale their fragrance, or gathered armfuls of the dusty blue lavender growing in such profusion beyond the garden walls, with the sophisticated *femme du monde* they had known in Paris.

Although there was an element of play-acting in this guise, for once Margarethe really did not want to be recognised. The catastrophy that she had been dreading for years had finally overtaken her: Monsieur Antoine had lifted a corner of her veil and revealed the fundamental flaw at the heart of her masquerade. Margarethe was in retreat.

If she had been prepared to confront the implications of the incident, she might have been encouraged to brazen it out. It was, after all, no crime to fantasise, or even to masquerade. But the lashings of Monsieur Antoine's scorn had reminded her forcibly of the humiliation heaped on her by Rudolph years ago in Amsterdam. Her attempt to turn the tables on Rudolph had been a dismal failure; she had armed herself with the weapons she had identified as vital to an

effective counter-attack — fame, fortune, influential connections — but she had still lost Jeanne-Louise. If those
weapons had failed against Rudolph, they would surely be
equally impotent against Monsieur Antoine. They were
certainly not likely to impress those of her rivals and detractors in Paris who were even now chortling with malicious
glee at her discomfiture. Like a crab with a broken claw, she
felt exposed and vulnerable — the Château de la Dorée was
a convenient cleft in the rocks, and she had scuttled there to
hide.

For the first few months of her sojourn in the Touraine
Margarethe was barely aware of her surroundings. The spell
of unaccustomed solitude and tranquillity induced a le-
thargy she found hard to shake off. For as long as she could
remember, all her energies had been directed into the quest
for romance and excitement — she had spent ten years in
pursuit of gratification for her senses. Now she found herself
in no hurry to resume the chase; she was content just to let
things drift.

As Margarethe's panic subsided and her bruises healed
she found to her surprise that a life without parties, shops or
adoring crowds had a charm all of its own. Felix Rousseau
had been so overjoyed at having his idol to himself that he
had spared no effort to provide her with everything she
could possibly want or need. He had filled the house with
flowers, engaged a full complement of servants to wait on
her and, anxious that she should not be bored when he was
away in Paris, had bought her a horse so that she would be
free to explore her surroundings. He still had his bank to run
and could only get down to Esvres at weekends, but Margarethe did not miss him. Although the Touraine could hardly
have been further removed from Java, she found something

of the same pleasure in the peaceful French countryside as she had experienced amidst the tropical luxuriance of that remote island. Loosing her long black hair from its restraining pins, and exchanging her stylish gowns for simple cotton dresses she wandered through the grounds of the château and roamed the surrounding woods and fields in dreamy contentment. As the *châtelaine* of la Dorée she could go where she pleased, dress as she liked and do whatever she wanted — there was not a soul to object, disapprove or even comment.

But as summer turned into autumn, Margarethe found herself infected by the *tristesse* of the season. She became pensive and melancholy, and accompanied her new mood with suitably grandiloquent gestures. Her lazy strolls in the sunlight became headlong gallops across the windswept fields, followed by hours brooding in a room lit only by the flicker of a log fire. Contemplating her restless existence it occurred to her that, in other circumstances, she might have asked nothing more of life than to be able to raise a scatter of rosy-cheeked children in this scented sunshine. If only Jeanne-Louise could have been here with her, how she would have loved the gardens and the vineyards, the dogs and the horses. The gathering gloom of the imminent winter suddenly seemed to be haunted by spirits from the past and all the emotions she had denied, all the grief and misery she had so determinedly ignored, now seemed to be pleading for her attention, reaching out from the shadows with pale grasping fingers, trying to draw her down into their hell. Tormented by regrets and longings, Margarethe found the solitude, once so refreshing, now frightening in its intensity. The contrast between what was and what might have been grew more obtrusive as the winter progressed. The novelty of her rural idyll had worn off and it was hard to sustain her enthusiasm for a role played before an audience consisting only of polite, poker-faced servants. She needed company to keep the ghosts at bay and to rescue her from the mire of self-pity. Rousseau's frequent and sometimes prolonged absence, so convenient to start with, now seemed like neglect, if not desertion.

She had been in Esvres for more than a year when she decided she could bear it no longer. A timely letter from her lawyer saying that the courts had at last decided in her favour over the *Antar* affair and had instructed Monsieur Antoine to pay her damages of three thousand francs set the seal on her decision. As he stepped off the train from Paris one Friday evening in the spring of 1911, the long-suffering Rousseau was greeted with the announcement that his mistress was bored in the country and wanted to return to Paris.

Poor Felix — he was too generous and too much in love — responded immediately to this new whim by providing Margarethe with a stylish and very comfortable house in the smart Parisian suburb of Neuilly-sur-Seine. He was on the verge of a spectacular and comprehensive financial collapse and the purchase of 11 rue Windsor was his last extravagant gesture. His wife would later blame Margarethe for his downfall, but it was really just as much his fault as hers. His business had been suffering seriously from neglect during the past eighteen months and the establishment of his adored Mata Hari in grand style at the Château de la Dorée had been a phenomenally expensive undertaking. He had been able to refuse her nothing — he had offered her the world and she had very nearly taken it.

By the time she was established in her new home, Margarethe had shaken off the ghosts, put the past firmly behind her with a vow never to let it intrude again, and was once more busily concentrating on herself. When Felix took his leave of her with tears in his eyes she was content to let him go. His company would only be a constant reminder of the shameful weakness that had made her run away and of the period of painful introspection that had followed her flight. That weakness too was a thing of the past. Her reputation and her self-confidence had been restored by the court's decision in her favour, her strength was restored and she had no more need of him. She was once more back where she belonged.

Four years before, when she had returned to Paris from Berlin in 1907, she had discovered that time did not stand still while she was away. Faced with the same situation in 1911 the effect of this phenomenon on her wardrobe was of more immediate concern than the effect it might have on her career. Horror of horrors, all her clothes were out of date. Her hats, her dresses, her shoes, all would have to be re-placed — it was unthinkable that the famous Mata Hari should appear in last year's fashions. Felix had settled a generous sum on her before his crash and with all her old zest for spending money, she plunged into a buying spree. If the couturiers rubbed their hands with glee as they saw her coming, their underlings sighed resignedly; as one dressmaker would later recall, 'I made several outfits for Madame Mata Hari and she was one of my least favourite customers, because she always insisted on being the centre of attention and demanded that all the seamstresses should concentrate on her'.

Not until she was satisfied with her appearance did Margarethe start to consider tomorrow. Then, ostrich feathers bobbing and lace parasol dangling from elegantly-gloved wrist, she set off to discover what had happened in the city since she had been away. She soon had the answer — Diaghilev had happened. Multi-talented and larger than life, impresario, promoter, presenter and self-appointed spokesman for all the arts, Sergei Diaghilev had launched an inspired and carefully planned attack on the cultural capital of Europe. The first prong of this attack had been an exhibition of Russian paintings which he had brought to Paris in 1906. In 1907 he had organized a series of concerts of Russian music and in 1908 he had introduced Mussorgsky's opera *Boris Godounov* with Feodor Chaliapin in the title role.

Each of these ventures had been more successful than the last and Diaghilev was encouraged to proceed with the most ambitious one yet: the one with which his name will always be most closely associated, the ballet. He had assembled a company of such explosive talent from both the St Petersburg and Moscow Ballets that a lesser mortal would have been unable to contain, let alone organise, them. The Diaghilev Ballet incorporated the dancing genius of Vaslav Nijinsky, Anna Pavlova and Tamara Karsavina, the choreographic brilliance of Michel Fokine, the costumes and designs of Leon Bakst and Alexandre Benois and the music of Glinka, Borodin, Mussorgsky and Rimsky-Korsakov. In 1909 he introduced this glittering ensemble to Paris.

The programme for their first performance does not now seem very revolutionary, but it too was carefully designed — Diaghilev had no intention of bewildering, antagonising or shocking his audience until they were ready for it. But *Le Pavillion d'Armide* by Tchérépnine, 'The Polovtsian Dances' from Borodin's *Prince Igor* and a suite of dances to an assortment of music under the title *Le Festin* provided spectacle enough for a largely uninitiated audience. In association with Gabriel Astruc, Diaghilev had decided that the old and unfashionable Théâtre du Châtelet was not quite up to the occasion.

> He [Diaghilev] redecorated and recarpeted the whole house, tearing out seats to make boxes and, with the enthusiastic help of Astruc, making the foyers and circle into a garden … Astruc even saw to it that his first-night audience was decorative, offering seats in the grand tier to the most beautiful actresses in Paris. Fifty-two accepted and he took the greatest care to alternate blondes and brunettes. A poster was designed by Serov and an illustrated brochure commissioned from a young poet-painter, Jean Cocteau.

In the words of Serge Grigoriev, Diaghilev's *regisseur*:

> When the performance was over, it was clear that the audience had enormously enjoyed it and were deeply impressed by it as a remarkable spectacle. On that night Diaghilev had been able in fact to show Paris, what had been so long forgotten, that ballet could be a truly wonderful art. That first night was undoubtedly a revelation to the Paris public, and marked a resurrection of the ballet in the world outside Russia.

Since she had been in Paris at the time Magarethe must have heard all about this 'revelation', and may even have attended a performance of the Diaghilev Ballet. But she had been away for much of the succeeding two years, two years during which the extraordinary Russian had masterminded a veritable revolution in the public's attitude towards dance. The success of his 1909 season had been followed by even greater triumphs in 1910 and now the Diaghilev Ballet was back in Paris for a third season which promised to put the first two in the shade.

The secret of Diaghilev's phenomenal success lay in his inspirational enthusiasm for ballet as a medium and his meticulous attention to detail. Under his expert guidance designers, choreographers, dancers, and very often composers too, worked closely together from the inception of each new production, and this harmony brought an added dimension of atmosphere and integrity to every performance. To an audience who, if they thought of them at all, imagined ballet dancers to be a little more than talented puppets and their art to be precise, sober and as dry as dust, Diaghilev's productions were indeed a revelation. When the curtain rose on the first performance of *Schéhérazade*, the opening bars of Rimsky-Korsakov's score were drowned in a burst of applause. The richness of the setting — vivid blues and greens against a brilliant orange backcloth — was matched and then surpassed by the breathtaking virtuosity of the dancers. All preconceptions and reservations were swept away; ballet had been brought down from its intellectual pedestal and revealed as emotional, exhilarating and eminently enjoyable.

The effects of this catharsis spread like wildfire; Margarethe returned from her sojourn in the country to find that suddenly everything in Paris had a Russian flavour and vivacity was the mood of the moment. Languor was outmoded, posturing was *passé* and mystery had lost its appeal. None of which boded too well for the employment prospects of an 'oriental dancer' no longer in the first flush of her youth and beauty, who had relied on just these qualities for her success.

Even Margarethe's previously sensational willingness to remove her clothes in public was no longer a passport to engagements — there was no shortage of younger, prettier and more talented girls who were quite happy to do that at any time. Margarethe was fully aware of this and was overheard to remark wryly that these days she would probably cause a sensation if she danced fully clothed. But as she gradually absorbed the full extent of the changes that had taken place during her absence, it became harder to smile. Her every attempt to stage a comeback was met with polite but distant regrets that there was no demand for the talents of Madame Mata Hari; maybe if she was to develop a new style …?

But Margarethe could not permit her confidence to falter. For now she had a new worry. With the bottomless well that had been Felix's pocket suddenly run dry, she was getting through the money he had given her at an alarming speed. Her extravagance had in no measure diminished with her changing circumstances and she was no more able to economise than fly. It was time to find another wealthy protector.

To any but the most critical eyes Margarethe was still a great beauty, and at thirty-five she could hardly have been described, even by her worst enemies, as anything more damning than 'approaching' middle age. But when she suddenly found that her services were no longer in demand either as a performer or, more seriously, as a courtesan, she was convinced that her looks had gone. As she peered anxiously into the mirror the question must have been ringing in her ears — when you no longer have your beauty, what will you have left? The answer was not reassuring.

Bravely reminding herself that she had conquered her emotions, had risen above the pain and was just taking the step to satisfy her curiosity, Margarethe chose this moment to try and get in touch with her daughter. She wrote a polite, even deferential letter to Rudolph pleading with him to let them meet. Jeanne-Louise was thirteen by now and Margarethe had had no news of her for more than six years. Had anyone suggested to her that she was clutching at straws in the face of a lonely future she would have laughed them to scorn. But her attempt was doomed to failure. Rudolph had remarried in 1907, had had another daughter (called Norma in memory of his adored Norman), and was on the point of separating from his second wife — neither his own experiences nor Margarethe's choice of career had in any way changed his feelings towards her. He was as determined as ever to prevent Jeanne-Louise from going anywhere near her mother. Margarethe received no reply to her letter. And although she can hardly have been surprised at her failure, the emotional trauma even of making the effort served to plunge her deeper into despondency.

A dispassionate observer would surely have been saddened to see the lady who had once been described as 'la femme la plus célèbre d'Europe' now reduced to haunting hotel lobbies in search of clients. If the cream of Parisian society no longer wanted to know her, at least there was no shortage of visitors to the capital to whom she was still the famous Mata Hari and who were happy to pay for the pleasure of her company.

Unfortunately they could not pay enough — six hundred francs a night came nowhere near to covering the costs she incurred daily in household expenses, servants' wages, stabling and food for her precious horses, not to mention her own personal expenditure on such necessities as clothes, jewellery and entertaining. In desperation she was reduced to frequenting *maisons de rendez-vouz*; the proprietors (or more frequently proprietresses) were usually willing to guarantee her one thousand francs a night in acknowledgment of the benefits to the establishment of her reputation. Margarethe's cloaked figure became a familiar sight on the doorstep of the notorious 14 rue Byron or, cruelly, 5 rue Gallilée just round the corner from the scene of her sensational debut, the Musée Guimet.

* * * * *

His triumphant association with Diaghilev had meanwhile lifted her old friend Gabriel Astruc to a state of great excitement. Possibly the success had gone to his head; maybe he imagined that it had given him the Midas touch and that no project with which he was connected could possibly fail. Or perhaps he was just trying to share some of his success with a client he had not seen for a while and whom he had heard had fallen on hard times. Whatever his reasons, in January 1912 he secured an engagement for Mata Hari to dance at none other than La Scala in Milan.

Margarethe's reaction to news of the engagement was one of stunned amazement. She could not have been more astonished had Bleriot invited her to fly his aeroplane. Since she would have had to have been superhuman to take such a prospect in her stride, and she was not superhuman, there were two other possible reactions. She could panic and run, or she could let the whole thing go completely to her head and tip her gently into a world of fantasy. Characteristically she adopted the latter course. Airily she told Astruc that she was happy to accept the engagement, although it was at such short notice that there was no question of her being able to rehearse much, let alone put in the strenuous practise her long months of leisure had made an imperative.

She was to portray Venus in a cameo role as part of a new ballet, *Bacchus and Gambrinus* with music by Marenco and, rather as a violinist may perform his own cadenza in someone else's concerto, she was to perform her 'Princess and the Magic Flower' in the fifth act of *Armida*, an opera by Gluck. The part of Venus required little more than one or two graceful poses which presented her with few problems — all she had to do was let down her hair and look seductive. As for her dance as the Princess, well, she had lost none of her skills in the creation of atmosphere; La Scala had a generous costume budget; and by the time the audience had sat through four and a half acts of the opera they would be ready to regard any diversion as a welcome relief.

Diaghilev's Ballet Russe had not yet reached Milan — indeed their debut there did not take place until 1920, and even then they would dance to half empty houses and indifferent audiences. Their reaction to Margarethe's performance, too, was lukewarm and the press, where they noticed her at all, were sparing in their praise. The *Corriere della Sera* admitted that her dancing showed 'strength of expression' but complained that it was 'mournfully slow'. But by now she was beyond caring — it was as if she felt her appearance in such an exalted arena had raised her above criticism, above any need even to acknowledge the existence of the press and their comments. One good thing did result from her performance at La Scala: among the audience that first night was a rich old roué whose blood was fired by her reputation. Thanks to him Margarethe at last had her opportunity to perform the dream-dance from Strauss's *Salome*, in a private performance in the courtyard of the old man's palazzo. With his extravagant praise ringing in her ears, she then floated back to Neuilly on the crest of a. wave of self-confidence.

If it struck Margarethe as at all strange that invitations to share her genius with the world did not come flooding through the door, she probably put it down to the well-known phenomenon that no genius was ever fully appreciated in her lifetime. And being a genius did not exempt her from having to pay the bills. Sighing at the persistence of her numerous creditors, she was struck by a brilliant idea. Why wait for some bashful entrepreneur to pluck up enough courage to approach her? A talent such as hers could flourish in any surroundings — even in the open air.

The London *Tatler* of 24th September 1913 carried a double-page spread of photographs urtder the heading 'Lady MacLeod Dances in the Light of the Moon to Her Friends'. The caption at the bottom of the page reads:

> Lady MacLeod, professionally known as 'Matu [sic] Hari' was brought up in India, the country which inspires so many of her dances. Recently her ladyship gave a wonderful *soirée d'art* at her magnificent hotel at Neuilly, near Paris, to which only a few special friends were invited. The dances which she performed were most suggestive of religious rites and love and passion, and were brilliantly executed.

The photographs show Margarethe still to be a very beautiful woman, and the caption confirms that she had not lost her power to captivate. She had hired the celebrated Indian musician, *Ustad* Inayat Khan, to accompany her on the sitar, and her costumes and appearance were more strongly Indian than ever. But her gentle expression, demure appearance and stylish poses suggest a new sadness. She was older, certainly, and probably not as supple or as sexy as she had been, but her only real fault was that she had become unfashionable. The reporter for the *Tatler* obviously found her performance a delight, but then he (or she) had probably never seen Mata Hari dance before and had no reason to dismiss her as outdated.

Whether she thought of this new venture as a money-spinner or was just indulging her own fancy it is hard to tell. Hard, too, to know what the *Ustad*, the neighbours, or the audience thought about this al fresco entertainment. Their reactions were probably a mixture of respect for the great star she had been and embarrassment at what they saw as her increasing eccentricity, with no doubt a measure of irritation on the part of the neighbours thrown in.

By a strange coincidence, one of those neighbours in Neuilly was none other than Isadora Duncan. The American dancer had bought an extraordinary studio in the suburb in 1908 but had never used it for more than a few days at a time. It had been built by the mural artist Henry Gervex who had insisted on the interior walls being three storeys high to accommodate his paintings. On a high balcony in one corner of this huge empty space Isadora had constructed a small, windowless apartment, the floor covered with black carpets, the walls draped entirely in black velvet sprinkled with gold-framed mirrors, for use as a living and sleeping area. The rest of the space served as her dance studio. Now she had decided to spend several months here with her two small children. Had the wind been blowing in the right direction, Isadora might have been able to hear the strains of incongruous music floating through the suburban air. The thread of coincidence which wove its way through the careers of the two dancers would be uncannily sustained right through bereavement to untimely death. Isadora's two children would both be drowned after a motor accident in 1913 when they were respectively seven and five years old, and Isadora herself would die in a car accident at the age of forty-nine. But there is no record of the two ever meeting.

Whatever the motives behind he latest bizarre development in her career, there can be little question that Margarethe's ever-precarious grip on reality was slipping fast. Her next move was to announce to Gabriel Astruc that she wanted to dance with the Diaghilev Ballet.

This time it was Astruc's turn to be astonished. The Diaghilev Ballet was at the height of its creative, artistic and popular success. The company was in constant demand and this year alone had engagements planned in Berlin, Dresden, Vienna, Budapest, Monte Carlo, Paris and London. Although Anna Pavlova had left to pursue an independent career, Tamara Karsavina had been joined by Mathilde Kchessinska and Ida Rubinstein as prima ballerinas, so it is unlikely they were looking for more dancers. Even if they had been, only the most highly trained and talented, the very cream of all that the Imperial Russian Ballet had to offer, would ever have been considered for a position with the Diaghilev company.

It was the company's reputation for liberalism and modernity that led Margarethe to believe she had something to offer them, the scandal and excitement that surrounded them, rather than their artistic aspirations, that drew her like a moth to a candle. The controversy that greeted their more startling productions, together with the faint breath of scandal that seemed to hang over the impresario and his brilliant protégé, Vaslav Nijinsky, must have been strongly reminiscent of her own early days as the sensation — and the toast — of Paris.

Nijinsky had by now severed his connections with the Mariinsky Ballet company of St Petersburg and committed himself entirely to Diaghilev. In fact he had been asked to resign from the Mariinsky for refusing to wear trunks over his tights in a performance of *Giselle*. A watching member of the Imperial family had been outraged at the sight of the dancer thus 'displaying his figure too distinctly' and Nijinsky was in disgrace — an incident almost certainly contrived by Diaghilev in order to get Nijinsky released from his contract.

Diaghilev, for his part, was relying increasingly on Nijinsky as choreographer as well as dancer - his innovative and highly controversial *L'Aprés-Midi d' un Faune*, was in the final run-up to its first performance. Michel Fokine was not unnaturally deeply hurt by being cast aside in so cavalier a manner, he had, after all, choreographed the spectacularly successful *Spectre de la Rose* as well as the Diaghilev classics, *Schéhérezade*, *Firebird*, and *Petrushka*. Tensions within the company were running high when Margarethe sent Astruc to negotiate a deal for her to dance with them. Diaghilev had more than enough to worry about without having to audition dancers he did not need and he brushed off Astruc's suggestion impatiently. Astruc, sweating slightly at thus being caught between two explosive temperaments, pressed him. As a favour to a.n old friend Diaghilev agreed that Margarethe could audition, but he himself was far too busy to see her — he told Astruc to make an appointment with his designer, Leon Bakst.

The first performance of *L'Aprés-Midi d'un Faune* was given at the Théâtre du Châtelet on 29th May 1912. It was greeted by a shriek of public outrage. *Le Figaro* quickly axed its ballet critic's article in praise of the work and thundered instead about the 'erotic bestiality' of 'those who make fun of us in the name of art'. The premiére was attended by Auguste Rodin, described by Diaghilev's manager Serge Grigoriev as 'very old and helpless, leaning for support on Diaghilev's arm'. But the sculptor was not too old for a verbal leap to the defence of his old friend in a long article for *Le Matin*. In fact both Nijinsky and Diaghilev were genuinely upset at having misjudged their public and unwittingly compromised their reputation, and future performances of the ballet were carefully modified.

But the scandal over *L'Aprés-Midl d'un Faune* only served to reinforce Margarethe's notion to join them, and she spread the word that she was about to make her debut as Diaghilev's new star — the only thing still to be arranged was the date of her first performance. The audition with Bakst left her with no such grand illusions. Arriving for the appointment she was outraged to find herself foisted off with Bakst instead of being greeted by the maestro himself. Her rage soon became fury. Bakst, who had probably been told by Diaghilev that the interview was being held as a favour to a friend and was a waste of time professionally, decided to enjoy himself at the expense of the 'oriental dancer'. Instead of asking her to dance he asked her to undress. Thinking that this might well be normal procedure in an audition (something she had never before had to undergo), Margarethe complied. Bakst, presumably after having a good look at the famous body, thanked her most politely, suggested that she get dressed again, and only then, without having asked her to dance a step, told her that there was no question of her dancing for the Diaghilev Ballet. Margarethe was mortified.

* * * * *

In the year that followed this humiliating encounter she accepted whatever engagement she could find, however lowly or obscure. She danced at l'Université des Annales, where her performance served to illustrate a lecture on Indian art. She abandoned her Indian theme completely and appeared at the *Folies Bergère* in a show with an entirely Spanish theme. She even travelled to Sicily to top the bill in a small provincial music-hall for a fee that only a few months before she would have scorned as absurd. But the strain was beginning to tell. She put on weight, her glorious black hair was streaked with grey and her face assumed a perpetually anxious expression. As nothing succeeds like success, so nothing guarantees oblivion more surely than failure.

And still the bills came flooding in. Margarethe economised: half her servants were paid off, part of the elegant house at Neuilly was put under wraps, her beloved horses were sold and some of her more valuable pieces of jewellery discreetly pawned. She was disgusted to find that her old friend Astruc apparently no longer had the time even to make an appointment with her, but he was finding it hard to forgive the embarrassment she had caused him *vis-à-vis* his infinitely more successful client, Diaghilev. And while Margarethe was over the hill and going down, Astruc was still firmly ensconced at the top. It was easy enough for him to make sure their paths did not cross.

Not without a hint of petulance Margarethe reflected that France had let her down; Paris no longer wanted to know her. And not without a brave measure of defiance she reminded herself that Paris was not the only city in the world. In February 1914 she closed the house at Neuilly, paid off all the remaining staff except her personal maid, and set off for Berlin. Who knows what changes she would find after an absence of seven years; her fame might still be intact and among her acquaintances in the city there would surely be old friends who could help her.

Coincidence, which would later play such a cruel role in deciding her fate, allowed her now to meet up with one old friend who was pleased to see her again and another who was in a position to help her. The first was Alfred Kiepert, still in the Westphalian Hussars and with more gold braid than ever decorating his uniform. The second was none other than her old flame from Madrid, Jules Cambon, now the French Ambassador to Berlin. Since 1912, when his brother Paul had been appointed Ambassador to London, the Cambon *frères* had been uniquely well-placed to act as the eyes and ears of France's President Raymond Poincaré at a crucial moment in European affairs.

International tensions had been steadily rising throughout Europe for months, rumours of war fluttered through every conversation, the subject hovered uninvited over every gathering and tiptoed into a million nightmares. But the population seemed to be indulging in Margarethe's favourite pastime of playing ostrich: nobody was prepared to admit that war was a real possibility — it could not happen, it would all blow over, the pedlars of gloom were exaggerating. Neither was it just the frivolous or ill-informed who refused to face up to the situation. Intelligent, well-educated and politically aware men and women of every European nation, who knew full well the tensions that smouldered so dangerously close to the surface, were genuinely unable to believe that Europe would go to war. As the sun shone and the spring danced into cloudless summer, scholars studied, lovers courted, children played and artists painted as if they had not a care in the world.

But there were those who knew. And as the representative of one of the Great Powers in the capital city of another, Jules Cambon had no illusions about the gravity of the international situation. He knew the real reason behind President Poincaré's intended 'courtesy' visit to St Petersburg and the topics he planned to discuss with the Tsar. He had a good idea, too, of the main subjects under review between Kaiser Wilhelm and the ill-fated Archduke Franz-Ferdinand when the former decided to call on his Austrian neighbour. He was well aware of the fact that while the principals at all these meetings would make great play of genial wining and dining, behind the green baize doors the minions were already scuttling about their business in a fever of preparation. Spies were sent out to listen and report, military attaches compared notes and swapped figures and, under urbane and smiling exteriors, diplomats in every capital gathered crumbs with an assiduity that would have been the envy of any housemaid. The Cambon brothers were most definitely not among those who dismissed the belligerent noises emanating from deep inside the German nation as mere sabre-rattling, and from his vantage point in the heart of the Kaiser's empire, Jules was sending out a stream of reports and warnings to the French Government on the nature and strength of the German threat.

Yet somehow, despite the vast weight of responsibility that lay on his shoulders, Jules Cambon still managed, as only a Frenchman could, to charm the very birds off the Berlin trees. When Margarethe asked him if he had any contacts in the theatrical world who might engage her to dance in Berlin, he found time to make several introductions. All of a sudden it seemed as though her career might not, after all, be over. In May she was offered a contract to dance in an operetta at the Metropole Theatre. The offer could not have come at a better time, it boosted her flagging confidence, put a new spring in her step and smoothed away the anxious wrinkles; at last she was to dance in Berlin.

Gleefully anticipating a triumphant comeback, Margarethe moved into the smartest hotel and sent her maid back to Paris to collect her theatrical costumes. Since *Der Millionendieb* was not due to have its première until September there was time for some good living first. Had she been less self-absorbed, she might have noticed that the residents of Berlin seemed to be affected with something of the hysteria that gripped the citizens of Paris.

As it was Margarethe found herself in greater demand than at any time for five years. Engagements for breakfast, lunch, tea and dinner, parties every night, invitations to the theatre, the opera and the ballet, and, best of all, requests for private assignations and the willingness of her patrons to pay generously for her favours. She happily accepted her new popularity as affirmation that her looks and desirability were intact and blossomed like a newly watered plant. She dyed the grey out of her hair, shed the extra pounds, carefully painted out the tell-tale lines round her eyes and prepared to resume her role as s.ociety's darling.

*   *   *   *   *

When war was finally declared at the beginning of August 1914 the initial reaction of the man in the street was one of indignation. People from all walks of life would look back at that moment and remember, incredulously, how 'the war at first seemed an infuriating personal interruption rather than a world-wide catastrophe' — a sentiment which echoed Margarethe's feelings precisely.

AN UNINVITED GUEST

If the individual reaction to the outbreak of war was indignation, the collective reaction was one of quite ferocious nationalism. From the moment that war was declared, woe betide any German discovered walking the streets of Paris. Angry crowds with violence in their hearts and bloodlust in their eyes surged along the *boulevards* in search of targets for their rage. Shops and businesses with German or Austrian names were ransacked, no *Brasserie Viennoise* or *Café Klein* had a chance of surviving the onslaught, and the police had no power, nor any great wish, to restrain them.

Rumours that the owners of the Maggi chain of dairies were serving poisoned milk to the children of Paris resulted in every one of their depots being burned to the ground. Hoardings advertising Kub bouillon were said to have secret messages to German spies in the city printed on the reverse and were promptly reduced to matchwood. Well-informed sources revealed that advertisements posted many months ago along every main road in France were in fact coded signposts directing the invaders towards Paris. Bona fide Frenchmen with foreign-sounding names hastily pinned to their windows some form of official identification such as a birth certificate or military call-up paper, to stay the hand outside holding the brick.

In Berlin public reaction was just as frenzied, the only difference being that here nationalist fever had erupted even before war was declared. Right up until the last minute Margarethe was swept along on the wave of excitement that raged through the city. She was in a state of such high glee at her sudden return to popularity that she found it very easy to share the elation of others. But her presence in Berlin at this precise moment would be crucial to the case of those who would soon accuse her of being a German spy. Over and over again she would be grilled about why she was there, who she knew, what she was doing in the German capital on the very day that Germany declared war on France. Again and again she would protest that she was there in her professional capacity as a dancer, that she knew a great many people in Berlin as she had lived there for several months in 1906, and that she had been as amazed as anyone by the sudden explosion of chauvinism in the city.

During one of the interrogations preceding her trial Margarethe would recall the day when she first became aware of this: 'One night towards the end of July 1914, I was having a meal in a private dining room with one of my lovers, Police Superintendent Griebel, when we heard the noise of a demonstration.' Reluctant to curtail what had promised to be a most rewarding evening, Griebel had taken his companion along with him when he went to discover the cause of the uproar. 'An enormous crowd had gathered in front of the Emperor's Palace - they were demonstrating wildly and shouting "Deutschland über Alles".'

Within a few days she was to witness a storm of anti-foreign fury as vicious as anything in Paris. The French, Russians and British, whether residents or visitors, were hounded mercilessly by the baying mob. Even for a citizen of a country that was to remain neutral for the duration of the war, it was a terrifying experience. The dangers of remaining in Berlin were real enough, but they were initially overshadowed for Margarethe by the news that the Metropole Theatre had closed its doors on the very day war was declared — her triumphant comeback would never happen. She was alerted to the wider implications of her situation by a sudden and dramatic change in the behaviour of her friends. Until a few days ago she had seemed always to be in the centre of a merry throng of revellers; now that throng had vanished, melted away by the violent heat of chauvinism. If to be foreign was the worst crime of all, to be associated with foreigners was considered very nearly as bad — not even Margarethe's most ardent admirer was prepared to risk his reputation by standing by her.

Her dismay turned to alarm when, on 4th August, she went to the Metropole to pick up the furs and jewellery she had left in the care of the costumier. The mild, even obsequious, little man she had known had been transformed by events into the most arrogant of Prussian despots. Stopping only to inform her that her possessions had been confiscated, he slammed the door in her face. It was the sort of situation that the Mata Hari of last week would have risen majestically to handle. But the Margarethe of today was very frightened. She had survived quite happily for thirty-eight years without giving a single thought to such mundane matters as international affairs and politics but now it was obviously time to sit up and take notice. Even she could see that circumstances rendered it impossible to travel directly from Germany to France, and, congratulating herself on her perspicacity, she therefore headed for Switzerland intending to travel on to Paris via Zurich. But, as she was to discover, from now on nothing would ever be that simple.

To one who had travelled blithely throughout Europe and even further afield without hindrance, and certainly without any form of identification, for more than fifteen years, it came as a complete surprise to be stopped at the Swiss border for lack of official papers. Before 1914 the only country to insist that all those crossing its borders must be in possession of a passport was Russia. Even after the outbreak of the war full passports were not immediately introduced and it was usually sufficient to have some form of official identification. But Margarethe had no papers of any kind, and the Swiss border guards told her that although her baggage had already gone on ahead, she herself was not allowed to pass. On 7th August she found herself back in Berlin not only without friends but without any clothes except the ones she was wearing.

*   *   *   *   *

While Margarethe and the other foreign nationals in Berlin were scuttling around trying to find a way out of Germany, hostilities were gathering pace. On 4th August Germany announced to Belgium that, for 'security' purposes, she was about to be invaded. King Albert of the Belgians immediately appealed to the British for their promised support and Prime Minister Asquith promptly protested to Germany that their action was in breach of their agreement to respect Belgian neutrality. When this protest was brushed aside on the evening of the same day by the German Chancellor, there was no going back. At midnight Britain joined the conflict.

The German Chief of General Staff, Helmuth von Moltke, had already set in motion his own modified version of the famous Schlieffen plan. This involved concentrating the bulk of the German army on a mighty sweep through Belgium and into France from the north, thus encircling and trapping the main bulk of the French forces which were expected to be gathered along the German-French border further south. Had von Moltke followed Schlieffen's original plan, German troops would also by now have been attacking the Dutch frontier. As it was, the full weight of this assault, falling on the comparatively short German-Belgian border and in particular the fortified town of Liege, was launched on the night of 5th August.

Within a matter of days more than three million men, French, Belgian, British and German, were lining up for what came to be known as the Battle of the Frontiers. The battlefield would reach from Liege in the north down the length of the French-German frontier as far as Mulhouse near the Swiss border. Obviously no civilian would be allowed anywhere near any of these frontiers, far less be allowed to cross them. The only possible way out of Germany seemed to be through Holland — and Margarethe found herself faced with the prospect of returning to her native land for the first time in ten years.

But she still had no travel or identity papers, nor did she have any money with which to buy herself a ticket. To the Mata Hari of last week this, too, would have presented no problems. But it was a slightly different matter when you had to turn on the charm wearing clothes you had not changed for a week and without the help of either your maid or your make-up. The only thing to do was to brazen it out. And since this time she was looking for a saviour rather than a lover, her plight might even be to her advantage — it would certainly make a change to be appealing for once to the highest instincts in a man.

Head held high, then, Margarethe smoothed out the creases in her dress as best she could and went to join the anxious group of expatriates gathered for mutual reassurance in the foyer of the Cumberland Hotel. It was her good fortune that the gravity of the situation did bring the higher instincts of many people to the fore, among their number an elderly Dutchman who not only paid her hotel bill but also provided her with a train ticket to Holland. Thanks to his disinterested generosity Margarethe was able to leave Berlin on 14th August. She travelled to Frankfurt where the Dutch consulate issued her with the necessary travel documents and by the 16th August she was back in Amsterdam.

*   *   *   *   *

It was many years since Margarethe had dreamed of a triumphant return to Holland — of flaunting her success before Rudolph and his powerful friends, and of using her wealth and position to reclaim Jeanne-Louise. Her angry desperation had burnt itself out long ago and her plans for revenge somehow seemed to have got lost along the way. But if she had contemplated an alternative scenario for her home-coming, it surely would not have been like this - exhausted, dishevelled and with little more in the way of possessions than when she had left.

Fortunately for Margarethe's pride, her arrival passed almost unnoticed; her countrymen had other things on their minds. The German invasion of Belgium had acted on neighbouring Holland as a boot in an ant's nest. Their pain-stakingly constructed and resolutely maintained shield of neutrality suddenly appeared paper-thin in the face of such calculated aggression. The streets of Amsterdam were thronged with ashen-faced people in search of information. Every division of the Dutch army had been ordered to the defence of the frontier with Belgium; soldiers were heading for their units; bewildered officials were attempting to restore calm; civilians of all sorts were begging for news and reassurance from anyone who would listen.

The turmoil subsided into shocked silence with the news, a few days after Margarethe's return, that Liege had fallen, that the Germans had marched through Brussels and had now reached the dense forest country of the Ardennes. Fear crept into the very souls of those who had filled the streets with noise; they withdrew, shivering, to their homes; they closed their doors and huddled to themselves, speaking in whispers and jumping at the least unexpected noise. If in France tongues had to be guarded for fear of listening Germans and in Germany the situation was reversed, in Holland contact with any foreigner was feared lest it compromise the nation's neutrality and result in her being drawn into a conflict that was none of her making.

Dutch neutrality was more vulnerable than that of, say, Switzerland or Spain because of her strategic geographical position. The military advantages the occupation of Holland would give to Germany were considerable. 'With Holland in the power of Germany', wrote one English journalist, 'Apart from any act of war, we could not defend India, nor our colonies, nor our trade routes, nor our coasts'. No less considerable would have been the military advantages to the Allied Powers had the Netherlands cast its lot with the Allied cause against Germany. The stream of food and military supplies passing into Germany through Holland from the outside world would at once have been cut off. The Allies also would have obtained the tremendous military advantage of a flank attack upon the German military forces in Belgium and northern France. As the Dutch historian, Amry Vandenbosch, pointed out, the dangers to Holland of joining either side were equally apparent. 'Had she taken the side of the Central Powers a swift and telling blow would at once have been struck at her overseas possessions and her overseas trade, and by joining the Allied Powers she would have invited an invasion from Germany and shared the lot of Belgium. To steer a straight course of strict neutrality was Holland's sole choice.'

Margarethe had the uneasy feeling that in this lethal game of musical chairs she had better claim her seat fast. From being a victory pennant worn with pride, her carefully cultivated cosmopolitanism had become if not a brand of shame at least a conspicuous question-mark. But blending into a background in which she no longer felt at home was not easy for one whose stock-in-trade had for so long been flamboyance. She spoke Dutch hesitantly and with a marked French accent and her habits and manners were decidedly exotic. The degree of suspicion which this produced was amplified by her reputation. Her exploits in the capitals of Europe had not passed unnoticed among her compatriots whose ideas of propriety had changed little during her absence.

In an effort to gain their acceptance Margarethe struggled to adapt. She even managed to enjoy the novelty of dressing up like a governess in demure, high-necked, sober-coloured dresses and hats that would have had her Parisian milliner throwing up his hands in horror. As she had discovered during her sojourn in the Touraine, there was nothing like a little play-acting to fend off boredom or frustration. She also noticed with a wry smile that this very modesty appeared to fascinate the worthy burghers; those who would never have dared approach a 'scarlet woman' found it quite acceptable to offer their protection to an outwardly respectable and obviously lonely lady.

A succession of lovers who were prepared to pay for a taste of Paris's leftovers solved her immediate financial troubles, and by the end of September she was living in an approximation of her preferred style in Amsterdam's Victoria Hotel. The initial panic in the city had subsided, the German advance had passed on through Belgium and into France, and Holland's frontiers were felt for the moment to be reasonably secure. Those who had so recently refused to believe that war was a possibility were now convinced that it would all be over before the New Year.

With this in mind, and perhaps acknowledging that her performing days were numbered, Margarethe decided to resume her career straight away. On 14th December 1914 she danced for the first time for a Dutch audience in a ballet called *Les Folies Françaises* to music by Francois Couperin. The Theatre Royal in The Hague was packed to the doors. Everyone wanted to see the notorious Mata Hari — if she had scandalised Paris, she must be truly sensational. But once again, as with her performance in Madrid, the audience was sadly disappointed. She performed her famous dance of the veils but this time she retained the veils. Many a disillusioned Dutchman went home that night wondering what all the fuss had been about. On the 18th December she gave a second performance, this time in Arnhem where Rudolph was still living. He is reputed to have refused an invitation to attend on the grounds that if she planned to show off her body he was not interested, he had seen it all before. It was the last time she ever danced in public.

Characteristically, instead of taking this lukewarm response to her performance as a hint that her career was drawing to a close, Margarethe chose to lay the blame on her audience. Obviously nothing had changed in the years since she had left Holland: the Dutch were still as bourgeois and disapproving as ever and, even after her triumphant success in Paris, did not consider her worthy of their admiration. Their indifference stung her to fury. How dare they turn their backs on her, who did they think they were to sit in judgement over one who had been fêted in almost every capital of Europe? Were they still prejudiced against her because of the scurrilous stories Rudolph had spread about her all those years ago? Could their memories be as long as that?

There was no question this time of running away. But neither was she prepared to go down on her knees and beg for their approval. If Rudolph was immune to both her wrath and her charm there must be someone in his arrogant, complacent world who was not. Someone who could be enticed into compensating her, unwittingly if necessary, for all she had suffered at Rudolph's hands. The magistrate who would later be responsible for putting her on trial for espionage would be drawn to the conclusion that Rudolph's cruelty had left Margarethe with a burning desire to avenge herself on all men. Until now that had not been the case. She had used men, certainly, but she had willingly allowed them to use her in return and had derived pleasure and satisfaction from their company. This time, though, she was out for revenge. If she could find the right man and persuade him to give her an inch, she was poised to snatch the full mile.

She found him. Baron Edouard van der Capellen, a Colonel in the Dutch cavalry, was possessed of a monstrous ego and an even larger fortune — a promising start. But he was qualified for the role she had in mind on more counts than that; the most striking of which was the uncanny resemblance between his family and Rudolph's.

Baron Edouard's grandfather, a Frieslander like Margarethe herself, had been one of the leaders who initiated the restoration of the House of Orange after the fall of Napoleon. Already a Vice-admiral, he had been rewarded for his endeavours by being incorporated in the nobility of the new Kingdom of the Netherlands as *Jonkheer* in 1815 and was appointed Grand Marshal of the Court of the prince of Orange, later King William II, in 1822. Of his nine children four had later held appointments at court and one, Jules, the youngest and Edouard's uncle, had followed his father into the Dutch navy and also risen to the rank of Admiral.

Baron Edouard himself was fifty-two years old, seven years younger than Rudolph, tall and fair with a large, fleshy face and drooping jowls that gave him the look of a bored and rather lofty bloodhound. The onset of war, by thrusting the armed forces into sudden and unaccustomed prominence, had presented him with a gratifying vision of the Baron as Conquering Hero. The prospect had put a new spring in his step and set the adrenalin pumping — Margarethe could not have chosen a more propitious moment to put her plan into action.

It was disappointingly easy. When Margarethe launched her attack she found the door wide open. The Baron soaked up her flattery like a sponge, accepted her wide-eyed admiration as no more than his due and his monocle misted up in the most satisfactory way when she turned on the charm. Within a month of their first meeting she was installed under his protection in a pretty little house in The Hague.

Of all her schemes, in many ways this was Margarethe's most successful. The next three years of her life would take her to higher heights and deeper depths than the most hair-raising of roller-coasters, yet through it all she would cling like a limpet not to the Baron himself but to her relationship with him. She had decided to make him compensate for all Rudolph's sins and she would abide by that decision. Even in the last desperate days before her death she would refuse to ask for his help fearing that if he knew what sort of trouble she was in he would close his purse-strings to her for ever.

But it was not always, easy. The Baron was moody and autocratic. In his eyes a mistress was a possession: he could drape her in silks and place her on a pedestal or he could treat her like a whore whose only function was to satisfy his lust; if he beckoned she must come running, if he walked away she must be there when he came back. Although subservience did not come naturally to her, Margarethe accepted his tyranny with as good a grace as she could muster. The generous allowance he paid her more than compensated for his foibles.

The gathering momentum of the war also served to ease the pressure on a relationship that under other circumstances would surely have been too fragile to last. The Baron's ever-longer spells of duty with his regiment on border patrol gave Margarethe time to breathe and an opportunity to spend his money. She refurbished the house and brought her wardrobe as up-to-date as conditions would allow, then looked around for the next diversion. So absorbed had she been in her own plans that it came as a shock to realise that there were no other diversions to be found; life with the Baron might be an effort, but life without him looked like being a colossal bore.

While her compatriots were prepared to accept the inevitable shortages and inconveniences of war as a small price to pay for the maintenance of their neutrality, Margarethe felt cheated. There was no glamour in deprivation, no excitement in safety. Boredom, frustration and the strain of constantly trying to live up to the Baron's expectations made her think longingly of the days when she had answered to no one, and when a Dutch magazine ran an article on her glittering career illustrated with a photograph of 'Madame Mata Hari' dressed in the height of fashion, it was almost more than she could bear. She pasted the picture sadly in her scrapbook, noting the date, 13th March 1915, ten years to the day since her debut at the Musée Guimet. Suddenly she was overwhelmed with nostalgia. She cursed the wretched war for wrecking her career and forcing her to stagnate in this dreary backwater, mourned all her possessions still locked away in the house at Neuilly, and ground her teeth with rage at the thought of her valuable furs and jewellery confiscated in Berlin. Above all she missed Paris.

* * * * *

In the first months of the war the *Ville Lumière* had been in a state of siege, facing the very real prospect of invasion and occupation. After the joint French-British defeat at Mons, the invading German forces had advanced through Arras, Cambrai and Reims until, by the beginning of September, they were in sight of the Eiffel Tower. A measure of their proximity to the capital was demonstrated when two regiments of infantry were sent by taxi from Paris to reinforce the Sixth Army on the Marne (the first instance, incidentally, of troops being moved to a battlefield by motor transport).

In the city itself the hatches had been well and truly battened down. The government left for Bordeaux taking with them twenty trainloads of officials, state papers, gold reserves, money and art treasures. The sumptuous apartments of the aristocracy and the beau monde were abandoned with unseemly haste as their occupants fled to safety. The redoubtable Mrs Clarke, one of the surprising number of English women who had decided to stay in Paris, waxed quite lyrical over the transformation to her beloved city.

Paris has stiffened her back to the rigorous necessities of martial law and the attitude suits her well. She wears very few fine feathers these days and her jewels are put away altogether. Her gardens bloom and her fountains play and the glory of the sunset gilds her domes and turns her river into a liquid stream of light. But there are no night-time revelries, and the poetry that is born of the fumes of absinthe is no longer written; for the cafes close at 8 o'clock and the restaurants at 9.30. All the theatres are shut and music is never heard either in private or in public.

With the French victory in the Battle of the Marne, the immediate danger to Paris had been lifted. There followed a series of engagements which would extend the Western Front from Switzerland in the south right up to Belgium's channel coast. The last of these desperate battles of 1914 was the one that, more than any other, would come to personify the bloody, muddy horror of the whole war: the first battle of Ypres. 'Trenches were dug, barbed wire was strung and positions were fixed in those dark and dreadful days, and they marked a line from which the Western Front would shift by no more than ten miles in either direction for the next three years.'

As the idea began to take root that the war, after all, was going to be a long one, the spirit of Paris started to reassert itself. There were still those who argued that it was totally inappropriate even to contemplate a return to normality. Was it not realised that the worst hostilities the world had ever seen, the outcome of which would decide the nation's very existence, were taking place a mere day's journey from the capital? But by November the situation in the capital had relaxed sufficiently for the *septembrisards* to start moving back. Thus scornfully labelled by those who had stayed put, these were the Parisians who out of prudence, snobbery or just plain fear, had left for Bordeaux with the government. As one of them would shamefacedly admit, 'We, the bourgeoisie, have always said that the great danger to Paris was a revolution among the working-classes, the mob. We were proved wrong, the mob stood steady when the bourgeoisie did not'. The government, too, returned to the capital, lending strength to the case of those who argued that it was time the city came back to life, time for the shops and theatres to re-open and for music once again to be heard along the *boulevards*.

The argument never really got off the ground because Paris was changing anyway. By virtue of its position the city was becoming the vast clearing station of the by now stabilised Western Front. Thousands upon thousands of soldiers passed through, stayed for a while and then moved on again. A rising flood of wounded, too, moved into, through and out of the city. Paris had a duty to do all it could to boost the morale of these brave lads who had endured, and would again endure, unspeakable horrors in the name and cause of its continued freedom.

In November the French Interior Minister Louis-Jean Malvy authorised the re-opening of the theatres. Although the nights would remain dark and quiet and only matinee performances were permitted, during the hours of daylight something of the pre-war bustle returned to the streets. Café tables were moved back out onto the pavements and lunchtime concerts returned to the public gardens. Although long queues still formed for bread, coal, eggs, milk and, above all, for information, Parisians once more felt able to smile. Indeed they were encouraged to do so. For with this resurgence of vitality came a new and intense spirit of patriotism. Defeat was a forbidden word. The personal misery and grief that lurked beneath every smile, the constant fear for husband and brother, father and son that twisted every heart, must not be allowed to show. Widows dared not weep openly for their lost husbands, but were expected to hold their heads high and be proud of their sacrifice for France. Despair was preempted by being labelled treasonable — pessimists, pacifists and defeatists were castigated for bringing encouragement to the enemy. Even to complain about rising prices was unpatriotic.

This conspiracy of optimism was compounded by the reluctance of soldiers on leave returning from the Front to talk about their experiences. Though their nights might be spent grappling in the barbed-wire clutches of a recurring nightmare, they were not going to waste their few precious days in Paris dwelling on these horrors. They wanted to laugh, to joke, to enjoy the camaraderie of their fellows and relish the luxury of having escaped for a while from the

119

brain-numbing carnage of the battlefield.

The newspapers, too, carried absurdly optimistic reports of the progress of the war, arguing that it was their function to boost the morale of military and civilian alike and at all costs to avoid offering a propaganda victory of any kind to the enemy. They carried reports on such lighthearted topics as the re-opening of the music-halls, the increasing popularity of the cinema as public entertainment and, the headlines that would catch Margarethe's eye, the new productions showing at the Opera-Comique, the Comédie Française and the Odéon.

In The Hague there was little gaiety, forced or otherwise. Far from being the crossroads of Europe, it felt to Margarethe more like the end of the earth. The Dutch, unlike the French, had no need to whip themselves into a patriotic fervour, they had no victory to aim for nor defeat to avert. There was no great danger with which to flirt, no call for energetic flag-waving, no crisis-induced camaraderie. During the course of the war the defence of the border would cost over 40,000 Dutch lives, but neutrality guaranteed that the country be spared the worst of the horror, the wholesale slaughter of the trenches. And since the pendulum did not swing to the depths, it also did not swing to the heights. Although the maintenance of that neutrality involved Dutch officialdom in an absorbing balancing act, it involved the great mass of the Dutch people in little more than a grim endurance test.

August 1915 brought Margarethe's thirty-ninth birthday and her frustration turned to desperation. Not content with having forced her into premature retirement, this awful war had now kept her a virtual prisoner for a whole year. The excuse she gave for going to Paris was surely too vacuous to convince even the preoccupied Baron; no one in their right mind would undertake such a long and uncomfortable journey just to collect a few cases of china. But although her motives were certainly self-indulgent to the point of idiocy, they were not remotely sinister. The Baron was heading back to the frontier and might be away for months; the prospect of yet another long stint of twiddling her thumbs till he came back was too awful to contemplate. Stoicism was not in her nature, austerity was not her style. Let others submit — she had had enough.

* * * * *

The German occupation of Belgium forced anyone wishing to travel from Holland to France to make the journey by sea. Since none of the French channel ports was open to civilian shipping, this meant a voyage of several days from Amsterdam, via one of the English channel ports, across the Bay of Biscay to Vigo in Northern Spain. From there the traveller took a train via Madrid to the Spanish-French border at Irun or Hendaye and finally boarded a French train to Paris.

It was nearly two years since Margarethe had last been in Paris and she was unaware of how drastically the city had changed. Determined not to arrive looking like a provincial matron, she shook her smartest outfits out of their mothballs and prepared to make a grand entrance. But she was in for a shock. One of the earliest casualties of the war had been the *Parisienne's* obsession with her clothes — now austerity was the order of the day.

The extraordinary fashions that had prevailed in the prewar years — absurd hobbling skirts that forced you to walk with tiny tripping steps; enormous, wide-brimmed hats festooned with ostrich feathers and hung about with an elegant spider's web of embroidered veils that dangerously obscured the vision — had no place in a world where practicality ruled supreme. Skirts had become fuller and shorter to accommodate a swift, purposeful walk; fabrics were plainer and colours more subdued in sympathy with the national mood. And just as it had become unpatriotic to display grief, so it became unpatriotic, and tasteless, to worry about anything so superficial as your appearance when everything you held dear, your loved ones, your home and your very country were in constant peril. In this cradle of haute couture, fashion had ceased to exist — now there were just clothes.

It was probably a zealous member of the Ligue pour la Guerre d'Appui who drew the attention of the French Security Services to Margarethe's arrival in Paris. In an attempt to match their efforts to those of the military, the civilian population of Paris, and in particular the women, were contributing to the national cause by any means they could devise. The suspicion that had instantly attached to any foreigner at the outbreak of war had broadened to include any individual whose endeavours on behalf of France were less than manifest. No factory hand or agricultural worker, however genuine and compelling his reason for not being in uniform, escaped the watchful eye of these self-appointed 'parasite-catchers'. Ex-soldiers who had been invalided out of the army, even wounded *poilus* (the French equivalent of 'Tommies') whose injuries were not outwardly visible, could not help noticing the sidelong glances and hearing the stage whispers of sharp-eyed doubters wondering why they were not at the Front. The campaign against those suspected of dodging their duty became an obsession. The stream of anonymous denunciations rapidly became a flood until by November 1915 they were coming in at the rate of ten thousand a month and a special court had to be set up in Paris just to deal with them. In this terrible climate of suspicion was born the Ligue pour la Guerre d'Appui.

The members of the Ligue, brainchild of the writer and journalist Leon Daudet, were committed to the exposure of all enemies of France. Any unusual activity, unscheduled visit or unguarded conversation, indeed any behaviour that seemed remotely suspicious, they instantly reported to the authorities. While the existence of the Ligue was an effective deterrent to any would-be shirker, its prime targets were not malingerers but spies. For the twin brother of fanatical nationalism was spy-mania. According to historian Constantine Fitzgibbon:

In the age of high nationalism it was in the matter of spies that the latent hysteria, mostly in England and France, where it was in part attributable to the Dreyfus affair, assumed epidemic proportions ... This sort of hysteria very rapidly vanished among the fighting troops in the West and the stupidest and cruellest forms of super-patriotism did not long outlive the enormous casualty lists ... though the gap between the French, British and German fighting men and the flagwavers safe and sound at home widened. But the spy-mania remained, and in some measure at least was deliberate government policy.

The activities of the Ligue were, indeed, encouraged by the French Government. The War Minister, M. Millerand, launched his famous slogan 'Taisez-vous, méfiez-vous, les oreilles ennemies vous écoutent!' in an effort to alert the public to the danger of spies. From time to time reports would appear in the press of a traitor caught and punished, a spy unmasked and shot. It was useful propaganda, fulfilling what the historian Richard Wilmer Rowan described as:

> ... the most complex requirements of their [the propagandists'] calling — namely, to make the enemy seem (1) utterly savage and demonic, (2) ever more powerful and threatening and yet (3) never more than temporarily victorious. To belittle a foe's achievements while continually exaggerating him as a threat was necessary because both the morale of the 'home front' and the zeal of the raw recruits must be simultaneously stimulated. And there was no better way of accomplishing this neat blend of quake and bravado than by magnifying the influences gathering behind all the German efforts.

Margarethe's arrival in Paris in December 1915 drew the instant attention of the ladies of the Ligue. Everything about her — her questionable reputation, expensive clothes, grand manner — set their hackles rising and their nostrils a-quiver. Here was a dubious character indeed; the authorities should be warned about this one. Thanks to the multiplicity of stories Margarethe had invented about her past, the Prefecture of Police were unsure about her exact origins. According to a card in their files she had been born in Belgium — not enough reason in itself to regard her with any great suspicion, but it confirmed her as a foreigner. The Ligue considered their doubts to be justified and went off to find their next victim. Within a few days of her arrival Margarethe's card had been stamped 'To Be Watched'.

What the members of the Ligue did not know was that her card would have been stamped even without their efforts. For thanks to a diligent immigration officer in Folkestone, the English port at which her boat had called on its way to Vigo, the Deuxième Bureau had already placed a large question mark against her name. On 9th December 1915 the following memorandum, marked *Secret*, had been entered in the Aliens Registry at the London office of MI5.

ZELLE, Margarethe Gertruida

The above named, a Dutch woman, left Folkestone for France on 3.12.15. When in England she stays at the Savoy Hotel. She is the mistress of Baron E. van der Capellan, a Colonel in a Dutch Hussar Regiment. When war broke out she was engaged at the Scala Theatre in Milan. She then left Milan and travelled through Switzerland and Germany to Holland. She then lived in Holland till the present time at a hotel in Amsterdam till August last and then in a house of her own at The Hague. She hopes to get engagements on her return in London and the provincial theatres.

She appeared most unsatisfactory and should be refused permission to return to the UK.

DESCRIPTION

Height 5'5", build medium stout, hair black, face oval, complexion olive, forehead low, eyes grey-brown, nose straight, mouth small, teeth good, chin pointed, hands well-kept, feet small, age 39. Speaks French, English, Italian, Dutch and probably German. Handsome, bold type of woman. Well and fashionably dressed in brown costume with racoon fur trimming and hat to match.

Copies to: Southampton, Havre, GHQ I(b), MI6, HQ, IGC, Home Office, Permit Office, Scotland Yard.

Although neither the author nor the recipients could possibly have been aware of it at the time — and the subject herself never even knew of its existence — Margarethe's ultimate fate was probably decided by this memorandum. But for the time being it was just one of many similar warnings issued on any traveller whose conduct did not entirely satisfy the watchful authorities.

By a combination of German carelessness and British good fortune, twenty-two German spies — almost the entire network — had been rounded up and imprisoned in England on the day after the declaration of war. This coup was a tremendous boost to the morale of the British Intelligence Services, but to let it become public knowledge would have been to calm the fears and reduce the watchfulness of a nation that must at all costs be kept on its guard. Instead, the official, though secret, line was to increase national vigilance by constantly exaggerating the quantity and efficiency of German agents on British soil.

This strategy, and the knowledge that the network would inevitably have been rebuilt with all possible speed, ensured that spy-mania was as alive and kicking in Britain as it was in France and Germany. Every foreigner in the country was suspect and those trying to enter by the channel ports most suspect of all. None would have been given permission to set foot on shore without the most convincing of reasons and even those in transit would have been subject to careful scrutiny. The faintest breath of suspicion was enough to condemn the person in question as 'undesirable'.

The immigration officer in Folkestone who questioned Margarethe had to be guided by his instincts. Had he had any concrete reason for labelling her 'unsatisfactory' he would certainly have mentioned it to his superiors. From the content and tone of his memorandum it is possible that he took exception to her 'bold' manner. However, the nature of the job even in peace time requires that an immigration officer be good at detecting both lies and attempts to impress. And Margarethe did both in answer to his questions. She had never been to England and had therefore never stayed at the Savoy Hotel — she probably knew it by reputation as the best hotel in London and hoped to impress her questioner by mentioning it. Her claim to have been in Milan at the outbreak of war was just a clumsy attempt to avoid having to admit she had really been in Berlin, an admission that might reasonably be expected to raise even more questions. Although he had no way of verifying any of her statements her questioner was left with a distinctly unfavourable impression of Madame Zelle. And that, again, was enough.

But Margarethe had been allowed to continue her journey, blissfully unaware of the fatal question mark that had been raised against her name. Copies of the memorandum were circulated to all interested parties and knowledge of its contents probably arrived in Paris at about the same time as she did. At that stage Margarethe's incomprehension of the prevailing mood of Paris was almost total and the significance of the sideways looks might well have escaped her. But style she understood, and as a professional partygoer it did not take her long to realise that she had arrived at this party seriously over-dressed. Far from disconcerting her, however, the realisation gave her just another excuse to go shopping. The unfortunate agents who were detailed to watch her were doomed to long hours loitering on pavements as she set about adapting her wardrobe.

This time Margarethe was disconcerted. The streets of Paris had changed almost beyond recognition. Most of the shops had re-opened after the immediate threat of German invasion had been lifted, but with a much reduced, and noticeably less subservient, staff of assistants. Enticing window displays had been replaced by patriotic tableaux draped with the national flag and by posters announcing fund-raising events for the benefit of wounded soldiers. No more motor buses trundled along the streets, no luxurious private cars, and even the ubiquitous horse-drawn *fiacres* were rare. Those that did remain were likely to be limping along behind some gaunt and toothless nag — for every able-bodied horse as well as every civilian motor vehicle had been requisitioned by the army. But if civilian traffic had virtually disappeared, military traffic was considerable. The unwary pedestrian was in constant danger of being crushed by speeding cars flying the tricolor, or by great grey lorries, loaded with foodstuffs, uniforms, wire netting, barbed wire, ammunition and every possible kind of war material rushing through Paris on the way to the Front.

And as with the traffic, so with the pedestrians. Margarethe had never in her life seen so many men in uniform. This was the war as it was never seen in The Hague. This was the action that was passing them by in Holland. Although to the Parisians life was calmer and more normal than it had been for many months, the newcomer from the neutral Netherlands found the atmosphere of tension and drama positively intoxicating. Even the discovery that shopping for clothes in this new Paris was no longer the pleasurable pastime it had once been, failed to suppress her high spirits. Quite the contrary — having only three items to choose from where once there would have been thirty made her feel quite virtuous; the uncomplaining acceptance of such paucity could be her own contribution to the war effort.

Such willingness to make sacrifices did not, however, mean she was prepared to abandon certain standards. She had always stayed in the best hotels and that was not going to change. The boredom of her watchers was somewhat alleviated by their amazement at the quantity and diversity of her gentleman callers at the Grand Hotel. Her accusers would find sinister significance in the fact that most of them were foreign, although logic might have pointed out that this was an effect of rather than a cause for suspicion; the gentlemen of the beau monde might be reluctant to relinquish their sophisticated internationalism, but they were as concerned as their less affluent fellow-citizens to avoid unnecessary contact with anyone whose loyalty might be suspect. They might feign a lofty disregard for parochialism but their patriotism was never in doubt. At the first call of the bugle they had grabbed the nearest champagne bottle, linked arms with their fellow-revellers and headed for the Front as cheerfully as if they had been heading for the next party — and once there they fought with the same determination they had previously applied to the pursuit of pleasure. Their departure to the war and the subsequent closing of the salons knocked the final nail into the coffin of the Belle Epoque.

Fortunately for Margarethe there were enough foreigners in the city to fill the gap. At this distance she felt under no obligation to remain faithful to the Baron and she had a wide choice of patrons. To judge by the rapidity with which she found a man willing to take on the role, she had certainly not lost her touch. Within a few days of her arrival she was living in the company and at the expense of the Belgian Marquis de Beaufort.

It is easy to condemn her insensitivity to the gravity of the situation. But it must be remembered that war on this scale was an unknown phenomenon. Previous wars had been spasmodic and very localised, with only the military being directly involved. A war that so directly involved and affected a civilian population was an entirely new concept. The people of Paris were by now facing the second winter of just such a war; but they still could not comprehend the full extent of either the conflict or the efforts and sacrifices yet to be made. However they did have eighteen months start on Margarethe and they had been plunged straight in at the deep end. Her only experience of the war so far had been a few frightening days in Berlin. As far as she was concerned war was for soldiers and had very little to do with her; she did not know — and had never had reason to consider — that she was expected to behave differently during a war. Although in Holland many women were contributing to the war by nursing the wounded and comforting the bereaved, there had been no indication that they had any other great role to play.

But her naivety in this respect did not mean that she was insensitive to the atmosphere in Paris. A woman whose livelihood depends on her ability to attract and gratify men can only succeed if she is fully aware of the qualities of other women. And it was the changes in the attitudes of the women of Paris that accounted for the most fundamental change in the city itself. With the departure for the battlefield of all able-bodied men, women were discovering for the first time a sense of their own worth. On their shoulders now rested all the responsibilities of home and family; they took over, because they had to, the roles that had traditionally been their husbands', their brothers' or their fathers'. In whichever direction their endeavours took them, the war had the effect of wrenching them away from the home and hearth where they had been traditionally confined for centuries. Initially this disruption to their lives was accepted with resignation as a temporary aberration. But it soon became, for a great many women, not only a habit but a need and sometimes even a pleasure. With their menfolk mobilised, women began to get used to the idea that they were on their own, that they had to make decisions, take responsibilities and accept the consequences on their own.

And as they adapted to these new conditions they became aware of another pleasure, of knowing that for the first time in their lives they did not have to rely on someone else to provide for them. They were themselves becoming the providers and in the process were gaining an undreamt-of measure of independence. By the end of the war there would be no occupation previously reserved for men that had not been successfully tackled by women. Certainly there had been working women in Paris before the war. But an official survey reported that by as early as 1915 ninety out of every hundred women had been forced to take on the role of bread-winner and head of the household. Work was no longer a matter of choice or a means of earning a little extra pin-money, it had become a necessity.

There were women working in banks, businesses and post offices, as clerks, messengers and secretaries. There were women newspaper vendors, street cleaners and barbers. On the railways, in the métro and on the trams there were women ticket-collectors and even women guards. The hundreds of hospitals that had sprung up all over Paris to accommodate the endless stream of wounded required a whole army of nurses and auxiliaries to staff them. And most important perhaps of all were the thousands of women who worked in the munitions factories. The French Chief of Staff and Commander-in-Chief General Joffre would testify to the significance of their contribution with his famous remark, 'If the women working in the factories had downed tools for twenty minutes, the Allies would have lost the war'.

The effects of this revolution were naturally most marked amongst the working classes. But the *grandes et petites bourgeoises* were as determined as the *travailleuses* both to contribute to it and to benefit from it. Those who had no need to take a paid job flung themselves whole-heartedly into good works. The French Red Cross, under whose aegis most of the new hospitals operated, was inundated with volunteers. One branch of the Red Cross, Les Dames Françaises, boasted the wives of no less than five government ministers as its joint presidents, while another, the Societé de Secours aux Blessés Militaires had a committee consisting almost entirely of *duchesses* and *comtesses*. One observer was amused to note that 'there is a good deal of snobbism connected with these societies, and political intrigue is not without its importance in their ranks', but went on to admit that 'the work they do is good, they are very rich and they have provided a stupendous amount of material for the soldiers during the war'.

Just as these good ladies had previously craved the reputation of 'patroness of the arts and giver of the most sumptuous parties' they now rivalled each other for the title of 'patroness of the *poilu* and provider of the most bounty'. The ladies of leisure who had been used to whiling away the empty hours in the creation of an elegant tapestry firescreen or an embroidered cushion cover had long since abandoned the *petit point*: now they knitted sturdy balaclavas and warm socks, they scoured the shops not for trinkets and ornaments for their own gratification but in search of little luxuries to send to their husbands or sons at the Front — cigarettes or tobacco, a small pot of jam or tin of paté, notepaper, chocolates or a bar of soap. The relish with which they tackled their new role was obvious, the energy they brought to the unfamiliar tasks remarkable, and the wide-eyed Margarethe found their preoccupation disconcerting. It seemed that she was the only person in Paris without a role to play in this war. Not only that, but she seemed to be the only woman in Paris who did not have at least one relation directly involved in the fighting.

In the early months of the war, before the system of giving each soldier a regular spell of leave had been established, the sending of packages and letters had been the only permitted contact between home and Front. For many women the prospect of such indefinite separation was intolerable and, since the distance between home and Front was often very short, the bolder ones decided to take the matter into their own hands. There was no blanket ban on women travelling to the war zone, but those who were allowed through were carefully vetted. According to one general, the ban only covered 'legitimate' women. It was thought that although a visit from a wife or mother might give momentary cheer to a fighting soldier, in the long term it might have a detrimental effect on his morale by reminding him too forcibly of the comforts of home and family. A visit from a *poule*, on the other hand, would have no such demoralising effect — on the contrary such women provided a necessary and indeed beneficial respite from the rigours of the battle-field. This bizarre distinction gave rise to some ludicrous charades: where prostitutes had always striven to pass themselves off as respectable, now the most refined and proper of women were trying, with varying degrees of success, to pass themselves off as prostitutes, sporting garish make-up and shockingly low-cut dresses in order to be allowed near their husbands.

With the introduction of regular rosters of leave, the traffic was reversed. The trains that had taken the lonely women to the Front now delivered war-weary, travel-stained and sometimes shell-shocked *permissionaires* back into the loving arms of their families. For the eight or ten days duration of their leave these exhausted men were smothered with all the tender care of their wives and mothers that had had no outlet for the eight or ten months of their absence.

Emotions on both sides were running too high for normal behaviour to be possible — the soldier could no more shake off the bravado that was necessary for his survival at the Front than could his wife forego the opportunity to cosset him like a helpless child. The war demanded a commitment from each one that was too intense to be set aside for such a brief interlude.

The soldier knew that he had to return in just a few short days to his ordeal; to sleep, if he was lucky, on a damp straw mattress; to wash rarely and in cold, often muddy water; to face fear and fatigue, injury and possibly death in a fight that seemed doomed to last forever. He could not permit himself to lower his guard and to drop his protective shield of indifference in case he had no strength to resume it when the moment came.

The women, for their part, found their passion to assuage

and compensate for the horrors endured by their menfolk too strong to be satisfied by such fleeting opportunities for expression. Their frustration led them to assume yet another role — that of *marraine*, or godmother to any unfortunate soldier who had no family to care for him. All over France women of every social class and every age group were adopting 'godsons'. Some would confine themselves to just one, others would take on several dozen; they wrote to them, knitted for them and invited them into their homes for their leave. And while there were certainly some women who took advantage of this arrangement — courtesans who saw it as a means of continuing their remunerative prewar occupation or lonely spinsters on the look-out for a husband — for the most part it was a rewarding experience for everyone involved, and made a significant contribution to the feeling of national unity and fellowship that would last for the duration of the war.

It is hardly surprising that Margarethe felt excluded from all this *bonhomie* and togetherness. There is a world of difference between standing out and being the odd one out — somehow she had to become involved. And how better than by picking up her career where she had left off and returning to the stage — many of the theatres were open and all these brave soldiers would surely benefit from the diversion and entertainment she could provide. From her elegant suite at the Grand she wrote a note to Gabriel Astruc. Rumour had reached her that Diaghilev was in Paris recruiting dancers for an American tour — would Astruc let the maestro know that Mata Hari was in town, free either to perform in Paris or to travel to America, and equipped with a completely new programme of dances that he would surely find irresistible.

While waiting for his response, she visited the main

theatres to catch up with the latest shows, have a look at the opposition and assess the possibilities. With each performance she attended her spirits fell and her optimism gradually evaporated. The theatres were certainly open, although only for matinee performances, and they were packed to the doors every day. But their whole character had changed.

The controversy that had surrounded the re-opening of the theatres in the early months of 1915 had never really subsided. There was still a large and vocal body of opinion that condemned such frivolity and declared that the time, energy and money involved could and should have been placed at the disposal of the war effort. They had not been convinced by the arguments of those in favour of re-opening: that in Paris alone seventy-five thousand people depended on the theatres for a livelihood — not just performers, but musicians, dressers, stage-hands, carpenters, painters, costume designers, stage-managers and cleaners. Was it fair to deprive all these people of an income just to protect the sensibilities of those who were fighting, particularly as most of them were women or elderly men trying to provide for their families, or *poilus* whose injuries prevented them from returning to active duty? Would it not be more practical to think of the theatre primarily as a place of work and only secondarily as a source of entertainment? With the added argument that the prestige of Paris was at stake and that the enemy must not be allowed to think it had succeeded in bringing the city to its knees, the pro-opening lobby had won the day.

But they were exquisitely sensitive to the slightest misinterpretation of the stand they had taken. They welcomed the suggestion that a fifteen per cent levy should be made on all box office takings for distribution among relief agencies and they reserved a quarter of their seats for wounded soldiers who would be allowed in free of charge. And, most devoutly of all, they guaranteed to stage only the most patriotic and morally uplifting of presentations. The anti-opening brigade had to accept these assurances and indeed many were soon won over. The theatres and music-halls became the arenas for what were, in effect, patriotic rallies.

The first hint of what was in store came when Margarethe visitedthe Comédie Française; proud posters proclaimed that the performance was in aid of the Secours National aux Blessés. Her apprehension increased as the curtain opened to reveal Marthe Chenal draped in the folds of an enormous Tricolor; to a great roar of approval the statuesque singer proceeded to give an emotional rendering of the 'Marseillaise' — by the end of the first verse the entire audience had joined in and the last verse was almost drowned in a tumult of tears.

Everywhere she went it was the same. At the Opéra and the Odéon, the Théâtre des Capucines and the Opéra Comique the audience sang 'La Marseillaise', 'La Brabançonne' or, the song that became the French equivalent of 'Tipperaray', 'On les Aura'; and the company presented such gems as 'La Fille du Regiment', 'La Patrie' or 'Les Enfants de la République'. Performances were sometimes interrupted by an actor, dressed specially for the moment in combat gear, holding up his hands for silence and announcing the latest news of this or that triumph or disaster at the Front. Collecting tins were passed among the audience with exhortations to dig deep for the Red Cross or for prisoners of war, for orphans,widows, wounded heroes or for the defence of the nation.

For once Margarethe did not need to be told — she knew

that she had no place here. Theatres were no longer in the business of entertainment and audiences no longer looked for diversion or light relief from behind the footlights. Gone were the elegant groups of gentlemen in dinner jackets and their bare-shouldered and bejewelled *petites-amies*, the genteel laughter and the social tittle-tattle; vanished, perhaps forever, those delightful days when the latest sensation would be showered with carnations in celebration of her beauty and have invitations pressed on her by ardent admirers whose silk-lined cloaks swung nonchalantly from velvet-clad shoulders.

The stark contrast between the idle, glittering past and the grim, functional present was too shocking to be ignored. As her performance in Arnhem had been her final appearance in public, so Margarethe's letter to Astruc was her last attempt at a comeback. Time and the war had conspired to end her career for once and for all.

$$* \quad * \quad * \quad * \quad *$$

All this while she was being watched. In the grip of the same fervour that motivated the members of the Ligue, her watchers saw significance in her every step. The subject of an unceasing surveillance, she was 'considered suspect on account of her indiscriminate relations with numerous officials of all ranks, all ages and all nationalities'. If nothing concrete could be held against her, then there was always the possibility of guilt by association: 'During the last few days she has become very close to a wealthy and highly suspicious Rumanian by the name of Koanda. This man has a record as a fraud and a swindler, and a deportation order is about to be made out against him on the grounds that his activities are contrary to the national interest'. The fact that Rumania was at this stage still a neutral country, although it would eventually enter the war on the side of the Allies, and that fraud was by no means peculiar to, or even particularly relevant to a war situation, did not enter into the matter. Had their reports mentioned nothing more damning than that Madame MacLeod was suspected of having measles, it would still have been that one word 'suspected' that jumped off the page and into official consciousness.

The watchers could have come right out in the open for all the difference it would have made to Margarethe's behaviour, for she had not the slightest inkling that she was under suspicion. An awareness of their interest might have mystified her or irritated her but it would not even have prompted her to examine her conscience. Secret agents, spies, classified information — these were as remote from her thoughts and as irrelevant to her life as barbed wire, trenches and bombs. If she had thought about them at all it would only have been as component parts, indistinguishable from a thousand others, of this vast, vindictive monster that was the war.

The effort of facing up to the failure of her attempt at a comeback left Margarethe drained and distracted. She could not even summon the energy to collect the possessions that had ostensibly been her whole reason for coming to Paris in the first place. In the month since she had arrived in her favourite city she had received a succession of punishing blows to her pride and to her plans. She had miscalculated at every step — the eagerly anticipated party had turned out to resemble nothing so much as a beleaguered scout-camp, there was no sign of anyone she knew there, and not only had she arrived unsuitably dressed, but it now transpired that she was both uninvited and not particularly welcome. Although she was not much given to introspection, she must have been aware that her disillusionment with Paris was the latest in a long line of similar disappointments. She had travelled with high hopes to Madrid, Berlin, Vienna, Egypt, Paris, Berlin again, then Holland and now back to Paris, but none of these places had lived up to her expectations — with every anticlimax her optimism was becoming a little harder to sustain.

As Margarethe was contemplating her predicament, the watchers were warming to their task. There was a definite hint of pique in the report they handed in to the offices of the Deuxième Bureau on 11th January: 'We have to inform you that before we were able to complete our investigations Madame MacLeod left Paris'. Travelling once more via Spain but managing to avoid another interview with the British Immigration Services, Margarethe returned, chastened and dejected, to Holland. The Baron was due back in The Hague soon — he at least would be glad to see her.

A SLIGHTLY NAUGHTY GAME

Whereas the best equipped and most active international espionage networks of today are those of the two superpowers, the United States and the Soviet Union, that was very far from being the case during the First World War. The considerable resources of the Russian Secret Service in the years leading up to the Bolshevik revolution were understandably focussed on internal dissent and upheaval. To the Americans, on the other hand, the concept of anything as innately covert as a secret service ran counter to their vision of the United States as 'The Land of the Free'. From an international point of view the values of the Monroe Doctrine still discouraged statesmen and politicians from getting involved in European affairs. Though this aloofness would be turned on its head in the later years of the war, even then the American Secret Service was negligible by comparison with those of its European allies.

The intelligence service in France at the beginning of the war was still smarting from the public humiliation it had suffered over the Dreyfus affair. Strenuous efforts had been made to root out the corruption that had led to a totally innocent man being arrested, tried, convicted and deported for selling military secrets to the Germans. The new brooms were determined to prove not only that the Deuxième Bureau was now a model of rectitude and discipline but also that it was a powerful force for the protection of the country.

The British Intelligence Service, for its part, still enjoyed an enviable reputation for efficiency — a reputation that had been enhanced by its early success in rounding up the German spy network in Britain at the outbreak of the war. Its origins lay in the historical necessity for Britain, as both a small island and a colonial power, to defend its vital sea-lanes and shipping routes; its efficiency was in large part due to its having been developed under the auspices of the Royal Navy. At this stage in their histories both the British Secret Service and the French Deuxième Bureau were concerned more with military than with political intelligence, a bias that they shared with their German counterparts.

But neither of them would have been a match for the Abwehr, as it came to be called, had this impressive organisation not suffered from one debilitating national weakness and one serious physical disadvantage. Paradoxically its weakness lay in the complacent assumption that the German military forces were too powerful to need any assistance from what was considered a subordinate department. According to Colonel Walther Nicolai, the General Staff officer who commanded the German Secret Service throughout the war, 'strong scepticism prevailed in the army commands regarding the possibility and the usefulness of espionage. This went so far that one army command, on the advance through Belgium, left the intelligence officer behind in Liege as needless ballast'.

The other disadvantage was geographical and only became apparent as the war progressed. Spies on both sides operated on three levels; at the lowest level there were the small-time, paid informers who could provide information on such things as public morale, troop movements, rail networks and transport facilities; then there were the spies with specialist knowledge who could report on communications, armaments, fortification levels in strategic areas, and technological advances that might constitute a threat; and thirdly, rarest and most valuable of all, there were those infiltrators at the highest level who could hope to learn something of the enemy's plans from as near as possible to the horse's mouth.

At the second and third level honours were probably about even between the two sides. If anything the Germans would have had the edge as far as high-level intelligence gathering was concerned had it not been for their misplaced confidence in their military invincibility. A Frenchman, Paul Lanoir, wrote an anguished exposé of the German Intelligence Service just before the war, in the hope of making his compatriots take the threat more seriously. In his book he revealed that a card index was kept in Berlin of every officer in the French armed services — against each name were entered details of the officer's private life with special reference to any personal quirks or weaknesses that might make him vulnerable to blackmail. The deficiency in the German network, however, was at the lowest level of espionage and was only revealed when the Western Front stabilised during the course of 1915.

Their difficulty lay in the fact that for the whole of the war the Western Front lay in French and Belgian territory. The German army was therefore living, working and fighting on enemy soil. Every French or Belgian national who suffered the *peine forte et dure* of German occupation behind the frontline became a potential supplier of information to the Allies. The Germans had no such partisan volunteer force on which to call. Their informers behind the French lines were therefore almost always working either for money or under threat of blackmail — patriotism rarely came into it, and their reliability was consequently open to question. When a shortfall was noticed in the ranks of these low-level informers, the word would go out that more had to be recruited.

The headquarters of the German Intelligence Service were in Berlin but its spies were controlled and recruited from strategically placed centres in, amongst other places, Switzerland, Holland and Spain. In these neutral countries the embassies not only of Germany but also of the *Entente* allies became the nerve-centres of countless espionage operations. Since in theory embassies are physically the territory of the country they represent, the activities that were carried on behind their closed doors could not be said to contravene the neutrality regulations. The Military or Naval Attachés on the staff of all these embassies were almost without exception either spies or spymasters. When a member of the German Diplomatic Corps in Madrid, Geneva or The Hague was seen suddenly to be widening his social circle in all sorts of unaccustomed directions it usually meant that a recruitment drive had been signalled from Berlin.

Just such a man was Karl Kramer. A long-time member of Colonel Nicolai's Intelligence Service, Kramer spent the war years as Press Attaché at the German Consulate in The Hague. In May 1916 he was introduced to Margarethe at a dinner party — and was quick to recognise a potential recruit. Four months in Holland had done nothing to restore her battered morale: the Baron was away again and Margarethe was feeling neglected, unwanted and thoroughly miserable — to have taken another lover in his absence would have caused a scandal certain to reach his ears. Although her trip to Paris had been both fruitless and frustrating, her few weeks there had made The Hague seem bleaker than ever by contrast. Ironically, shortages in the neutral Netherlands were more severe than in France and, since Margarethe's return, living conditions had steadily deteriorated. This was partly due to the British naval blockade of the Channel which, although aimed at Germany, inevitably prevented the import to Holland of vital food supplies. Butt an already grave situation was exacerbated by the influx across the border of both civilian and military refugees from occupied Belgium, an influx that would continue to grow over the four years of the war despite all German efforts to stem it. Eventually their concern over the usefulness of this border to the Allied armed forces and their secret services led the Germans to erect a high-voltage electric fence along the length of the frontier — a drastic measure that only served to increase the ingenuity of those determined to cross it.

The German border guards were, however, under strict instructions not to violate the neutrality of the Netherlands and, with a few grim exceptions, these instructions were obeyed. The Dutch, in turn, were aware that if their neutrality was to be respected by both sides then they had to keep at least some of the rules themselves.

> … [civilian refugees] met with much compassion and generosity, and many of them were spontaneously received into families. The refugees however were not

only civilians. There were also a large number of soldiers and our neutrality obliged us to disarm and intern them. The government set up internment camps without delay … it will be understood that it was not easy to find food for so many guests.

As Queen Wilhelmina of the Netherlands was quick to point out to her often confused subjects, 'neutrality in the sense in which it is used in international law does not simply mean that one stands aloof. It is a defined legal status which the neutral country has adopted, and the parties at war are obliged to respect its rights'. The phlegmatic monarch then went on to reassure them that she understood the dilemmas this stance would inevitably impose: 'This neutrality implies well-defined obligations for every Dutchman. The duties of neutrality are absolute and leave no room for human feelings. This situation can easily lead to tensions and struggles in the individual. At heart man is never neutral, he always has a preference … and the practical application of the rules has to be left to personal judgement.'

Although personal judgement was not one of Margarethe's most successful attributes, it was nevertheless one which she continually and determinedly exercised — sometimes with disastrous results. The most fateful of all her misjudgements followed on her second meeting with Karl Kramer. But as she would explain to her interrogator, when the German Press Attaché made his approach she thought she knew just how to handle him. 'One evening in May 1916 1 was in my house in The Hague. It was late and my elderly maid, Anna Lintjens, had gone to bed. Someone knocked at my door and I went to open it myself. I recognised M. Kramer who had written to say he would call but had not said why.'

As far as Margarethe was concerned there was only one possible reason for a man to call on her late at night; and Kramer's appearance placed her in something of a dilemma. Since she had few morals she would have had no qualms about the morality of entertaining other lovers in the Baron's house, but word of any such liaison would be sure to reach the Baron and, once again, she dare not jeopardise the security of her future for the sake of a few hours of pleasure. But for all her resolution it was hard to break the habits of a lifetime — she could not bring herself to shut the door in the face of an admirer. Kramer was invited in.

While Margarethe was still trying to work out how to reject his advances without hurting his feelings it became apparent that she had misread his intentions. When he revealed the true purpose of his visit she did not know whether to be insulted or flattered: 'M. Kramer knew of my connections with France and he asked me whether I would be willing to undertake some small commissions in Paris that would be much appreciated by the people of Germany'.

Early on in her career Margarethe had learnt that it was unsophisticated to appear surprised by anything or anyone. But Kramer's proposition was so totally unexpected that for a moment all she could do was stare at him in amazement. Kramer was quick to fill the pause: 'If you are able to help us I am authorised to offer you twenty thousand francs'. Margarethe recovered her poise at the mention of money, but the offer carried all kinds of implications that she would need time to absorb — she regained the initiative and postponed any decision by dismissing the figure as too paltry to be worthy of serious consideration. 'M. Kramer agreed with me, but he added that if I could give him proof that I was efficient then I would be able to earn much more. I said I would need a few days to consider the matter; he said he quite understood and asked me to contact him when I had made up my mind.'

Kramer then complimented Margarethe on her international reputation, let her know that he was impressed by her wide circle of acquaintances and allowed a hint of deference to creep in when he mentioned how uniquely well placed she was to have an influence on international affairs. Then he withdrew, leaving Margarethe partly indignant that he had not after all been lusting after her, partly relieved that her resolve had not been put to the test and found wanting, and wholly bemused. However, once she had recovered her breath and given the matter a little careful thought she realised nothing could be more logical than to take advantage of Kramer's proposal to settle an old score: 'I remembered my valuable furs that had been confiscated by the theatre in Berlin, and I realised this would be the perfect opportunity to reimburse myself for their loss. Therefore I wrote to Kramer and accepted his offer'.

But try as she might she would never be able to convince her prosecutors that this was her true motive. And just as they could not, or would not, accept her story so she could not, or would not, accept that it was her naive belief that she could double-cross the German Secret Service that would give them a firm foundation on which to build their case.

But all this was far in the future as she sent word to Kramer that she was ready to accept his offer. Kramer quickly scuttled round to her house armed with the twenty thousand francs in cash and some of the more legendary tricks of his trade. Margarethe admitted to being intrigued when he produced from his briefcase three bottles of invisible ink, 'two were transparent in colour and the third was blue-green'. The liquid in the first bottle was to dampen the paper, that in the second was for writing the message which could then be erased with the contents of the third bottle. It all seemed like a slightly naughty game. Playing along, she confided in Kramer that although she could envisage no problems over using the inks, she might be a little reluctant to sign any messages sent in this way with her own name. Kramer had thought of that one — any information she had to send should be addressed to him care of the Hotel de l'Europe in Amsterdam and should be signed merely 'H21'. He himself had no need to use an alias — the name Kramer was as common in Holland as Smith in England or Durand in France and was therefore anonymous enough.

Technology was already making quite an impact on intelligence gathering. Marconi's twenty-year-old invention of the wireless telegraph had come into its own as an invaluable means of communication; the telephone was established as a vital link in the chain; and an entirely new species of human — the cryptographer — had sprung into being to enhance the value of these channels. Each effective invention, however, rapidly acquired an effective countermeasure. Radio telegrams were being intercepted, telephones were being tapped and messages in code or cipher were being waylaid and decoded. But as yet this technology was available only to the select and well-trained few. Kramer had no intention of using Margarethe as anything more elevated than a paid gatherer of low-level information. As such, she would have no need of elaborate equipment — invisible ink would suffice. His instructions to her were of the simplest: 'go to Paris and send back any information you can pick up that might be of interest to us'.

Espionage and sexuality have been inextricably mixed since Delilah, in the pay of the Philistines, used the power of her sexuality to persuade Samson to reveal the source of his legendary strength. Certainly there have been countless instances of expert female agents infiltrating strategic bedrooms, patiently working their way into the affections of a highly-placed official until they gain access to his innermost secrets. Both sides in the First World War employed just such agents, with varying degrees of success. But this was intelligence gathering at the second, specialist level. Had she been working at this level Margarethe would have been given a specific, individual target; she would have spent weeks learning everything there was to know about him and months manoeuvring herself into a relationship close enough to give her the opportunity of exploiting it. Few men bright enough to hold a position giving access to classified information would at the same time be fool enough to share this information with a casual bedfellow.

A far more common link between espionage and sexuality is the use of the latter as a weapon of blackmail. Evidence of marital infidelity or, more effective still, sexual perversion has always been a powerful lever with which to force the miscreant to betray secrets. But for this purpose Margarethe was disqualified by her reputation as one of the most successful courtesans of her time. Few Frenchmen of her acquaintance would have crumpled under the threat of being exposed as one of her lovers — although the day was long gone when they would have considered sharing the bed of Mata Hari as something of which to boast, few reputations could have been so fragile as to feel threatened by the revelation. And not even the most damaging and vicious of the rumours that had whistled about her head for ten years had ever contained even the merest hint of perversion.

Kramer, therefore, was just enlisting Margarethe as a paid informer. She would be working on the same level as the waiters, shopkeepers and cleaners already employed by the Germans to keep their eyes and ears open, albeit in more glamorous surroundings. Where they would be expected to rifle through the contents of official waste-paper baskets, or report on who was meeting who for coffee in this or that discreet restaurant, she would be expected to take advantage of her social position to gain access to the homes of the affluent and influential. They might drop the occasional indiscreet remark in the privacy of their own apartments or let slip a careless word in the company of their intimate friends. All Margarethe had to do was pass these back to Amsterdam, and for this she would be amply rewarded.

Her claim that she had no intention of spying for Kramer can probably be re-interpreted as meaning she had no intention of sticking her neck out for him. The idea of being a spy might even have appealed to her imagination — after all it would give her her very own role to play in the war as well as offering a suitably enigmatic alternative to her previous career as a 'mysterious oriental dancer'. But it would have been totally out of character for her to have leapt into diligent action on Kramer's behalf — even for money. Her knowledge of the workings of the German Intelligence Service was non-existent; she had no inkling of the vast, ruthless machine that was grinding away over Kramer's shoulder and she probably reckoned it would be quite easy to fob off the unremarkable little Press Attaché with occasional tit-bits of gossip. If she did trip over some gem of secret information (and, more relevant and ever more unlikely, if she recognised it for what it was), well, she would be happy to pocket the generous reward. But she was most certainly not going to put herself out in the process. Kramer had given her a valid reason for returning to Paris and it is unlikely she gave the matter any more serious thought than that.

After a brief visit to The Hague the Baron rejoined his regiment and Margarethe was free to leave once more for Paris. Her new passport was issued on 15th May 1916 but, much to her indignation, she learned that her request for a visa for England had been refused. Although she had planned no more than a fleeting visit to London as a pleasant diversion on her way back to France, she saw this refusal as just one more infuriating curb on her personal freedom. So she went to the Foreign Office in The Hague and asked them to press her case. Obligingly, the Foreign Office sent a cable to the Netherlands Legation in London: 'Well-known Dutch artist Mata Hari, Netherlands subject whose real name is MacLeod-Zelle, wants to travel for personal reasons to Paris where she lived before the war. British Consul Rotterdam declines to put visa to passport though French Consul has done so. Please ask British Government to give orders consul Rotterdam that visa may be issued. Cable'. A week later the Netherlands Legation sent their reply: 'British Authorities have reasons why admission to England of lady mentioned is undesirable'.

Once again completely unknown to her, the memorandum in the Aliens Registry in London had been joined by another. Dated 22nd February 1916 and also labelled *Secret*, this one was even more uncompromising than the first.

ZELLE,M.G.
(Mata Hari)

Ref: Circular 61207/MO5 E

This woman is now in Holland. If she comes to this country she should be arrested and sent to Scotland Yard.

Copies:Ports (7), Home Office, Scotland Yard, MI1C, Havre, GHQ 1(b), HQ.IGC, Permit Office.

Dutch intelligence officers were keeping a close watch on all their country's conspiring visitors in a further attempt to safeguard their neutrality. They are even said to have kept themselves better informed about the machinations of British, French and German 'diplomats' than any of the belligerents. So their attention would have already been drawn to Margarethe by Kramer's visit. Although the British did not reveal the contents of this second circular to the Dutch authorities, the fact that the visa had been refused was enough to make them wonder whether Kramer's late night call on Margarethe might have been more than just a social one.

Shrugging off the disappointment, Margarethe boarded the *Zeelandia* on 24th May on the first leg of her journey back to Paris. She later claimed that one of her first acts on leaving Holland was to take Kramer's little bottles of invisible ink out of her handbag and drop them deliberately into Amsterdam's deep water canal. But her gesture of defiance was either lost on or missed by her new watcher. For once again she was under surveillance — this time from a zealous Dutchman instead of two bored French *flics*. Although the name of Henry Hoedemaker did not appear on the official lists of any intelligence service, he put it about that he was working for the British. His job, he claimed, was to patrol the Channel on the lookout for spies entering or leaving Holland.

If he was an agent he was a spectacularly inefficient one, with few if any of the essential qualifications for the job. In fact so conspicuous and indiscreet was he that Margarethe's travelling companions were able to warn her that she was the object of his scrutiny. It is far more likely that he was a self-appointed vigilante in the grip of spy-mania — one of those ubiquitous busybodies whose nuisance value is tolerated by those he decides to help only on account of his infuriating habit of so often being right. On board the *Zeelandia* Margarethe was at her most charming — the other passengers would remember her as a delightful travelling companion. When Hoedemaker, who was chronically unable to keep his mouth shut, confided to one of them that he had searched Margarethe's cabin the information was immediately passed on. Even recalling the incident twelve months later under interrogation, the memory was able to arouse Margarethe's wrath.

> I asked him in front of several witnesses whether he had been into my cabin, and he denied it. I then asked my witnesses if he had boasted to them of having been there. They confirmed that he had. I demanded that he apologise to me. When he refused to apologise I struck him in the face so violently that blood spurted from his mouth. The other passengers cheered my action.

When the ship docked at Vigo in northern Spain, Margarethe strode ashore still seething with indignation at

Hoedemaker's behaviour. An American fellow passenger from the *Zeelandia* warned her that Hoedemaker was a dangerous man to cross — and that he would be sure to cause difficulties with the immigration service, if not in Vigo then certainly at Hendaye where they would cross from Spain into France. Margarethe did not care. Her travel plans were not about to be upset by an insolent and bad-mannered nobody. There was no trouble at Vigo or Madrid, but at Hendaye Hoedemaker tried to get his revenge. Margarethe had to suffer the indignity of being thoroughly searched by the border police and then interrogated before finally being told she would not be allowed into France.

It was even more humiliating to discover that the taciturn policemen seemed impervious to her charms; neither her most winsome smile nor the mention of friends in high places could make them change their minds. So Margarethe pulled out all the stops. Her old flame Jules Cambon had returned to Paris from Berlin in October 1915 to become Secretary General of the Ministry of Foreign Affairs at the Quai d'Orsai, one of the most influential posts in the war-time administration of France and one that had been specially created for him. Margarethe withdrew as far as San Sebastian and wrote to Cambon asking for his assistance. It would have taken several days for the letter to reach Paris and several more before she could hope to receive a reply so, instead of posting it, she returned to Hendaye and flourished the missive in front of the police. This time they were impressed and she was allowed to proceed.

The incident with Hoedemaker had few repercussions — it is relevant only in that it serves to demonstrate how blind she was to the implications of having accepted Kramer's money. Had she really intended to spy for Germany the experience at Hendaye, as a foretaste of things to come, would have left her shaken and not a little apprehensive. As it was she felt neither threatened nor compromised because her conscience, as she saw it, was clear. To those who, courtesy of a thousand spy stories, have gained an insight into the world of espionage her naivety does appear incredible. In mitigation it can only be said that, in common with ninety-five per cent of her contemporaries in the days before the birth of the genre, her ignorance of the shady world she had entered was total.

With Kramer's twenty thousand francs in her pocket Margarethe booked into her favourite hotel, the Grand, on 16th June. Within forty-eight hours the *flics* from the Deuxième Bureau were back in position on the pavement. There was no sign of the Marquis de Beaufort but no shortage of alternative company. The list of visitors to her room, each one carefully noted by the watchers, was as varied as ever and included one Jean Hallaure, a young lieutenant in the French cavalry whom she had first met during her abortive reconnaisance trip to Paris in 1903 and who would play a significant if unwitting role in her ultimate fate.

Much to Margarethe's relief, Paris and the Parisians seemed noticeably more cheerful than they had been at the beginning of the year. Vera Brittain, in her piercing elegy *Testament of Youth*, put the atmosphere into its true perspective: 'France was the scene of titanic, illimitable death, and for this very reason it had become the heart of the fiercest living ever known to any generation. Nothing was permanent; everyone and everything was always on the move; friendships were temporary, appointments were temporary, life itself was the most temporary of all'. The continuing stream of soldiers in transit through the city added their zest to the frenzy - with the result that the streets had a cosmopolitan bustle that verged on the jaunty.

One *poilu*, returning to Paris on leave after several months at the Front, felt quite put out at the international invasion of his city:

> The onlooker has a job to distinguish between the thousands and thousands of soldiers of every race, origin and skin colour, from every army, of every social class and in every kind of uniform imaginable. The calm English, the ever-smiling Italians, the Belgians — a little slow and always looking as though their uniforms had been made for someone else; the Canadians looking completely at home, the astonishing kilted Highlanders, the surly Serbs, the heavy, severe Russians with theatrical half-boots whose blue eyes seem to reflect the nostalgia of the steppes; Portuguese, Japanese, Hindus, Brazilians, New Zealanders, Australians — amongst this motley the poor French soldier has no chance to shine.

The Marquis de Beaufort finally arrived in Paris for a short spell of leave in the middle of July. He moved into the room adjacent to Margarethe's in the Grand Hotel, but his days as her main attraction were numbered. While waiting for him to appear Margarethe had looked into a pair of those 'blue eyes that seemed to reflect the nostalgia of the steppes' and, for the first time in her life, she had fallen in love.

Her detractors, both at the time and since, have dismissed her passion for Vadime de Masloff as that of a middle-aged woman pathetically clinging to an illusion of youth, sometimes citing her choice of a lover young enough to be her son as proof that she was now reduced to paying a gigolo to satisfy her craving for admiration. But whatever their provenance or promptings, her feelings for the Russian were as genuine, as exciting and every bit as painful as if their ages had been reversed. In all her years of parading lovers before the world, she had never once mentioned either loving or being in love with any of them. Yet she was prepared, on the eve of her fortieth birthday, to broadcast her love for a man nearly twenty years her junior, despite the derision such a declaration would inevitably attract.

Those same detractors have pointed to the continuing stream of visitors to her room at the Grand to justify their scepticism — how could she claim to be in love with Masloff while she was still distributing her favours so widely? The daily reports from the watchers to the Deuxième Bureau could be said to prove their point:

> 12th July Lieutenant Hallaure, 15th–18th July Marquis de Beaufort, 30th July Commandant Yovilchevitch from Montenegro, 3rd August Lieutenant de Masloff, 4th August Captain Meriani of the Italian CRI, 16th August Captain Gerbaud, 21st August an unidentified English officer, 22nd August — [two this time but not simultaneously] — Irish officers James Plunkett and Edwin Cecil O'Brien, 24th August French General Baumgarten, 31st August Scottish officer James Stewart Fernie.

But the length of the list could also be said to demolish their argument — a woman who can attract such a wide variety of lovers can hardly be suspected of having lost her charm. As she herself would endeavour to explain, her passion for uniforms was as lively as ever.

> I love officers. I have loved officers all my life. I would prefer to be the mistress of a poor officer than of a rich banker. My greatest pleasure is to sleep with them without thinking of comparisons between the different nationalities. These gentlemen sought me out and I said 'yes' with all my heart. They went on their way content — I kept only Masloff. I adored him.

Vladimir de Masloff was just twenty-one years old and a Captain in the 1st Russian Special Imperial Regiment, one of the few units of the Russian army to see action on the Western Front. This spell of leave was his first visit to Paris, the city so beloved of the Russian aristocracy. French had long been the preferred language of the pampered and now so threatened elite of Moscow and St Petersberg, French fashions were thought to be the height of sophistication, French paintings the only works of art outside Russia worth collecting and France the only place to go to escape the rigours of the Russian climate and the provincialism of Russian society. Members of the Imperial Family were virtually honorary citizens of both Paris and Monte Carlo. Vadime's father, a General in the Russian army, was not a member of the aristocracy but his adoption of the French 'de' in his name reveals that he at least aspired to those sophisticated and fashionable heights. Young Vadime was well aware that by reaching Paris, even at this late and unpropitious moment, he was fulfilling cherished inherited ambitions.

The horrors of the Front so closely followed by the thrills of Paris already had Vadime's head reeling. When, within the space of a few hours, he was introduced to and almost immediately seduced by an elegant and infinitely charming woman who by her own account was also a world-famous artiste, he must have thought he was dreaming. But if so, it was a dream from which he was in no hurry to wake up. His stock amongst his colleagues soared when they saw him in such illustrious company, and he was no more immune than the next twenty-one year old to the glamour of an affair with an 'older woman'.

But for Margarethe it was not just an affair. It was a cataclysm. In all the years since the failure of her marriage to Rudolph she had equated 'feeling' with 'suffering'. Through the triumphs and disasters of her career and throughout her restless quest for the greenest pasture, she had shied away from any but the most superficial emotions. Now, for the first time, she was confronted by a man and a relationship that threatened to bring her protective wall of indifference crashing about her ears, to run riot through her deepest feelings and scatter her composure to the winds. And there was not a thing she could do to prevent it.

As with so many of her lovers, she had been drawn first to Vadime by his uniform: the high necked tunic, jodhpurs and gleaming Cossack boots had been intriguingly foreign. But under this romantic exterior she had discovered an intense and melancholy boy: alone, far from home and family, frightened but too proud to show it, who gazed at her in awe as at a goddess, loved her with impetuous passion and then slept in her arms like a child. It was an irresistible combination. Almost before she realised it her feelings for Vadime had turned from a trickle of attraction through a surge of passion into an overwhelming obsession.

All her reservations were swept away, all her resolve

forgotten; somehow this outwardly unremarkable Russian soldier had breached her defences. Suddenly emotion was the most natural thing in the world — all the love she might have given to Rudolph, all the care and devotion she might have lavished on Norman and Jeanne-Louise, all the tenderness and concern that had been denied an outlet for so many years were now Vadime's for the asking. For the remainder of his leave they spent every possible moment together, eating, drinking, laughing, loving, walking in the Bois or strolling along the banks of the Seine, with eyes for no one but each other. Margarethe took Vadime to a studio where they were photographed together standing arm in arm. On the back of the picture she wrote in flowing letters 'Souvenir of some of the most beautiful days of my life with my Vadime who I love more than anything in the world'.

When his leave came to an end Margarethe could hardly bear to let him go. When, less than two weeks later, she had word that he had been wounded on the Somme her immediate reaction was to drop everything and go to him.

His wounds were serious but not fatal — shrapnel from an exploding shell had hit him in the face blinding him in one eye and his throat and lungs had been seared by poison gas. But he was one of the lucky ones. The transporting of thousands of wounded men every day from battlefield to hospital was a logistical nightmare. In a blistering article in the *Echo de Paris* the journalist Maurice Barres launched a frontal attack on faulty administration in the *services sanitaires* and the inadequacies of the system.

Tetanus and gangrene have killed far too many of our soldiers, and they have all too often lost limbs, or even their lives, from the failure to transport them quickly to hospital ... The wounded have been put into cattle trucks, more or less clean, on to straw that is full of germs, they have lain for days on end with no food, no drink, no surgical help. Some have travelled the length of France when they should have been sent to the nearest hospital; others have been left on the battlefield because it was a human impossibility for the number of doctors and stretcher-bearers on the ground to get them away in time; others have been put into cold damp churches waiting for the help that came too late.

Barres cited as an example the case of one soldier, wounded at Peronne on the Somme, who 'remained three days in the ambulance; then he was sent to Montrouge in Paris, where he spent half a day; from there he was taken to Niort where he stayed three days; from there to Marseilles where he spent three hours before being taken back to Paris'.

Vadime fared better. Within twenty-four hours of being wounded he was being cared for in a military hospital. But Fate was again playing tricks on Margarethe; instead of being taken to one of the hundreds of hospitals in Paris her blue-eyed boy was taken to Vittel, a health-spa at the foot of the Vosges mountains — deep in the Zone des Armées. Not only would she need special permission to travel there but her innocuous interest in a militarily sensitive area would give her accusers another very handy peg on which to hang their case. Desperate to get to Vadime's side Margarethe ignored the obstacles, concentrating instead on assembling her strings and selecting the most appropriate one to pull. Her old friend Lieutenant Jean Hallaure had held a desk job in the War Ministry since being seriously wounded at the

Front and, without thinking of the morality of using the services of one lover to enable her to reach another, Margarethe decided to enlist his help in getting the required pass for Vittel.

Questioned later as to why he had been willing to give her this assistance, Hallaure explained that Margarethe had told him she had been unwell for a while and wanted to go to Vittel to take the waters. He claimed to have realised that this was just an excuse; but his job at the War Ministry did not give him access to classified information and he was therefore unaware that she was under any kind of suspicion — he had believed her real reason to be that she wanted to go to Vadime. On his recommendation, therefore, Margarethe presented herself at the office of the War Ministry on the boulevard St Germain where she could apply for a passport for Vittel. The officer charged with her interrogation would become familiar with the plaintive cry, '1 didn't know that the building also contained the office of the French Counter-Intelligence Service'.

A TERRIBLE
CONFUSION

With characteristic inconsistency Margarethe would later declare first that she met Captain Georges Ladoux completely by accident on the stairs of the building, then that she met him when she opened the door of his office by mistake, and sometimes that he was the person she had been told to contact about her permit for Vittel. Whatever the truth of the matter, it was a portentous encounter.

Georges Ladoux had been appointed by General Joffre to head the counter-espionage service in June 1915. Although he was a professional soldier and had spent several years in charge of training schoolboy cadets before going as an instructor to the Military College at Saint-Cyr, his talents were ideally suited to a behind-the-scenes existence in the shady world of espionage. He had contributed frequent articles to the left-wing journal *Radical* and congratulated himself on being the friend and confidant of artists and intellectuals. He had a passion for intrigue and a reputation for making even the simplest of matters excruciatingly complicated for the pure joy of unravelling them. This had the unfortunate effect of making it impossible for his colleagues and subordinates to understand either the man or his methods, which in turn would lead to him being arrested in October 1917 for complicity with the Germans. Presumably he was able to clarify things to the satisfaction of the courts, for he was acquitted of all charges and reinstated. But at the time of his meeting with Margarethe he was at the peak of his labyrinthine deviousness and, as chief of the Cinquième Bureau, well aware that Margarethe was under suspicion.

Writing his memoirs nearly twenty years later Ladoux would recall: 'It was in August 1916 that I met Mata Hari for the first time and it seems like yesterday. I can see her now, dressed despite the summer weather in a dark coloured suit and a broad brimmed straw hat decorated with a large grey feather'. Ladoux offered her a chair and sat back to enjoy himself — it was just the sort of situation he relished.

Margarethe perched on the edge of the offered chair and regarded Ladoux speculatively, wondering how best to handle the man upon whose goodwill depended her ability to reach Vadime. She saw, 'a fat man with a very black beard and very black hair and spectacles — tall and fat. Fatter than a man of fifty should be. He smoked all the time. He always had a little cigarette in his lips'. Taking her courage in both hands she explained to Ladoux that she needed to travel to Vittel to complete a cure started several months ago for a kidney complaint. She understood that Vittel was now in the Zone des Armées and that she would therefore require a permit before she could travel there.

Ladoux smiled beatifically. Her request was the clearest indication yet that she was indeed working for the Germans. As he explained: 'There was something very troubling about Mata Hari's request — particularly as her sudden wish to take the waters of the Vosges came only a few days after the decision had been taken by GQG to establish an airfield in the area from where bombing raids could be launched on German factories'.

But he had a plan. Mata Hari would be allowed to go ahead with her plans to take the waters of Vittel and to visit her Russian lover (of whose existence Ladoux was fully aware) and his agents would follow her every inch of the way. To those who would question the wisdom of permitting a suspected enemy agent to enter a prohibited area he would maintain that this was a very astute move — she only need take one step out of line for them to have their proof.

But he was careful. If she was indeed a German agent her suspicions would be instantly aroused should such a request be too readily granted — enough time must elapse between her application and its fulfilment for it to look as though thorough checks were being made. Ladoux explained the formalities and suggested she call again in a few days to hear the outcome. Margarethe had to be content with that, but it was hard to disguise her impatience. In an agony of restlessness she filled the next few days as best she could by scouring the shops for some new clothes to take with her to Vittel. Vadime must be in need of cheering up and he would appreciate her looking her best.

Ladoux, on the other hand, used the time to develop his plans. His penchant for the unorthodox had led him to recruit a motley collection of unlikely characters as his agents, many of whom were drawn from the artistic world. The stage director, Lugne-Poe, was sending him snippets of information from Scandinavia where he was touring with his company of actors. Mistinguette, Margarethe's celebrated successor as star of the *Folies Bergère*, was living in an apartment on the boulevard des Capucines rented by Ladoux and from where she could report on the activities of

Almereyda, a journalist suspected of preaching mutiny amongst the rank and file of the army. His meeting with Margarethe had started him thinking. If it could be proved that she was not a German agent, then it was worth considering whether she could be of some use to the Cinquième Bureau. Her connections were undoubtedly widespread and strategically interesting; intelligence reports had shown her to have an extravagant lifestyle that needed generous financial support — it might be worth sounding her out. It could do no harm to let her know he was interested in the possibility of employing her to work for France — if she really was working for the Germans such knowledge could even increase her self-confidence to the extent that she might betray her true colours in Vittel.

Poor Margarethe. So absorbed was she in building herself a secure future with Vadime that she could not see the remorseless hordes massing around her. Thanks to the regular allowance she was still receiving from the Baron in Holland and to the balance of Kramer's money, she had no immediate financial worries; but her emotional happiness was teetering on the edge of an abyss. The only man she had ever loved was lying wounded in some far-away hospital bed — her place was by his side, holding his hand, soothing his fever and caressing away his pain. The longer it took her to reach him the more miserable he must surely become, and the greater the chance that in his misery he might turn to other arms for comfort.

Three days after their first meeting she was back in Ladoux's office seeking news of her permit. Once more he ushered her politely to a chair and, carefully phrasing his questions to make them appear routine, asked her first about her feelings towards France. She replied firmly that she had always been a francophile. According to Margarethe the conversation, conducted in a typically arch manner and accompanied by significant looks and pregnant pauses, then went as follows.

> He said to me 'you can do so many things for us if you like' and he looked me in the eyes. I understood. I thought a long time. I said 'I can'. He said 'would you?' I said '1 would'. He said 'Would you ask much money?' I said 'yes I would'.

Ladoux remembered it slightly differently, claiming that he mentioned the fact that she was under surveillance from the British who suspected that she might be a spy but that he, Ladoux, had no such doubts about her. The inconsistencies scattered through the accounts each one would later give of this conversation and of their subsequent dealings with each other have been interpreted in diverse ways both by those who were involved in her trial and prosecution, and by subsequent interpreters of the story. To those with an interest in condemning her, Margarethe was inconsistent quite simply because she was making it all up and to those who suspected Ladoux of duplicity his version was an attempt to prove the correctness of his behaviour. An equally likely hypothesis seems to be that by the time she was called upon to report on the conversation Margarethe, not surprisingly, was in a terrible muddle about who said what to whom and why, and Ladoux was unable, even twenty years later, to abandon his lifelong passion for obscurity. Whatever course their conversation really took, the upshot was that Margarethe finally got her permit and agreed to visit Ladoux again when she returned from Vittel.

Although priority was obviously given to military traffic, throughout the war civilians could and did travel around France by train. One civilian traveller, making an excursion from Paris to visit relatives in Orléans, recalled that such wartime train journeys were always more or less of an adventure.

Everybody is liable to arrest in these days, even French-men, for we all have spies on the brain and it is not to be wondered at. For this reason it is as well to be provided with a superfluity of identity papers rather than too few. There is no glory in being arrested as a spy and there is much inconvenience; therefore we decided to arm ourselves with every identification paper we could gather together — birth and marriage certificates, passports, *permits de séjour*, identity cards and any amount of letters from 'persons of irreproachable distinction'. The result was we were never asked to show so much as an envelope, but the inner satisfaction that we could do so if necessary was comforting.

For all the paraphernalia and discomfort involved in making any such journey, there was something of a holiday atmosphere on these civilian trains. But the view from the train as it passed through areas that had been under German occupation was a sobering one.

We thought we could distinguish the marks of the German horses' hoofs on the roadside; we imagined the terror of any inhabitants who might have remained in the village as they watched the enemy's troops ride past; many of the houses were the homes of poor people and to see them lying there nothing but heaps of stones, iron and charred wood is a dismal sight.

Margarethe did not get her pass until the end of August, by which time her patience was very nearly exhausted. She had received a plaintive postcard from Vadime in which, with the perennial Russian passion for diminutives, he begged his 'beloved Marina' to come to him — although he was now recovering well he was still very much in need of sympathy and affection. By now he must surely be losing faith in her. And even if he was not, every day that passed made it more likely that his wounds would have healed sufficiently for him to have to return to active duty. When she finally set off from Paris Margarethe's relief and delight more than compensated for the rigours of the journey. She arrived in Vittel on 1st September 1916.

Before the war Vittel had been renowned as a sedate and gracious health spa, where jaded bon viveurs could stroll the *boulevards* waiting for the restorative waters to work wonders on their battered constitutions, and where every elegant hotel garden nurtured groups of pale convalescents timidly testing their recovery in slow, measured paces round the flowerbeds. The war had changed all that. The faded, querulous gentlefolk could no longer justify indulging their *maladies de richesse*; their places in the dappled shade of the chestnut trees had been taken by a kaleidoscope of walking wounded. Every man who could move was encouraged to take the fresh air: men with arms in slings, hands swathed in bandages, heads enveloped in a cloud of gauze leaving only two holes for the eyes, men on crutches guiding men who had been blinded and amputees in rickety wheelchairs being trundled about by their dot-and-carry-one comrades, they joked and smoked, played endless games of cards, wrote letters to their loved-ones and dozed in the sun. The genteel hotel rooms had been transformed into stark, functional and often overcrowded hospital wards that echoed with the groans and cries of the wounded and dying.

As the crow flies Vittel is less than seventy-five miles from Verdun. The brutal battle that had raged round that hapless town since February was temporarily in abeyance as the focus of action had transferred to the Somme. But it has been estimated that seventy per cent of the French Army fought at Verdun at one point or another during 1916; French casualties numbered some 500,000 men killed or wounded, and the facilities not only of Vittel but of every medical centre in Western France were stretched to the utmost.

By the time Margarethe had picked her way through these bizarre crowds to Vadime's hospital her relief had turned once more to anxiety. What if Vadime had been hiding the truth from her? He could have been wounded far more seriously than he was prepared to admit — maybe he had been mutilated beyond recognition. In response to Margarethe's anxious enquiries a harassed nurse directed her out onto the terrace. She scanned the rows of faces, oblivious to the appreciative whistles and good-natured cries of 'come and hold my hand', 'you can mop my brow any time you like' and 'where have you been all my life, darling' which greeted her from their ranks. And then she saw Vadime. He was pale and thin and wearing a black patch over his left eye, but he was on his feet and walking rather shakily towards her along the terrace.

To those who witnessed the touching reunion there was nothing remarkable in their obvious love for each other.

Many a stranger relationship blossomed in those extraordinary times and nowhere more often than in the military hospitals. To the wounded, exhausted, mud-encrusted men, coming from the squalor of the trenches to the cool, white, calm of a hospital, there was something almost mystically attractive about the gentle women who cared for them. To the women who tended their wounds and patched up their hideous mutilations these men were so heroic, their injuries so severe, their courage so limitless and their uniforms so attractive that it was only a short step from admiration to love. Every hospital had its tale of unlikely unions born of this reciprocal attraction. At Chaillot a twenty-three-year-old soldier from the 107th Infantry, blind in both eyes and with both arms amputated, was led to the altar by a little white-haired lady old enough almost to be his grandmother - the joy on their faces was so radiant that his comrades were moved to club together and buy the couple a house in Normandy. A prim, middle-aged school teacher in a small country village near Lyons married a once dashing young officer in the Hussars whose face was so mutilated he was forced to cover it completely with a mask. By comparison with these remarkable relationships the love between a twenty-one-year-old boy and a sophisticated *femme du monde* old enough to be his mother aroused not the slightest comment or surprise.

Vadime and Margarethe could not but be affected by the atmosphere of Vittel. Against a background of such suffering every emotion was heightened: joy was more sublime, love more precious and the thought of loneliness made infinitely more unbearable by the threat of imminent separation. Their time together was brief; after ten days Vadime's wounds were considered to have healed sufficiently for him to return to active service. In the grim knowledge that the average life expectancy of an officer at the Front was just five months; that many of his friends had already died; and that his family were thousands of miles away, Vadime swore his undying love to Margarethe — his parting words were a proposal of marriage and her farewell a radiant acceptance.

Georges Ladoux was eagerly awaiting his agents' accounts of Margarethe's activities in Vittel, and he was only marginally disconcerted to discover they had nothing significant to report. Her behaviour, they told him, had been irreproachable. She had stayed on in Vittel for a few days after her Russian lover departed and had returned to Paris on 13th September without making a single suspicious move or contact. So be it. Now was the time for a more positive approach. When, as agreed, she called at his office a few days after her return Ladoux got straight down to specifics: was she still willing to work for France and if so how much would she expect to be paid? Margarethe, who was dreaming about her future with Vadime, replied airily that if her work proved satisfactory she would expect one million francs. Considering that this sum represented the combined salaries of a dozen of his top agents, Ladoux managed to keep a remarkably straight face.

He would later claim that he still suspected her of being a German agent and was just giving her sufficient rope to hang herself: 'To gain her confidence it was necessary to seem to be asking her to work for the French. The conversations she had with me were intended to calm her fears'. Gently letting out the rope, he asked her how she thought she would be able to serve France. Her reply, according to Ladoux, showed she had as inflated an idea of her influence as of her worth.

> Rising theatrically to her feet and apparently plucking her ideas out of thin air as she spoke, she said 'The Germans have always adored me. If you could only have seen the way they treated me in Berlin — like a queen; unlike in France where I am not thought to be very respectable. Their desire for me had them grovelling at my naked feet. In Berlin I was the mistress of the Crown Prince [presumably thanking her lucky stars that she had never denied the rumours] and he would be thrilled to see me again. A coup like that would surely earn me one million francs'.

Another few yards of rope: 'But Mata Hari, nobody with your contacts with France could hope to get anywhere near him'. If Ladoux was reporting the conversation faithfully and not just twisting the facts to justify his later actions, Margarethe then obligingly placed her head right in his noose by stating that she knew someone who could arrange it all for her: 'his name is Kramer'.

The name exploded like a firecracker in the ears of the counter-espionage chief. But once again Ladoux managed to keep a straight face. The Allied Intelligence Services knew all about Kramer but his links with Margarethe, although rumoured, had never been confirmed. By admitting her connections with him Margarethe had confirmed his suspicions — she must be a German spy. But still he had no intention of arresting her. So set was she on earning her million francs and living out her grandiose fantasies that she seemed oblivious to the implications of her remark — there was still a chance he could use her. Ladoux therefore explained that he would not be able to pay her anything at all until she had proved that she could be trusted, nor would she receive any of the trappings of a spy — no contact address, no code number, not even any money for expenses. All he could promise was that she would earn twenty-five thousand francs for every enemy agent she was able to deliver to him. But he was curious to know why she was willing to undertake such a risky mission. Her reply rings truest of all the statements he claims she made: she needed the money. She was planning to marry a Russian officer from a good family and there was a better chance of them approving the match if she could show them she was a very rich woman.

For all her lofty remarks about the Germans 'grovelling at her feet, hardly able to control themselves', it is obvious that it was now Margarethe who was grovelling, not before Ladoux but before Vadime. She was still not confident of her ability to hold on to him, even with his proposal ringing in her ears, and was desperately arming herself with every possible magnet. Her charms might fade a little more slowly if she was worth a million francs and she was prepared to risk everything in order to get her hands on the money.

According to Margarethe's testimony, Ladoux told her to go back to her house in Holland and await further instructions; but she had a few loose ends to clear up before she could leave Paris. Vadime had unexpectedly passed through the city on his way to a new posting and during their one precious night together they had agreed that she should lease an apartment for their future meetings and, who knows, even for their future life. She must make it habitable and equip it with a few comforts in case Vadime had the opportunity to use it while she was away. Then, since Ladoux had refused even to pay her expenses, there was the small matter of arranging finance for her journey. Through the Dutch Legation in Paris she sent a cable to Anna Lintjens, her maid in The Hague, asking her to arrange for five thousand francs from her allowance from the Baron to be sent to her. The contents of the cable were inspected by the Deuxième Bureau. 'Aha' they whispered to themselves, 'Anna Lintjens — that must be one of Kramer's aliases' and they duly noted the fact in their files. They appear not to have appreciated the irony, were this the case, of Mata Hari financing her first mission for the French out of German intelligence funds.

The money arrived in Paris on 4th November and, armed with this and a visa permitting her to leave France for Spain and Holland, Margarethe headed south the next day. A few days after her arrest Ladoux would write a letter setting out the background to her case to Pierre Bouchardon, the military magistrate charged with investigating the whole affair. In it Ladoux would claim that sending her back to Holland was just a ruse to get her to Spain: 'we had our suspicions that she was in the service of the Germans but we had to prove it, and for that it was necessary to arrange for her to spend some time in Spain where our intelligence services are particularly well organised'. But the 'particularly well organised' intelligence services obviously failed to realise what was expected of them. Instead of arranging for Margarethe to 'spend some time' with them, they had her followed on her journey through Madrid and on to Vigo and then watched her set sail for Holland on board the *SS Hollandia*.

This time Margarethe had no intention of leaving the *SS Hollandia* until it reached its destination. The failure of her last application for a visa to visit Britain still rankled, and in any case she was eager to get on and prove her worth to

Ladoux. Indeed, no call at an English port was scheduled. But Fate decreed otherwise. As guardians of the Channel, British naval authorities had the right to stop and search every vessel passing through. Word had reached them from Whitehall that amongst the passengers was thought to be a woman suspected of spying for the Germans. A Royal Navy frigate was therefore despatched to intercept the ship and escort it into Falmouth harbour.

The ship's cargo, accommodation and passengers were thoroughly inspected. As she would later testify, Margarethe was vastly indignant to find herself the object of their particular attention.

> The ship was invaded by policemen, soldiers and women officers whose job it was to search the women passengers. Two of them searched my cabin, even going to the lengths of unscrewing the mirrors off the wall. I was interrogated by an officer who questioned me as to my identity — then he fixed me with a strange look and pulled a photograph from his pocket of a woman dressed in Spanish costume with a white mantilla. The portrait looked a little like me except that the woman was shorter and heavier than I am.

When the officer had asked whether this was not a picture of her, she had been able to laugh off the suggestion. But he had not been convinced and Margarethe was asked to disembark. She was taken into the custody of an officer of the Cornwall constabulary, escorted to London by train and handed over to Scotland Yard. With her introduction to Assistant Chief Commissioner Sir Basil Thomson, who was in charge of counter-espionage at Scotland Yard, Margarethe achieved the hat-trick. Now she could claim with complete accuracy that within the space of five months she had made contact with all three intelligence services: the German through Kramer, the French through Ladoux and now the British through Sir Basil Thomson. It was quite an impressive list for a middle-aged, small-time, would-be agent for she-couldn't-quite-decide whom, who had yet to be the slightest use to any of them.

Thomson was very much in the Noel Coward style of English gentlemen. An old Etonian and Oxford graduate, he was witty, urbane, immaculately dressed and, beneath the suave exterior, dedicated to his job. This included responsibility for the Irish Special Branch as well as counter-espionage — even in those days surely more than one man could be expected to handle. Nevertheless, when Margarethe was brought in to Scotland Yard on 13th November 1916 it was Thomson himself who conducted the interrogation. Her worst fears were allayed by his first question, for he demanded to know whether her name was indeed Clara Benedix. When Margarethe replied indignantly that it most certainly was not, that her name was Madame Margarethe Gertruida Zelle MacLeod, also known as Mata Hari, and here was her passport to prove it, Thomson had to withdraw to consider his next move in the light of this startling information.

Scotland Yard had been acting on what they thought to be reliable information stating that Clara Benedix, a known German spy working in Madrid, had been travelling on the *SS Hollandia*. After mulling it over for the night, during which time Margarethe was confined to a cell in Scotland Yard, Thomson unwittingly betrayed a characteristic which he shared with his French counterpart, Georges Ladoux. As

Ladoux, convinced of the infallibility of his case, had decided that 'Anna Lintjens' was an alias used by Kramer, so Thomson decided that Clara Benedix and Mata Hari must be one and the same person, although which was the alias he was not quite sure. A glance at his files had shown him that the lady in his custody, whatever name she was using, was under suspicion of espionage. He sent a cable to Spain asking for confirmation that Clara Benedix had, in fact, boarded the *SS Hollandia* and the next morning he called Margarethe up to his office for some preliminary questioning while he waited for a reply.

If she was indeed Margarethe MacLeod, he told her, then his department knew a thing or two about her. This in itself was no cause for alarm, Margarethe reminded herself, it was only natural, after all she was a famous woman. Thomson went on to reveal that he was in possession of certain facts, one of which concerned a sum of 20,000 francs. Had anyone given her such a sum before she had gone to France? No. Was she sure? In Holland? This time Margarethe admitted that she had taken 20,000 francs out of her bank account to take with her to France. Thomson thought he could discern a link here, and asked her from which bank she had withdrawn the money. When she told him that it had been the Londres Bank he cast his fly and watched for a reaction. 'Londres Bank is the bank of the German Embassy'. If he expected her to rise to this conspicuous bait he was disappointed. Margarethe shrugged, 'I don't know'. Thomson tried again. 'We have information that Mata Hari received 20,000 francs from the German Embassy'. This time he just got the shrug. Although the extent of his knowledge must have shaken her, she was well versed in the art of disguising stage fright. To her relief Thomson seemed content to let it rest there for now. After asking her some more or less routine questions about her past he had her escorted back to her cell.

Pacing the floor in alternate bouts of righteous indignation and panic, Margarethe decided to settle for outrage as the best defence. With Thomson's permission she wrote a letter to the Dutch Ambassador in London begging him to help her.

> Excellency, I most respectfully request you to come to my assistance as quickly as possible. I have been implicated in a terrible confusion. I am Madame MacLeod, nee Zelle, a divorcee. I am *en route* for Holland from Spain, in possession of a valid passport, but the English police pretend that it is false and insist that I am not Madame Zelle. I am in a terrible state of nerves, imprisoned here at Scotland Yard. I beg you to come to my aid. I live in The Hague, at 16 Nieuwe Uitleg, and I am as well known there as in Paris where I have lived for some years. I am completely alone here and I swear to you that my affairs are all strictly in order. It is just a misunderstanding, but I implore you to help me.
> Sincerely, Margarethe Zelle MacLeod.

Thomson decided to sit on this epistle for a while. He wanted to find out as much as possible about his captive before she was whisked away, as a neutral had every right to be, by the Dutch Ambassador. At their next interview he showed her a picture and asked if it was of her. This time Margarethe was able to confirm that it was indeed. 'Yes. That is the picture M. Rudeaux took of me.' Then, taking the initiative, she told Thomson she hoped he was now satisfied that she was not Clara Benedix. Feeling more expansive this time, Thomson explained his predicament:

> Well rather a curious thing has happened. We have our doubts about all this. We have got to get evidence from Spain as to whether you are a separate person from Clara Benedix, or whether you are one and the same. We have also been in touch with our people in Holland. They tell us that Madame Zelle is suspected of being a German agent, that Mata Hari truly is a German agent and so is this Clara Benedix. So you see my problem.

It was outside the brief of the stenographer recording the interview to comment on such things as tone of voice, expressions or reactions — he recorded merely what was said. But it is not hard to imagine the impact Thomson's words must have had on Margarethe. They gave her her first real hint of the scope of the shady world into which she had had the temerity to stray, and her first premonition of its power to contaminate. It was beyond her powers of rational thought to absorb all the implications of his remarks — but of one thing she was now certain. If Scotland Yard had enough information about her to suspect her of being a German agent, without her having carried out one single little mission on their behalf, then she was clearly in very deep water indeed. There was no longer any point in pretending she was just involved in a case of mistaken identity. It was time to discard a few veils.

If Thomson's remarks had had the required impact on Margarethe, her next words were equally effective. 'Now I have to tell you something that will surprise you. I thought it was too big a secret. This Captain, Captain Ladoux, asked me to go into his service and I promised to work for him.' Thomson's mask of imperturbability remained intact and he confined his reaction to a quiet rebuke. 'You ought to have mentioned this to me yesterday.' But her revelation put a whole new complexion on the matter. Before deciding where to go from there he realised he must establish the veracity of her claim.

For the best part of an hour he questioned her closely about Ladoux, where had she met him, what did he look like, did he speak loudly or softly, had she noticed any particular habits or peculiarities of speech that would prove conclusively that she knew him. He was well acquainted with his French counterpart and Margarethe's answers convinced him that she had certainly met the counter-espionage chief. Very well then, what about the work she had promised to do for him? Her explanation that she had been given no specific mission, but had been told merely to go back to Holland and await further instructions must have sounded lame even to Margarethe. So anxious was she to prove that she was on the right side, and so desperate to cling on to her opportunity to earn a million francs, that she then related (or invented) a story intended to bolster her claim to be working for the French. Her anxiety was beginning to have a detrimental effect on her command of the English language and on her ability to explain herself clearly.

When I was in Vigo I met the French Consul at the Dutch Legation. He said to me 'You love a Russian officer. You would give him the pleasure of sending a telegram to see if he is wounded, and work a little with me. Will you do something for the Russians?' I did not mention the French. He said 'Can you go to Austria?'

He said he wanted to know what reserves they had to fight. He said 'Do you know Austria?' I said yes I had danced in Vienna. I was to go there and await his instructions.

This garbled and unlikely tale had the opposite effect on Thomson to that which Margarethe had intended. The ramifications of the whole business were beginning to exasperate him and he fell back on irony: 'It would be awkward to have a levee of all the belligerent countries in your room'. The irony was lost on Margarethe who claimed to have no idea what he meant. Anxious to bring the interview to an end, Thomson finally asked her whether either Ladoux or the Consul in Vigo had given her any money. Margarethe admitted that they had not. 'Just a promise that if you were useful ...?' Something in his manner must have betrayed his scepticism for she rapidly back-pedalled on the Vigo tale. 'I would not make anything out of the Russian business.' But she had to convince him about Ladoux: 'If I gave Captain Ladoux plenty of satisfaction then I would be paid 1,000,000 francs.'

Thomson had had enough. His parting words as he left the room were 'well, we have sent a cable to Spain'. This time instead of being taken back to her cell, Margarethe was allowed to leave Scotland Yard. Her luggage, which had in the meantime been thoroughly searched and its entire contents meticulously listed by the police, was restored to her and she was told she could stay where she pleased, but that she would be kept under observation and very likely summoned for further questioning. Something, at least, could be salvaged from this harrowing experience, even if it was only the fulfilment of an old ambition: chin held high and loftiest expression to the fore, she demanded to be escorted to the Savoy Hotel.

That night Thomson fired off another cable about his erstwhile captive, this time to Ladoux asking him to confirm that Margarethe Zelle MacLeod, otherwise Mata Hari, was one of his agents. But if he expected the replies neatly to clear up the whole matter for him, he was to be disappointed. A cable from Spain revealed that a mistake had been made — the woman Clara Benedix was still in Madrid. A cable from Ladoux stated baldly 'never heard of her', and a note from the Dutch Embassy in response to Margarethe's letter (which Thomson had finally forwarded) confirmed that the lady in question was, indeed, a bona fide Dutch citizen in possession of a valid passport.

Thomson now had three options open to him. He could allow Margarethe to continue her journey to Holland, he could arrest her as a spy, or he could send her back where she came from. It was the cable from Ladoux which finally made up his mind. Thomson was well aware that spy-masters automatically denied all knowledge of their agents if they got into trouble, but Margarethe had proved beyond doubt that she had met Ladoux. Surely the least Ladoux could have done, as a colleague and an acquaintance of Thomson, was to acknowledge this. His enquiries had revealed the evidence against her to be flimsy to say the least, and probably insufficient to warrant charging her with the offence, so Thomson resolved to land the whole problem back in Ladoux's lap. He summoned Margarethe for the last time and told her he had decided to send her back to Spain. Seeing through her probably better than anyone else, he suggested quite gently as they parted that she would be doing herself a favour if she would in future avoid getting involved in matters that were really no concern of hers.

By the beginning of December Margarethe was back in Madrid.

PASS THE PARCEL

Had her mind not been wrestling with the thorny problem of how to get her hands on Ladoux's million francs, Margarethe might have thoroughly enjoyed Madrid. Certainly there were worse places to be in 1916. Spain, like Holland, Sweden and Switzerland, remained neutral for the duration of the war. Its destiny was not at stake whatever the outcome; its strategic geographical position at the entrance to the Mediterranean rendered the preservation of its neutrality vital to both sides; and its rich deposits of minerals — copper, mercury, wolfram and even coal — were a crucial source of supply for the foundries and munitions factories of Allied and Central powers alike.

The flourishing trade in these and other commodities and the profits that accrued, discouraged the Spanish middle classes from expressing any personal preference for one side or the other and doused any smouldering partisan leanings. Together with the Church, which would not advocate belligerency, the army, which certainly did not wish to be thrown into the slaughter, and the aristocracy, which saw involvement in the war as a threat to their continued financial and social supremacy, the middle classes therefore remained firmly in favour of maintaining Spain's neutrality. King Alfonso XIII was heard to lament 'the King and the *ca-*

naille are the only ones who love France'. But he, too, was walking on a knife-edge, caught between his wife, Victoria-Eugenie, a granddaughter of Queen Victoria, on the one side and his forceful and determinedly pro-German mother on the other. Domestic as well as national tranquillity was at stake and the King bowed to the *forces majeures*.

As a result of this even-handed approach Madrid became a thriving international market-place with an increasingly cosmopolitan population. Far from the theatre of war, it suffered few of the crippling restrictions and shortages which had extinguished the bright lights of Paris, Berlin and Vienna. By comparison with these erstwhile meccas of hedonism the atmosphere in Madrid was restraint personi-fied — traditional Spanish decorum (under the watchful eye of the Church) and the inescapably sobering influence of the war precluded the perpetration of those startling excesses so beloved of the pre-war beau monde. Yet there was an elegance and style to life in the city that in other circum-stances Margarethe would have fully appreciated.

This is not to suggest, however, that there was no excite-ment in Madrid. On the contrary, beneath the refined and gracious exterior there bubbled a veritable witches' brew of intrigue and conspiracy. For the largest and most efficient of all the intelligence networks were centred on the Spanish capital, operated beyond their own borders by both France and Germany. To Germany in particular, a country with no direct access to the Mediterrarean, Spain was the ideal place from which to conduct their 'secret war'. It was vital to the German cause that their submarine fleet operating in the Mediterranean should have access to Spanish ports for refuelling, and it was the responsibility of the German 'dip-lomats' in Madrid to ensure that this option remained open to them.

The Allies, of course, were well aware of the real function of the outsized German diplomatic mission to Spain. But as direct military action against their enemies was out of the question on neutral soil, it was a case of matching secret agent with secret agent. As the German contingent grew, so did the French; as German profficiency and effectiveness increased so it had to be equalled or surpassed by the French. It was in recognition of this fact that Georges Ladoux had contrived to send Margarethe to Madrid in the first place. He was, in effect, just passing the buck — just as Basil Thompson had intended to pass the buck back to him. But by returning her to Spain, Thomson was unwittingly serving the Frenchman's cause rather than landing him with a problem.

Instead it was Margarethe who had the problem. Her arrest and detention in London, alarming enough in themselves, had stymied her plan to prove her worth to Ladoux. If she were to return to Paris with nothing to show for her month's absence he might not be willing to give her a second chance. Her million francs, and the magical seal it was meant to set on her relationship with Vadime, seemed in danger of slipping out of her reach. She wrote to Ladoux asking for further instructions, but when no reply was immediately forthcoming, in her own words she 'decided to take the bull by the horns. What was to prevent me from using my time to make contact with the Germans? At that moment if I could have found a way to sleep with the German Ambassador, I would have done so. Daring challenges require daring action'.

Realising, perhaps, that the route to the German Ambassador's bed might be paved with insurmountable obstacles, Margarethe directed her attentions to his subordinates Hans von Kalle and Han's von Krohn, respectively the Military and Naval Attachés to the German Embassy. Her eternal passion for soldiers prompted Margarethe to concentrate on von Kalle who, as luck would have it, was infinitely better looking than his naval counterpart. From her elegant room at the Palace Hotel she penned him a commendably succinct note. '*Mon Capitaine*, I wish to talk to you. Which day and which time would suit you?'

Had her choice fallen on von Krohn both the reply and her whole future might have turned out very differently. For von Krohn already had a beautiful and very possessive mistress, Marthe Richer, who would have had something fairly sharp to say about another woman moving in on her patch — not because she was in love with von Krohn, who by her own admission was 'ugly, skinny, boring and blind in one eye', but because it had taken her months of hard work and scheming to reach her present privileged position. For Marthe Richer was exactly what Margarethe wanted to be — a French spy working for Georges Ladoux.

But there the similarity between the two women ended. Where Margarethe was naive, clumsy and motivated entirely by cupidity, Marthe was dedicated, meticulous and very brave. One of the few women in France at that time to have qualified as a pilot, she had presented herself to Ladoux and offered to work for him after her husband was killed at Verdun. Twenty years after the war she and Ladoux would collaborate, in an orgy of mutual admiration, on writing the story of their partnership, *Ma Vie d'Espionne*, in which is reproduced some of their more stirring conversations:

'There are some things, *mon capitaine*,' I told him, 'to which it is not possible for a woman to consent.'

Ladoux, stern faced, replied, 'But Marthe, think of the sacrifices being made by all those poor boys in the trenches'.

My heart sank. I protested, 'But what you are asking of me is total abnegation. It is a sacrifice greater than death'.

He was implacable 'The service demands it'.

I was forced to resign myself to the inevitable. I told him, 'The service demands a very great deal — but I will do my best'. He knew what it had cost me to say those words, and he tried to make it easier for me by showing me how much was at stake. 'There is something that will support you, Marthe. You must think of all the mothers in France who, thanks to your efforts, will be reunited with their sons who are fighting at sea. Baron von Krohn is responsible for those submarines whose torpedoes are sending them to their deaths. Your little moral objections cannot stand in the way of such a great task'.

The melodrama was intentional. She was trying to restore her reputation which had suffered severely when Georges Ladoux was arrested. Although he himself would be reinstated, some of the mud stuck to those of his operatives who did not have the same opportunity to clear their names. In fact Marthe Richer was one of the most successful of all female 'specialist' agents employed by the French during the war. Although she was thoroughly French, or as she put it 'more than French since I came from German-occupied Lorraine', her maiden name had been Betenfeld. With a name like that it had been comparatively easy to convince von Krohn that she was in fact a Swiss with great sympathy for the German cause. Having manoeuvred her way into his affections it was then only a short step into his confidence and by the time Margarethe arrived back in Madrid Marthe was living the perilous life of a fully-fledged double agent.

Marthe had a French codename, l'Alouette, the Skylark, and a German Secret Service codenumber, S32; amongst other coups she had been able to send Ladoux details of a trans-Pyreneean spy network operated by the Germans, had identified a top German agent working in France and had relayed to Paris details of a new and highly effective chemical used in the manufacture of invisible inks. In return Ladoux provided her with specially concocted 'secrets' carefully designed to convince von Krohn of her devotion and value to the Germans. But contrary to what Margarethe — and, to be fair, a good many other people as well — imagined, it was not a life of great glamour; as Marthe was at pains to explain.

> To be a spy during the war is not, as one might think, a question of throwing oneself into a romantic adventure, nor is it a matter of playing the *femme fatale* and turning heads, or of trading secrets for huge sums of money. To be a spy is to be a servant. What a terrible existence. Surrounded all the time by suspicion and distrust. Your mission is to make your enemy believe that you are a traitor. But this in itself makes your enemy wonder

whether you are not in fact a spy. And if you are successful then those who sent you to do this work also start to
doubt you. The double agent is caught between two fires
— and is also sometimes caught in the crossfire. I have
been in just that situation.

Her endeavours on behalf of France were neither fully
appreciated nor justly rewarded until the year after she had
published her memoirs. Until then she had been surrounded
by the very doubt and suspicion of which she was so well
aware. But in 1933 Marthe Richer was finally decorated
with the Légion d'Honneur. After the Second World War she
would be elected to the National Assembly, play a prominent role in passing a law to ban prostitution and live to the
ripe old age of ninety-two before dying in her sleep in 1982.

In December 1916, though, she could have had no great
expectation of even seeing her thirtieth birthday, let alone
her ninetieth. As a thoroughly professional operative she
was well aware of both the dangers and the value of her
work. Had Margarethe attempted to approach von Krohn,
Marthe would have made very sure she never got near
enough to jeopardise everything she had worked so pain-
stakingly to achieve. Indeed she might even have warned
her off any attempt on von Kalle either, thereby unwittingly
and indirectly saving Margarethe's skin. As it was, they
never even met — and Margarethe sailed blindly on to her
doom.

Her direct approach to von Kalle seemed to pay immediate dividends, for she received the polite response:
'Madame, I do not have the honour of being acquainted with
you, but would be happy to meet you here tomorrow at three
o'clock'. Margarethe was jubilant. She had never dreamed

it could be so easy. The following afternoon she donned her most seductive outfit and most coquettish smile and, at the appointed hour, presented herself at his door. Even months later, when she was languishing in prison surrounded by shredded fantasies, she refused to believe that von Kalle had been anything other than completely bewitched by her: 'I behaved in a manner guaranteed to make him fall for me — and he did'.

Von Kalle had welcomed her most courteously. They had exchanged pleasantries and Margarethe had stressed her friendly feelings towards Germany, telling him that she had spent many months in Berlin before the war. When she mentioned the name of her 'special friend' in Berlin, Alfred Kiepert, von Kalle suddenly remembered that they had, after all, met before. He knew Kiepert well — and was he not right in thinking she had attended some military ma-noeuvres in his company in Silesia, was it in 1906 or 1907? He was certain they had been introduced — she must please forgive him for not immediately realising that Madame MacLeod and Mata Hari were one and the same.

This was a bonus. Margarethe had no recollection of the meeting, although she did remember the occasion, but the link could only be to her advantage. After a few minutes reminiscing about mutual acquaintances, she had gone on to explain to von Kalle why she had called. She told him how she had been arrested in England under suspicion of spying for Germany (that would surely go a long way towards establishing her credentials) but it had transpired that the English had mistaken her for someone else. Did he know anything about this Clara Benedix? She would be intrigued to meet someone with whom she apparently had so much in common.

Von Kalle told her he did not have the pleasure of know-ing Fraulein Benedix. He was certain she did not work in Madrid. However he would be happy to make some enquir-ies of his colleague, Baron Roland. As the officer in charge of the German intelligence network in Barcelona, he might well be able to help. In her testimony Margarethe did not elaborate on the 'intimacies' that she claimed had followed von Kalle's casual release of this unsolicited gem of infor-mation. It seems highly unlikely that a man with his looks, brains and influence had to rely for sexual gratification on a chance visit from a middle-aged courtesan. If 'intimacies' did take place, and were not just a figment of Margarethe's vanity, it seems far more likely that von Kalle was playing her at her own game. Certainly the Military Attaché to the German Embassy in Madrid in 1916 was not the kind of man to be so easily duped. Indeed, he appears to have been wise to Margarethe from the start, and might even have invented his claim that they had met in Silesia as a ploy to gain her confidence. For, again according to her testimony, he then 'sat back in his chair and said, "I am very tired. I have just finished arranging for a group of German and Turkish officers to land from a submarine on the coast of Morocco, in the French zone".'

It is hard to imagine that anyone could be so dim-witted as to be taken in by this obvious plant. But Margarethe sus-pected nothing. Back in her hotel room that evening she wrote triumphantly to Ladoux in Paris. When he realised that she had managed to glean not only the name of the German Intelligence Supremo in Barcelona but also details of secret submarine operations in the Mediterranean he could surely no longer doubt her skill as an agent. He might even be persuaded to part with the first instalment of her million francs.

Signing off with a flourish, she turned her attention to her plans for the rest of the evening. Her presence in Madrid had not escaped the notice of several members of the bona fide as well as the 'honorary' diplomatic contingents stationed in the city. If the dazzling beauty that had propelled her to fame and fortune was a thing of the past, Margarethe MacLeod was still a very attractive woman; and when things were going her way could be extremely good company. Tonight she had promised to dine with one of the attachés to the Dutch Embassy, Cornelius de With, and they had arranged to meet in the foyer in her hotel. Her spirits, which had been flagging since her ignominious return from England, had been greatly revived by her triumph with von Kalle. Now they were boosted still further by the realisation that she still had the power to turn heads. De With was standing with two other men by the door of the foyer and there was no mistaking the admiration in their eyes as he introduced them. One was a colleague from the Dutch Embassy, Baron von Claesens. The other was the Military Attaché to the French Embassy, Colonel Denvignes.

De With and von Claesens were both lively and entertaining young men, so Margarethe did not pay much attention to the elderly Denvignes that evening. But the next day, when she was sitting in the reading room of her hotel, he reappeared. Making his way directly to her side, the 'doddery old Colonel', as she later described him, 'asked me if I realised why he was there. I guessed perhaps that he had come to see me and he admitted that was the reason. He asked me where I was going to be that evening and I said I had been invited to a gala dinner and dance by someone at the French Embassy. He replied that he had to go to an official dinner somewhere else, but that he would come and look for me afterwards'.

There had been no mistaking the look in Denvignes' eyes — Margarethe was familiar enough with lechery to recognise it when it drooled down her *decollétage* — but she had not encouraged him. As she later scornfully asserted: 'What would someone like me want with a lover like that?' But Denvignes was as good as his word, and by the time he joined the party at the French Legation later that night an idea was forming in her mind. As the French Military Attaché it was just possible he might be in a position to do her a service. She was a bit hazy about the hierarchy of the Deuxième Bureau, but if Denvignes was not Ladoux's superior, at least he might have some influence with him. If she could impress Denvignes with the information she had managed to winkle out of von Kalle, then he in turn might be able to put in a good word for her with Ladoux. Anything that might bring the million francs within reach was worth a try.

Her unexpectedly warm welcome must have had the Colonel's already rheumy eyes really watering. Excusing herself to her two *chevaliers*, she took Denvignes' arm and led him to a quiet seat in a corner of the room. After ordering him a 'reviving cup of tea' she put on her best conspiratorial whisper and repeated to him everything she had learned from von Kalle. At her most artless she assured the Colonel that if she had known he was in Madrid she would have taken this information straight to him instead of writing to Ladoux. What did he think she should do now?

Denvignes was so overwhelmed by the proximity of her cleavage that he was really hardly listening to what she was saying. But when she pressed him for his advice he managed to pull himself together — sufficiently at least to suggest that she return to his room with him so they could discuss the matter further. Margarethe protested that she could not possibly arrive at a party with one escort and leave with another, no matter how much she would like to do so — why did he not call at her hotel next morning when he had had a chance to think it over. Interpreting this as an invitation to an assignation of an amatory rather than an official nature Denvignes assured her he would do just that; and the following morning he appeared at her door while she was still having breakfast. He must have been a singularly unattractive man for her to have ruled out so completely any question of accommodating his desire; Margarethe was usually only too ready to use her body as the first weapon in any campaign. This time she used the inappropriateness of the hour as an excuse to fend off his groping hands and forced him to talk instead about von Kalle.

He asked her to repeat everything she had told him the night before, and this time he did appear to be listening — particularly to the story of the submarines in North Africa. When she had finished he questioned her closely; how many officers had been landed, was the submarine carrying arms as well as men, were other submarines engaged on the same operation? When Margarethe insisted that she had told him everything she knew, Denvignes told her that her next move was obvious — she must go back to von Kalle and try and get some more information. Even Margarethe was surprised at this: 'I said I would go when I had the chance, but told him I didn't imagine he was going to tell me much'. But the Colonel had clearly decided that that was enough business for one day — now he wanted to concentrate on pleasure.

Leading the conversation round to more personal matters

he asked her, with a knowing leer, to tell him about 'the various relations I had had with highly placed members of society. Then he let me know that he would like nothing better than to be allowed to share their privilege'. By this time Margarethe had her answer ready: 'I told him that my heart belonged to a Russian. I told him that we were in love and that the Russian, Captain Vadime de Masloff, had asked me to marry him'. But Denvignes' finer feelings, if he had any, were unable to compete with his passion for this once notorious and still captivating woman. If anything her touching confession inflamed him further. 'He presented me with a bunch of violets that he had brought with him and asked me to wear them between my breasts all day; then he would come and reclaim them in the evening. He begged me to let him have a ribbon from my petticoat, and insisted on taking it off himself, and he implored me to give him a handkerchief scented with the perfume I was wearing so that he would be reminded of me every moment of the day. He was behaving just like an indiscreet adolescent.'

The last thing Margarethe wanted to do was to antagonise him. So she agreed to wear his violets and let him take the ribbon and the handkerchief, coaxed him out of his pique with kisses and restored his good humour with promises. He had told her that he was leaving for Paris the next day so there was no time to waste. Although she had her doubts about the likelihood of a further meeting with von Kalle yielding any more secrets, she was prepared, even anxious to give it a try. Even if nothing came of it she would at least be carrying out the instructions of a second member of the French Intelligence Service — if that was really Denvignes' role.

Von Kalle appeared to be delighted to see her again; and

if Margarethe was feeling less than confident about her mission, his charm soon put her at her ease. Over an intimate dinner *à deux* he encouraged her to talk about herself. Margarethe was happy to oblige. But she knew the dangers and determined not to fall into any of his traps. So carefully avoiding any reference to Masloff and steering clear of subjects that might lead to her inadvertently revealing her connections with Ladoux or Denvignes, she talked about her early life. She told him about her childhood and her parents, her disastrous marriage and her great love for the art and religion of Java which had been the inspiration for her career. She talked of Holland, described her pretty little house in The Hague and boasted about her rich lover, Baron van der Capellen, whose generosity enabled her to lead such an interesting and varied life. And for good measure, she reminisced about her triumphs in Vienna and Berlin.

Seeing her host in such a convivial mood encouraged her, after a while, to change the subject — it was a classic case of 'that's enough about me, now let's talk about you'. In honeyed tones designed to penetrate the most flatter-proof of male egos, she breathed her wide-eyed admiration for the awesome responsibilities that his job must entail — she would be fascinated to hear more about it. That business about the submarine, for example, that must have been a very dangerous expedition. Was it a unique event, or were things like that happening all the time?

As she had anticipated, von Kalle reproved her gently for asking questions she must know he could not answer. But he did not retreat into a cocoon of complete secrecy. Instead he started to talk, in the most relaxed and natural manner but only in the most general terms, about his work. As the evening progressed, however, as the candles burned lower and the bottles of wine gradually emptied, he seemed to grow careless. There was mention of a French airman he had recruited to fly his agents into Allied territory, and there was a passing reference to a new formula for invisible ink that would soon be issued to some of his operatives. And there were compliments and kisses and sighs of pleasure until the wee small hours when he slipped a roll of money into her bodice and escorted her back to her hotel.

If Margarethe was pleased with the way the evening had gone, so too was von Kalle. While she was bustling round to Denvignes' hotel to report on her latest coup, the German Military Attaché was arranging for the second in a series of radio messages to be sent to Berlin.

The first message had been sent on 13th December, the day after Margarethe had called on him at his apartment. It said:

> Agent H21 of the Cologne Department, sent to France for the second time in March, has arrived in Madrid. She has pretended to accept an offer from the French intelligence Service to work for them. She wanted to travel to Holland from Spain but was mistaken for someone else and was arrested at Falmouth on November 11th. When the mistake was discovered she was sent back to Spain because the English continued to suspect her.

Although radio was by now widely used by both sides as an invaluable means of both local and international communication, its use was still limited by shortage of equipment and trained operators. Access to the airwaves was granted only to those with urgent information to transmit, and rigid rules governed the content of transmissions. A tale of interruptions to the travel plans of a minor agent would certainly not have qualified for inclusion. Yet von Kalle's telegram containing just such trivial information was coded and despatched without delay or question. In his definitive work *The Codebreakers*, David Kahn states that diplomatic messages exchanged between Berlin and Madrid were intercepted by the English and relayed directly to the French, and that one of the German codes in which they were sent was deciphered on the very day in which it came into service. Mr Kahn goes on to state that 'It was in this code that the German naval [sic] attaché in Madrid radioed to Germany several times concerning funds and instructions for agent H21 [Mata Hari]'. Since the information contained in von Kalle's messages was of little or no interest to the Germans, it can only be assumed that von Kalle knew, or guessed, that the code had been broken and that he was therefore sending the messages with the specific intention of letting the French read them.

There is no reason to suppose that Hans von Kalle was either more perceptive or more intelligent than Ladoux or Thomson. But although they had all in turn been suspicious of Margarethe, von Kalle had one great advantage over his French and English counterparts — he had seen her at work. He knew the exact extent of her contribution to the German cause — none at all — and he had been able to gauge her value as both a French spy and a potential double agent — again zero. He also knew for certain that which Ladoux and Thomson could only surmise, that the twenty thousand francs which had mysteriously appeared in her bank account in Holland had come from Kramer. But where they might have congratulated her on a neat swindle, von Kalle could hardly be expected to see it that way. As far as he was concerned she had double-crossed the German Intelligence Service, and he was not prepared to let her get away with it. However, there was a problem. In neutral Spain he had no power to arrest her. He could have dreamed up a plan to get her to Germany where his superiors could have dealt with her; but there was a far simpler option - he could get the French to do his dirty work for him. Not only would he be relieved of an irritating and time-consuming task, but by presenting Margarethe to them he might be able to divert the attention of the Deuxième Bureau from the activities of genuine and valuable German agents.

His first radio message, therefore, had been intended to identify her beyond question to the Deuxième Bureau. A second, drafted from the information she had so innocently given him in the candlelight and making reference to the money he had pressed discreetly into her bosom, was intended to prove to the French once and for all that she was indeed an active and fully paid up German spy. This one read 'H21 will arrange through the Dutch consul in Paris for another credit transfer to be sent to her servant and asks that Kramer in Amsterdam be informed. 1 have already given her three thousand five hundred pesetas'. Two days later, on 28th December, von Kalle would send the final message to Berlin revealing that agent H21 was about to leave for Paris and that she wanted the five thousand francs her maid was holding for her to be forwarded to her bank in the French capital.

Lonely, muddle-headed and breathtakingly incompetent, driven by the insecurity of loving a man twenty years her junior, Margarethe had become the package in a merciless international game of pass-the-parcel. As Ladoux and Thomson had done before him, von Kalle was just passing the buck. And he had made sure that when the music stopped it would be Georges Ladoux who would be left with the parcel in his lap.

But even now Margarethe was unaware that she was in any kind of trouble. The only small cloud on her horizon was that she still had received no reply to her letter to Ladoux asking for instructions. Assuming that he must be preoccupied with other weighty matters, she decided the only thing to do was to return to Paris and confront him with the indisputable proof of her skill as an agent. She had poured the story of von Kalle's indiscretions into Denvignes' slightly deaf ear and, in return for her promise to call on him as soon as she got back, he had agreed to put in a good word for her with Ladoux. As far as she could see her fortune and her future were assured.

NO WAY TO TREAT A HEROINE

1917. Whoever you were, wherever you lived, whatever your politics or your nationality or your age, your life was to some extent changed by the events of that fateful year. For some it would mark a new beginning — mighty heads had fallen in the closing months of 1916; in the haggard aftermath of Verdun and the Somme, General Joffre, the French Commander-in-Chief, had been encouraged to retire and was replaced by the volatile and bumptious young General Nivelle. The career of the German Chief of Staff, Erich von Falkenheyn, had also ended with the failure of these infamous campaigns to achieve their intended aims — his role and increasingly the power and influence that had once rested with the Kaiser, was taken over by Paul von Hindenberg and his alter ego General Erich Ludendorff. In England the exhausted Prime Minister Asquith had resigned, to be succeeded by Lloyd George and his coalition of radical Liberals and hard-line Conservatives. Tsar Nicholas II of Russia was clinging by a thread to his throne, while in Switzerland Lenin was coiled for the pounce. In the United States, too, things were changing. Within a few months Woodrow Wilson's strict policy of non-intervention would finally be abandoned and America would, decisively, enter the war on the side of the Allies.

For others, the millions of men and women excluded from this elevated game of general post, 1917 would be another year of endurance and deprivation, of inconsolable grief and futile, ugly death. They had no power to alter the course of the war — and no option but to follow the orders of those who had that power but not the compassion to use it. By January 1917 the war that had initially been expected to last only a few weeks had already lasted for nearly two and a half years. The longer it went on, the further away peace seemed to be; and the greater the sacrifices made, the more relentless the demands with which they were met.

As they looked ahead into the new year and saw no end to the misery, the men at the Front felt their cheerful bravery crawling inwards and turning to fierce anger. Anger at the enemy for refusing to be beaten; anger at their own well-fed staff officers in their comfortable headquarters for issuing absurd orders that would lead to yet more agony and death. Anger, even, at those civilians, far away from the fighting, who urged them on with eager, bright-eyed patriotism and demonstrated their own devotion with tales of sugar shortages, meat rationing and the impossibility of finding coal.

But those who fought did not have a monopoly on anger. The deprivation in society was real; the suffering and endurance and struggle were as genuine, if not as intense or as fatal, amongst the civilian population as amongst the military. The dichotomy created by this lack of common experience opened up an almost unbridgeable gulf between the two. When the *poilu* returned home on leave his family were now no longer 'those who love and weep for me and for whose sake I am fighting this war' but 'those who do not understand what it is like'. When a wife opened the door to her husband she was still overjoyed at his safe return; but he was no longer just 'my hero, my beloved, the man whose comforts and wishes are paramount'. For she too had been fighting a battle; to feed and cloth her family, to fix the roof, to pay the bills, to stand in endless queues for provisions and scour the streets for the very necessities of life. When every day since she had last seen him she had driven herself to the point of exhaustion just to keep the family's head above water, how could she be expected suddenly to transform herself into the serene and sympathetic spouse? He, too, had become 'the one who does not understand what it is like'.

Where once the war had been seen as a great and patriotic cause, in which every man and woman played a part, and for whose sake individual interests were willingly ceded to the common good, it was now being revealed as a monstrous, all-devouring tyrant. Vera Brittain was speaking for many when, in early 1917, she admitted that, 'one's personal interest wears one's patriotism rather threadbare … after all, it is a garment one has had to wear for a very long time, so there's not much wonder if it is beginning to get a little shabby'. Her words would have applied equally to hope. In the good old days neighbour had greeted neighbour with wishes of a 'happy' or a 'prosperous' New Year. In the years since 1914 these wishes had become for a 'victorious' or a 'peaceful' New Year. As 1917 dawned there were no such wishes — just a shrug of tired surprise that there should be any New Year at all. Looking forward was a pointless exercise — when all the world was dark what could you hope to see? There was no more talk of what might happen or what could be done 'after the war': indeed the wise man in 1917 dared not even think about tomorrow. Time enough for that if he survived today.

The pervasive gloom of the New Year was compounded by one of Fate's more spiteful tricks. For the winter of 1916–17 was the coldest in living memory. When Margarethe returned to France on 4th January she found the country frozen almost to a standstill and covered by a thick blanket of snow that reached as far south as Bordeaux and Toulouse. Paris was a nightmare. Ice had turned the streets and pavements into treacherous skating-rinks; even with their hoofs wrapped in sacking the few remaining carriage-horses slipped and skittered and fell trembling into the gutters, wrenching aged joints stiffened further by the cold and splintering brittle bones. Frozen pipes burst and sent cascades of water flowing down walls and pouring through ceilings and the intense cold turned it to ice before the flow could be stemmed or the flood dispersed. And there was no respite. For of all the shortages plaguing the long-suffering people of France, none was more severe or more painful than the shortage of coal.

Production of coal in the industrial north and north-east had all but ceased as the Western Front thrashed back and forth and then ground to a standstill through the middle of the main coal-mining areas. Ships carrying imported coal were one of the prime targets of Ludendorff's policy of unrestricted submarine warfare. Such coal as was available was instantly requisitioned by the military whose priorities were to fuel the factories and keep the troop trains running. The introduction of strict rationing for domestic supplies meant that each week the already struggling housewife had to devote the best part of a day to standing in yet another interminable queue, this time for a small sack of coal that might or might not arrive and which, if it did, she then had to hump sometimes several miles from the depot to her home.

In a desperate search for an alternative source of fuel, swarms of small boys scoured the alleys of Les Halles market for any kind of box or packing case that could be shredded to keep the fires burning. The peeling bark was stripped unceremoniously from the famous plane trees lining the *boulevards* and gangs of amateur lumberjacks raided the Bois de Boulogne in the hours of darkness to fell any tree small enough to carry home.

Nor was it just the poor who suffered. Coal was distributed strictly on a per capita basis — the larger your house, and therefore the bigger the area that had to be heated by the same small sack of coal, the colder it was likely to be. And the darker. For electricity, generated in coal-fired power stations, was the next victim. Supplies were sporadic and sometimes cut for days on end. The managers of even the grandest hotels were reduced to removing nine out of ten lightbulbs from their sockets lest their guests be tempted to squander the precious current. Paraffin, gas and petrol became covetted, luxury commodities. The following winter would, unbelievably, be even colder; in January 1918 the river Seine would freeze over for the first time in one hundred and twenty years. But the gift of prescience would have brought little comfort to the benighted Parisians as they shivered through January 1917 by the light of a few small candles.

*   *   *   *   *

Because of the intense cold, Margarethe decided not to go

to the apartment she had rented for herself and Vadime. Instead she booked into the Hotel Plaza Athenée where she could live, the war and the weather permitting, in reasonable comfort without having to worry about anything as mundane as frozen pipes. She confidentlyexpected that within a few days she would be so rich that she never need worry about anything again.

She could scarcely contain her excitement — indeed she already felt like a heroine. The information she had gleaned in Madrid would surely guarantee her the warmest of welcomes and the heartiest of congratulations from Ladoux; why, the whole of France would owe her a great debt of gratitude for her achievement. Having sent word to Ladoux of her return, she set out straight away to contact Denvignes and find out what progress he had made in promoting her cause with the Captain.

I went to look for the Colonel at his hotel, but I was told that he had just left. He was on his way back to Madrid, but there was a chance his train was still at the station. I went with all speed to the station and managed to speak to him before the train started. I asked him if he had been to see Captain Ladoux on my behalf and tell him how useful I had been.

His response was the first sign that things might not be going entirely to plan. Instead of greeting her with his usual blend of courtesy and ardour, Denvignes seemed positively embarrassed by her sudden appearance. As carriage doors slammed and guards' whistles blew, he pretended first not to have heard what she said, then that he had not understood but at last he could prevaricate no longer.

The Colonel told me he had been to see Captain Ladoux's superior officer. He had told him that I was an intelligent woman and mentioned that I was well connected in Madrid. Then he said that this superior officer had asked him if he knew of any approaches I had made to the German Military Attaché. He had denied any knowledge of such a thing. I was completely taken aback. When I asked Denvignes why he had lied, all he did was to murmur *mon petit, mon petit*. And then the train moved out of the station. I was left staring after it in amazement, at a loss to understand why the man who had so lately been on his knees to me was now behaving so differently and refusing to tell the truth about me.

She returned, cold, confused and just a little apprehensive, to her hotel. After a night spent racking her brains for a possible explanation for Denvignes' extraordinary behaviour, the morning found her angry and disgusted. 'I decided that he was refusing to help me out of spite. He felt cheated that 1, Mata Hari, would not become his mistress. Bah! It was bad enough when he wanted to play games with me — I suppose that he didn't dare to play these love games when he was a young man.'

But when she read the note handed to her by the hotel receptionist the following day her apprehension returned. It was from Captain Ladoux — and it was far from being the effusive summons she had expected. It read simply: 'Stay in Paris. You will be contacted within the week'. An hour later Margarethe was round at his office demanding to speak with him. A preoccupied receptionist told her that the Captain was out of town and was not expected back for some days.

Margarethe was at a complete loss. What was the matter

with everyone? What was she supposed to do now? This was no way to treat a heroine. As she picked her way nervously across the pavement of the boulevard St Germain she became aware for the first time of just how cold it really was. The faces of the passers-by were pinched and drawn. The voices of a group of young soldiers reached her from across the street — they were harsh, discordant, aggressive. They conjured up memories of the red-faced men who had lurched down the streets of Medan in far off Sumatra, jostling and leering and scaring her with sudden bursts of loud, humourless laughter; they too had been young men, and they too had been angry and frightened. The Margarethe of eighteen years ago, young, beautiful, romantic, had felt nothing but repugnance for such a public display of vulgarity. The Margarethe of today, had she not been so preoccupied, might have recognised and even sympathised with both their fear and their anger.

As the days passed and she still heard nothing from Ladoux her nervousness increased. Either because they were growing careless or because anxiety was making her more alert and observant, she became aware for the first time of the watchers on the pavement. Soon she was seeing them everywhere: she saw them in the foyer and on the street; they followed her when she went out shopping; and she even thought she caught sight of them in the corridor outside her hotel room. Quelling the urge to run and hide somewhere far from Ladoux, Denvignes, von Kalle and their whole beastly world of subterfuge, she decided to brazen it out. But the same preoccupied receptionist in Ladoux's office gave her the same response — the Captain was still away and might not be back for several weeks. No, they knew nothing about any surveillance. A visit to the police station was no more productive, and the police, though courteous, were no more helpful — the surveillance, if such there was, had nothing to do with them. Margarethe was ushered out of the building with the politest of suggestions that she should go home and stop imagining things.

Ladoux had promised that she would be contacted within a week, but the week passed with no word from him. Who was he ignoring her? Who had her achievement not even been acknowledged? Why, for God's sake, did someone not tell her what was going on? So twitchy had she become that when someone did knock on the door of her room on the morning of 13th January, she nearly jumped out of her skin. But when she asked who was there, a familiar voice replied, 'It is I, Vadime'.

His sudden and unexpected arrival plucked Margarethe out of one panic and dropped her straight into another. She could not let him see her in such a state of nerves, she must change her dress, do her hair, adjust her make-up — but she could not keep him standing on the landing like a stranger. A quick glance in the mirror, a few sharp pinches to bring the colour back into her cheeks, a hasty rearrangement of the pins in her hair, and she opened the door to her lover. But one look at Vadime and her vanity was forgotten. He stood like a ghost, trembling, too tired even to take the last few steps across the threshold of her room.

Margarethe led him in and closed the door. Then having helped him off with his greatcoat, she sat him down in a chair and poured him a glass of wine. For a long time he just sat there saying nothing, but her anxious fluttering seemed to rouse him from his daze. No, he had not been wounded again, he was just tired. Yes, he did feel a little unwell, but it was only a headache, nothing out of the ordinary, he had a headache most of the time these days. His throat? Well yes, it had been troublesome, the after-effects of the gas poisoning — he was meant to be going into hospital soon for further treatment. He was sorry to arrive unannounced, he hoped it was not inconvenient but he had nowhere else to go, did she mind?

For once someone else's needs were more important to Margarethe than her own. As well as being exhausted and far from well, Vadime was homesick and desperately anxious about his family. Problems with communications meant that news from Russia was sparse and fragmented; what there was told of food shortages, terrible casualty lists and increasing civil unrest. He had no money and no strength, he was tired, tense and very fragile — and at this moment he needed Margarethe's love and reassurance even more than she needed his. Although there was nothing she would have liked more than to be able to confide in and lean on him, she could not add to his misery by burdening him with her own problems.

So she told him nothing of her dealings with Ladoux, made no mention of von Kalle or the watchers and explained merely that she had changed her plans to go to Holland for fear that, once there, she would not be allowed to return to Paris. She listened to him talk, and then she let him sleep. There would be no passion on this night, just more tenderness and concern than Margarethe had ever shown to any other person in all her life. In the months to come she would look back on that night and wonder; she had found comfort and consolation in knowing that Vadime had turned to her in his misery - would she have felt the same if she had known that it was to be the last night they would ever spend together?

In the morning Vadime had to leave. His regiment was just passing through Paris; he must go with them. Margarethe promised to visit him in hospital as soon as he let her know where he was and resolved to call at her bank that very day to arrange for some money to be sent to him. They both wept as they parted.

True to her resolve, Margarethe called at her bank and arranged for three thousand francs to be sent to Vadime. As she emerged from the building she caught sight, once again, of the watchers on the pavement. This time rage and frustration got the better of her anxiety. As soon as she got back to her hotel she wrote angrily to Ladoux: 'What do you want of me? 1 am prepared to do anything you ask, I ask you no questions and I do not wish to know your agents. I am an international woman and you have no right to question my methods or my life — and no right to send your secret agents to pester me'.

But her rage collapsed and the apprehension returned as soon as she had sent the letter. It had been easy, while she had been busy, to ignore the occasional twinge of doubt about the wisdom of her involvement with Ladoux. Being once again in the middle of things, whisking from one capital to the next in search of the next introduction; dining with the powerful, being fêted by the influential and indulging in the odd bit of verbal sparring with the strategically placed; it had all been pleasantly reminiscent of those glorious days when she had been the toast of Europe. But now the inactivity, the loneliness, Ladoux's silence, and above all the endless waiting, were gnawing away at her confidence. Playing with fire had been exhilarating; sitting in a cold, dark, empty room in a half-deserted hotel with nothing but her thoughts for company most certainly was not. On the contrary — it was proving to be painfully, wretchedly revealing. For some reason that she could not yet quite understand, her plans and dreams had gone terribly wrong.

The doubts that she had denied for so long now crowded in on her, clamouring for her attention. There were hidden depths and treacherous pitfalls in the murky world of espionage that she had never even guessed at. Everything seemed to have been turned on its head. The situations and the people that she thought she had been using as a means to her own happy ending now seemed to be using her for their own, as yet unimaginable, purposes. She had strayed into a nightmare from which there seemed to be no awakening. Every possible way out was barred by the very people she had once thought to be her allies; but their once smiling faces were rendered almost unrecognisable by chilling expressions of complete indifference. All of a sudden it was hard to tell whether she was shivering because she was cold or because she was very frightened.

*   *   *   *   *

She had every right to be frightened. The silence from Ladoux and the delay in contacting her were intentional and calculated. He was not in his office — that much was true. But neither was he out of town on some other business. In fact he was concentrating almost exclusively on her.

Almost as soon as she had left Paris Ladoux had had cause to be devoutly thankful he had not committed himself to employing her as an agent. Her arrest at Falmouth had been just an unlucky coincidence — neither she nor anyone else could have foreseen that Margarethe MacLeod would be mistaken for Clara Benedix. But the cable from Basil Thomson had been acutely embarrassing. How could he possibly admit to employing as a French agent a woman whom Scotland Yard had suspected for more than a year of being a German agent? Even to have admitted contemplating such a thing would have been seen as a slap in the face for the British Intelligence Service. It was vitally important for both MI5 and the Deuxième Bureau that the high level of co-operation between the two organisations should not only be sustained but also that it continued to improve. If no less a person than the Chief of the French Bureau were to be seen ignoring repeated warnings from England, then that co-operation could be placed in jeopardy.

The decision to deny all knowledge of her had, in the event, made his life very much easier. Since nothing had ever been put on paper and no money had changed hands between them it would only ever be Margarethe's word against his own should the matter ever come under official scrutiny; and Ladoux was understandably confident that his word would carry the greater weight. He could now see that, by investigating the possibility of using her either as an agent or a double-agent, he had been wandering up a blind alley. A little vigorous back-pedalling would set him back on course and enable him to concentrate, without distraction, on his original plan — the collection of irrefutable proof that she was, indeed, a German spy. As chief of counter intelligence it had fallen to his lot on more than one occasion to send a trusted agent to his certain death for the sake of the grand design — it was a regrettable but unavoidable part of his job and he was not a man to shirk his responsibilities. His conscience was therefore not the least troubled by the idea of abandoning to her fate a woman he had only considered employing as an agent. Against a professional intriguer with a passion for the recondite, backed up by the considerable resources of the Deuxième Bureau, Margarethe had little chance.

Just as Margarethe's worst crime in von Kalle's eyes had been her attempt to double-cross and thereby make a fool of the German Intelligence Services, so her worst crime in Ladoux's eyes was that she had so nearly succeeded in making a fool of him by tempting him to employ her. It was the fact that the mistakes each side had made in their dealings with her had come so near to catching up with them, rather than any other crime that she might have committed, that made the two men so vindictive in their determination to bring her down. From the moment he had sent off his reply to Thomson's cable denying any knowledge of Margarethe, Ladoux had been intent on establishing her guilt and justifying his own actions. To have put pen to paper in reply to her letter from Madrid would have been to provide her with the very evidence of his momentary lapse that he did not want her to have. He was still receiving surveillance reports on her movements from his watchers — now he concentrated on analysing the information they contained with the selectivity and single-mindedness of a man who has erred and now has a chance to redeem himself. One of his best allies in the task would turn out to be Margarethe herself.

She had already admitted that she was well acquainted with Kramer, the Press Attaché at the German Embassy in The Hague. Her bold approach to the Military Attaché at the German Embassy in Madrid could therefore only be interpreted as proof of her close connections with the whole of the German Intelligence Service. The warmth of her reception and the intimacy of her relationship with von Kalle clearly demonstrated that the two were old and trusted friends; and when she had climbed out of von Kalle's bed straight into the arms of none other than the Military Attaché at the French Embassy there could be no doubt she was acting on von Kalle's orders. He had obviously supplied her with false information on the strength of which he, Ladoux, was supposed to confirm her status as a French agent.

Colonel Denvignes' unexpected infatuation with the 'dangerous woman spy' had threatened, for a moment, to upset all his plans. But, luckily for Ladoux, Margarethe's equally unexpected reluctance to become Denvignes' mistress had given him a chance to extricate the old man before he became irretrievably compromised. When Denvignes had returned to Paris Ladoux had taken him on one side and revealed the true nature of the woman whose cause the Colonel had been about to plead. It would be a shame, did the Colonel not agree, if his long and distinguished career should end in a public scandal? And yet surely such a scandal would be hard to avoid if the Military High Command were to learn of his relationship with an enemy spy?

Not surprisingly Denvignes was acutely embarrassed to discover that news of his indiscretion had preceded him to Paris. He hastened to reassure Ladoux that there had, in reality, been no relationship — a little mild flirtation, that was all. But Ladoux could take no chances. Less impressionable men than Denvignes had fallen victim to the charms of the famous Mata Hari; it was essential for him to be well out of reach of those charms when Margarethe returned to Paris. So he arranged through his superiors for Denvignes to be posted straight back to Madrid. The train carrying the chastened and unhappy Colonel had moved out of the station in the nick of time and Ladoux had heaved a mighty sigh of relief. For by now, thanks to von Kalle's radio messages from Madrid, his dossier was nearly complete.

These messages could have been intercepted at one of two places. Either, as David Kahn suggests, they were intercepted by the English in London and forwarded to the Admiralty department known as Room 40 for deciphering; or they could have been intercepted by the French themselves at their listening post on the Eiffel Tower. From there they would have been forwarded to the team of French code-breakers, headed by a Professor of German Studies, who were based in the town of Saumur on the Loire. In both these centres teams of cryptanalysts worked round the clock on breaking German codes and ciphers. As Constantine Fitzgibbon remarks in his *Secret Intelligence*, 'In an age that had not heard the word "computer" it was a matter of brain power alone, so exhausting and performed under pressure that nervous breakdown was not the exception but more usually the ultimate rule'. Despite the pressure the success rate both in London and Saumur was extraordinarily high.

What was sometimes even more difficult to gauge was the validity of the contents of the deciphered messages. Each side knew that the other was intercepting and trying to decipher their opponent's radio traffic, and a recognised way of making the task even more time-consuming and difficult was to bury the nuggets of real interest in great drifts of meaningless or misleading information. It was also obviously of vital importance neither to let your enemy know when you had broken his code nor, conversely, to let him find out that you were aware he had broken yours. As an additional ploy the Germans deliberately played down their own expertise in this field and feigned a lofty disregard for that of the Allies. The American Ambassador in London, Walter H. Page, was thoroughly taken in by this stratagem.

> One of the most curious discoveries, and one that casts an illuminating light on German simplicity, is the confident belief of the German Government that its secret service was in fact secret. The ciphers and codes of other nations might be read, but not the German; its secret methods of communication, like anything else German, were regarded as perfection.

The interpretation of deciphered messages was thus almost as important as the actual deciphering. In the case of von Kalle's messages to Berlin about agent H21 this interpretation was none of the analysts' concern. Once deciphered, the messages had simply been transcribed and sent to Paris. It was for Georges Ladoux to decide what interpretation should be put on the contents, and what action should then be taken. The American Ambassador to London was obviously not the only one to be deceived by the Germans' avowed confidence in the secrecy of their communications system. No warning had accompanied the transcripts to the effect that the code in which these messages had been sent was one which the Germans knew to have been broken. Ladoux therefore took the contents of von Kalle's radio messages at their face value, which, considering that they virtually handed him Margarethe on a plate, is hardly to be wondered at.

It was a good moment for the counter-intelligence chief. He now had positive proof that she was a German agent. He knew the name of her spy-master, Kramer, and her code number, H21; he had confirmation that she had been receiving regular payment from Amsterdam and could prove that she had been trying to infiltrate the French Intelligence Service. His work had been done for him. He no longer had to worry about his own little gaffe, but could concentrate on making the most of von Kalle's *bonne-bouche*.

But Ladoux was as ambitious as he was thorough. Secure in the knowledge that he had Margarethe well and truly hooked he was in no great hurry to reel her in. If he allowed the line to run free for a little longer there was a chance she might lead him to some of her contacts in Paris — and after all he was in the business of catching German spies. But he had no great faith in her zeal and was not prepared just to sit back and wait for her to leap into action on behalf of her German masters. By keeping her waiting, and guessing, he was giving the line just enough of a tug to worry her without scaring her into a panic-stricken leap for freedom: maybe the uncertainty would send her scuttling to those contacts in search of advice.

Her frequent visits to his office and the stream of notes demanding to see him proved that his silence was indeed worrying her. But her complaint that she was being pestered by his secret agents showed that she was also very wary. If he was to learn anything from her movements he would have to change his team of watchers and tighten up the surveillance.

When it dawned on Margarethe that within twenty-four hours of making the complaint the watchers had indeed vanished, she was more disconcerted than ever. If Ladoux was prepared to react so promptly to her request then why on earth would he not see her? The value of the information she had so cleverly collected for him in Madrid must surely diminish with every day that passed before it was acted upon. But her anxiety did not, as Ladoux hoped, send her rushing to the Germans for advice. Instead the only unexpected visit she made was to a house in the Paris suburb of Raincy and the only advice she sought was that of the fortune-teller who lived there. Ladoux's new team of watchers were far more discreet than their predecessors and Margarethe was never aware of their existence. But when they had twice followed her to the house in Raincy they were convinced they were onto something. Their enquiries, however, revealed that Madame Lucien was indeed a bona fide clairvoyant; and the only advice she had given Margarethe was to forget the million francs — she would never receive them. Which would explain, the watchers' report continued, why Madame MacLeod had left Raincy in a very bad mood and had not been back since.

The watchers had only two other pieces of information that could possibly be of interest to Ladoux. The first was that at the end of January Margarethe had moved out of the Hotel Plaza Athenée and into the Elysée Palace Hotel on the Champs Elysées. The only reason they could think of for the move was that she might find more potential clients at her new address. The second item of interest was that at the beginning of February she made contact with a friend from the past — a little lawyer by the name of Edouard Clunet. This was disconcerting news for Ladoux. Clunet's sudden appearance on the scene put a whole new complexion on matters. In the twelve years since he had last met Margarethe he had gained a sound reputation as an international lawyer. His loyalty and devotion to France were above suspicion so Ladoux could only assume that Margarethe had contacted him in his professional capacity. Since he was most certainly not prepared to allow Clunet to find ways of getting Margarethe off the hook he had better act quickly.

In fact Edouard Clunet had come back into Margarethe's life by chance. In the course of one of her abortive visits to Ladoux's office her eye had lighted on the brass nameplate on a nearby doorway. Maître E. Clunet, Avocat. She had hesitated. Many things had changed in the last twelve years — would her old admirer still be so devoted now that she was no longer a great star? Maybe he too I would turn his back on her when he realised what kind of trouble she was in. But there was just a chance that he would prove to be exactly the friend she needed. He was a lawyer, not a 'diplomat', he had never made any demands on her and he had proved a willing and sympathetic listener on several occasions when she had needed advice. Suddenly there was no one in the world she wanted to see more.

It was hard to know which of them had been the more surprised. If time had not been especially kind to Margarethe it had taken Clunet from upright, dapper middle age into dusty decrepitude. The death of his only son on the Somme a few months previously seemed to have added another ten years to his age and he looked almost too frail to stand. But the sight of his adored Mata Hari standing on his doorstep had brought tears of joy to his eyes. Almost overcome with emotion he had invited her in and within a few minutes she found herself pouring her whole sorry tale into his bemused ear.

Not surprisingly Clunet had been unable to make head or tail of her story. But his offer of assistance had been spontaneous and sincere — she must not worry, he would do all he could to help her. Although she had been dismayed to see him looking so old and worn, Margarethe had found it an enormous relief to be able to share her worries. Over the next few days she had also been wonderfully reassured to discover that Clunet was convinced from the start that the whole thing was a misunderstanding - of course she was quite innocent and it would only be a matter of days before they had everything sorted out.

But time ran out on the Maître. On 13th February Police Commissioner Albert Priolet knocked on the door of her hotel room with a warrant in his hand. It read: 'The woman Zelle, Margarethe, also known as Mata Hari, Protestant, born in Holland on August 7th, 1876, height 1.75m, able to read and write, is charged with espionage and passing intelligence to the enemy with the intention of furthering his interests'.

Margarethe was under arrest.

LE CAPITAINE RAPPORTEUR

She was taken under police escort from her hotel room straight to the Palais de Justice. There, in the tiny office he always referred to as his 'cupboard', she was interviewed by the magistrate responsible for investigating the case against her, Captain Pierre Bouchardon.

Bouchardon was a small, sallow and deceptively mild looking man, in his mid-forties, with mournful eyes that peered out from behind an enormous black moustache, and a decidedly jaundiced outlook on life. This latter was the result of two early disappointments in his career. The first had been when his ambition to become a doctor had foundered because, in his words, 'in mathematics I was possessed of an ignorance which defies description. In examinations my mark was always zero; and I know that were I to sit the same exam today [he was seventy at the time of writing] my mark would still be zero. It was therefore "Adieu" to medicine'. Having settled on a career in the law, he had then spent fifteen years as a magistrate on the provincial circuit mourning his failure to win a posting to Paris: 'It became, for me, a Paradise lost'.

The second great disappointment of his life had come at

the start of the war. 'I had been a Captain in the Territorial Infantry for ten years and now, by virtue of my seniority, I was appointed Commander of the battalion.' But within a few days the Colonel of the battalion made the horrifying discovery that his newest commander could not ride a horse. 'I had to admit to him that, before "the most noble conquest man has ever made" I have always stood in abject terror. I therefore had to command from the ground, and the other captains in the battalion never missed the chance of giving me contemptuous looks from their lofty mounts.' This discovery promptly put paid to his military ambitions. But it was also responsible for winning him his cherished posting to Paris. For the shocked but kindly Colonel suggested that the Captain might be happier with an appointment to the post of examining magistrate to the military courts in the capital, where he would be unlikely to encounter many horses.

For the first months of the war Bouchardon was engaged on purely military matters: 'desertion, insubordination, refusal to obey orders, taking leave without permission and a whole list of the other small crimes that accompanied the confusion of mobilisation'. But gradually he had found himself taking on more complicated cases which, as the war progressed, increasingly involved matters of national security. When, many years later, he published an account of his years as 'Capitaine Rapporteur' to the 'Troisième Conseil de Guerre', he admitted that not only was it written with the benefit of hindsight but also that his memory, at the age of seventy, might not be entirely reliable.

But if time had served to dim his memory it had had just the opposite effect on his tongue. Despite a long and ultimately successful career as an Assize Court Judge his *Sou-*

venirs are tinged with a bitterness verging on the spiteful. Every character in every one of his anecdotes, man or woman, hero or villain, comes in for the same mocking, derisory treatment; and the events described seem to have been selected as much for the opportunities they offered his sharp tongue as for their historical or professional value. His account of his first meeting with Margarethe admirably demonstrates his blistering descriptive powers.

> When she entered my office for the first time — it was 13th February 1917 — I saw a large, thick lipped woman with skin like leather and false pearl earrings. Was she, had she ever been beautiful? Without a doubt, if an old photograph was anything to go by. But the woman who was brought to me that day had suffered badly from the ravages of time. Eyes as large as eggs, bulging, tinged with yellow and threaded with livid red veins, flattened nose, huge mouth reaching almost to her ears, teeth like tombstones, hair greying at the temples where the dye had worn off, she bore little resemblance to the dancer who had bewitched so many men. But she had retained something of her physical elegance, she still moved with something of the grace of a tiger in the jungle.

Beauty may be in the eye of the beholder, and even Margarethe herself would no longer have claimed to be in her prime, but this was a cruel caricature more worthy of a Liane de Pougy or a Colette than of a pillar of the Palais de Justice. But, writing long after the event, Bouchardon was doing his bit to rake out any lingering embers of sympathy his readers might have felt for Margarethe. At the time, though, he was careful not to let his victim read his thoughts. Through all their dealings over the next four months Margarethe, who complained loudly and at length about almost everything else, never had cause to complain about his attitude, indeed she seems to have stood very much in awe of him, which is perhaps hardly surprising since he held her life in his hands.

Georges Ladoux's decision to have her arrested had signalled the end of his direct dealings with Margarethe. He bundled into a file all the information he had gathered on her activities and sent it, under a covering letter, to Bouchardon. Now it was up to Bouchardon to examine all the evidence collected by Ladoux and decide, on the strength of that evidence and his own enquiries, whether she should be sent for trial.

With her arrest all Margarethe's worst fears had been confirmed. Stunned into silence she had allowed Police Commissioner Priolet to escort her to the Palais de Justice without protest. But when Bouchardon asked for her name, address and date of birth she had forced herself to speak. 'In the haughty voice of an important person who has been improperly and unnecessarily inconvenienced, she explained who she was and then turned to leave.' With all the compassion of a small boy watching a captured beetle scuttle to supposed safety under the sole of his boot, Bouchardon let her get as far as the door. 'But she was no longer free. Already the stairway leading to the cells was opening before her feet.' He called her back. When he explained to her that, far from being allowed to leave, she was to be taken to prison and locked up, 'she just stared at me in horror, dumb with terror, eyes glazed and wisps of tinted hair trembling against her temples'.

But Bouchardon would soon discover that this beetle was not so easily crushed. A night in a padded cell in St Lazare prison forced Margarethe at last to confront the reality of her situation. In such surroundings there was no longer any point in fooling herself — some of the blame for this whole ghastly mess lay at her own door. But now at least she knew what she was up against, and at least the weeks of anxious, nervous waiting were over. Now she knew what the watchers had been doing and understood why Ladoux had refused to see her. Although the finer points of Ladoux's trickery were still obscure, she could see that she had been caught in a trap.

* * * * *

That same day a postcard addressed to Margarethe had been delivered to the Elysée Palace Hotel. It read '*Ma chère petite* Marina, in a few days I shall be evacuated to hospital, but I still have not been told which one. I will send you word. *Je t' embrasse*. Vadime'. It was collected, along with all her other possessions from the hotel, and taken to Ladoux's office. Margarethe never received it.

* * * * *

When she was summoned to Bouchardon's office the following morning, even the magistrate was impressed by the transformation. There was no trace of the abject, trembling creature who had been led away to a cell the night before. In her place was a clear-eyed, composed and deferential woman who sat calmly on the offered chair and answered his questions firmly but politely. Margarethe had pulled herself together, decided on her plan of campaign and would stick to it, through thick and thin and in the face of whatever he contrived to throw at her, to the bitter end.

Her night of reflection had forced her to acknowledge that her flirtation first with Kramer and the German Intelligence Service and then with Ladoux and the Deuxième Bureau had been, to say the least, misguided. But although she now heartily regretted ever having met either of them, she knew, as von Kalle had known, that she had never been of the slightest use to Kramer. Therefore she could, and did, lay her hand on her heart and swear, 'I am not guilty. I have never had anything to do with espionage. I am not a German spy'.

Bouchardon, for his part, was as convinced of his own objectivity as Margarethe was of her own innocence. 'Even though as a Frenchman I sometimes find it hard to disguise my feelings in front of those accused of spying, I have never forgotten that I am a magistrate and that I owe to everyone, whatever they might have done, the same impartiality.' But as her innocence was tinged with guilt, so his objectivity was tinged with prejudice. Bouchardon was no more immune than the next Frenchman to the current epidemic of xenophobia, and despite his frequent protestations to the contrary, was convinced from the start that Margarethe was guilty. 'She was a born spy. She had all the qualifications. Feline, supple and deceitful, accustomed to amusing herself at the expense of anyone and everyone, without scruples, attracting men with her body, devouring their fortunes, and then breaking their hearts.'

*   *   *   *   *

While they were talking another postcard was being delivered to the Elysée Palace Hotel. '*Ma chère* Marina. I am in hospital at Epernay waiting for the operation on my throat. If you could come to Epernay try and do so, there is a good hotel where you could stay and I would be very happy. Telegraph me your response. *Je t' embrasse*. Vadime.' This card, like the first, was picked up by Ladoux's agent and taken to the boulevard St Germain.

* * * * *

Unlike many observers of her self-centred stampede through other people's feelings, Bouchardon believed she was genuinely in love with Vadime.

> In her life there was perhaps one real passion. At forty years old she had become the mistress of a twenty-four year old [sic] Russian, Captain Wardine de Massloff [sic] who, she claimed, fought like a lion and whose whole body was covered in the scars of battle. Was she playing with him too? Or was she really in love for the first time? I am inclined to believe she was sincere. One of her first requests was for news of him.

With tears in her eyes she begged Bouchardon to find out where he was.

> I am so worried. I am haunted by the fear that he may be dying in hospital without me by his side. At least allow me the possibility of writing him a brief note to let him know what has happened to me. I don't want him to think I have deserted him. He might imagine that I left

Paris without getting in touch with him and he doesn't deserve to suffer because of me.

Bouchardon had no intention of granting her request. At least not immediately. But he made a note of Vadime's name and regiment for future reference — should she be reluctant to co-operate, her love for this man might turn out to be a valuable lever. In the meantime, her supplication gave him the upper hand. Determined to keep the advantage he picked up Ladoux's file and, signalling for her silence, kept her waiting while he re-read the covering letter.

Following the arrest of Mata Hari I have the honour of informing you of the reasons why the *Etat-Majeur de l'Armée* was interested in Mata Hari in the first place. Towards the end of December 1915 an informer told the Cinquième Bureau that MacLeod appeared suspect because of her relations with numerous officials that she chose indiscriminately of all ranks, all ages and all nationalities.

The *Etat-Majeur de L Armée* notified the security services that MacLeod left on or about the 10th January for Holland via Spain before their investigations were complete, but that during her stay in the capital she had been very close to a highly suspicious Roumanian called Koanda who had a record as a swindler and was then deported on the grounds that his activities were against the national interest.

At the end of June 1916 the Services in Spain signalled that Mata Hari was returning to France. The Security Services and the Prefecture of Police were warned and decided to mount a surveillance which continued up till the end of August. This surveillance revealed numerous indications of the indiscreet curiosity of Mata Hari but furnished no proof that she was working for the German Intelligence Service. It was necessary, in order to gain her confidence, to seem to be asking her to work for the French. The conversations she had with me were in order to calm her fears. We had our suspicions that Zelle was in the service of the Germans but we had to prove it, and for that it was necessary to arrange for her to spend some time in Spain. This was finally brought about after the British refused her entry and she had to return to Spain where she put herself at the disposition of the German Military Attaché. We were finally convinced of her guilt and thus she was arrested several days after she returned to France.

Reading this letter again with the subject sitting across the desk watching him, it seemed to Bouchardon to contain even less in the way of proof than it had the first time. For Ladoux had chosen to make no mention of his ace; the intercepted radio messages sent by von Kalle to Berlin. Even in his memoirs written twenty years later Ladoux gives no explanation of why he withheld this seemingly irrefutable evidence of her guilt. The only possible conclusion one can draw is that something had happened between the beginning of January when he received them and the middle of February when Margarethe was arrested to make him doubt their authenticity; maybe it had finally dawned on him that they were too obvious to be genuine, or possibly word had reached him that, at the time they were sent, the Germans had already known that the code used was one that had been broken by the Allies.

Whatever his reasons, Ladoux was obviously hoping that the strength of his own conviction, together with the circumstantial evidence of the surveillance reports and the fact that the British had been suspicious of her for more than a year, would be sufficient to condemn her.

But if Bouchardon had his doubts about the strength of the case he could build on the contents of Ladoux's file, he was satisfied that it gave him good reason to hold Margerethe in custody. Now that she was safely under lock and key he was in no hurry to bring her to trial. He would make his own investigations into her alleged activities. If they failed to turn up any conclusive proof of her guilt then there was always a chance that, under the constant pressure of imprisonment and interrogation, the accused might be tricked into betraying herself.

Bringing that pressure to bear straight away, Bouchardon had Margarethe returned to her cell without addressing another word to her. It was an astute move. Margarethe was furious. She had been all ready with her protestations of innocence, her sweet smiles of reason and her appeals to Bouchardon's better nature — and he had not even allowed her to open her mouth. Right. She would show him that she was not so easily ignored.

From the moment she was returned to her cell she started to complain. The cell was too dark, it was not properly ventilated, she was ill, she suffered from claustrophobia, she was cold, she had already developed a feverish cough and was spitting blood, and, over and over again, she wanted to see her lawyer. Her complaints were relayed to Bouchardon. Although he was not yet ready to allow Clunet to see his client he did arrange for the prison doctor to examine her, 'to report on her health and decide whether it was necessary to remove her to another cell'.

* * * * *

On the 15th February a letter addressed to Margarethe was handed to Ladoux's agent by the desk clerk at the Elysée Palace Hotel.

> *Querida* Marguerita, you can't believe how awful this hospital is. I only wish I had you beside me so I could murmur words of love into your ear. Alas the distance between us allows me only to dream of this. I see you in my dreams and sometimes it is so strong I forget it is only a dream. I love you. Your photograph which I hold to my heart, is a constant consolation. I send you my love and long to cover your wonderful body with crazy kisses. Your Vadime.

* * * * *

On the 16th February Bouchardon received the doctor's report on Margarethe.

> Margarethe Zelle is 40 years old, tall, well-built and seems vigorous. The cell which we visited is spacious, the walls are padded but the only ventilation is through a small, round, barred window about twenty-five centimetres in diameter.
> In the light of our examination we can state that the accused has no fever, her tongue is clear. She is emotional and nervous, but listening to her chest revealed no

abnormalities and her heart is sound.

CONCLUSION: The accused is suffering from no organic infection and no fever. She is in good health but on humanitarian grounds it is recommended that she be moved to a cell with better light and ventilation.

On the 17th February she was indeed moved to a better cell. Once again the wind had been taken out of her sails. But if Bouchardon thought he could so easily keep her quiet he was very much mistaken. From then on his office in the Palais de Justice was bombarded by letters from the prison on the Faubourg Saint Denis. Margarethe complained about anything and everything — she was still cold, there were not enough blankets, her bed was too hard, it was so full of vermin she dared not sleep on it; the food was cold, it was not enough, she was getting thin, the bread seemed to be smaller every day, it was so dirty 'that even dogs would refuse to eat it'; she was dirty, the conditions were appalling, she was not allowed to wash properly, there was no bathroom, she had no soap, she wasn't even allowed a hairbrush so that she could keep herself tidy.

But Bouchardon's patience was endless. Ignoring her more ridiculous demands he pointed out that, as she had money, she could provide herself with such essentials as a hairbrush, more blankets and extra items of food. He suggested that, instead of complaining, she should count her blessings. At least she was not forced, as less fortunate prisoners were, to spend several hours a day labouring in the prison workshop in order to earn themselves these little comforts. His patronising manner had Margarethe gnashing her teeth in frustration.

By this time poor little Clunet was beside himself. Since

the moment of her arrest he had laid siege to Bouchardon's office, pestering every clerk he met and dogging the magistrate's footsteps every time he moved from his room, pleading to be allowed to see Margarethe. Bouchardon brushed him off impatiently; the lawyer would be allowed to see his client when he, Bouchardon, was ready and not before.

Spluttering with indignation Clunet scuttled back to his chambers and reappeared the next day staggering under the weight of a huge legal tome which he thrust belligerently under Bouchardon's nose. The magistrate had no right to deny him access to his client; military law stated that prisoners under interrogation had the right to demand the presence of a lawyer, it was here in black and white. Sighing at the old man's persistence, Bouchardon agreed that Clunet be allowed to attend the next session of his interrogation. The following morning, 18th February, he summoned Margarethe once more to his office.

But in the meantime the magistrate had done his homework. As he would later explain to the Military Governor of Paris to whom Clunet would protest about his lack of access:

Maître Clunet is an old and naive admirer of the dancer Mata Hari. He brings to the defence of his client the ardour of a neophyte and has for her a strength of feeling I can hardly explain. Certainly the loyalty and patriotism of the advocate are above suspicion — it is just that the fact of his lively attachment to his client does not permit him to understand the gravity of the affair. Many of the matters under discussion with Mata Hari concern top secret, ultra confidential documents. With the best will in the world Maitre Clunet could not *garder la réserve que j' impose* and could not be sufficiently discreet and I therefore intend to stick to the letter of the law which only states that lawyers must be present at the first and last interviews with their clients.

Satisfied that he had found legal justification for his actions, Bouchardon allowed Edouard Clunet to accompany Margarethe to this first session, and then proceeded to cut short the interrogation, confine his questions to a minimum and return Margarethe to St Lazare before she had had a chance to state her case. He was well aware that the chances of Margarethe incriminating herself would be greatly reduced were Clunet sitting by her side keeping a watchful eye on both his questions and her answers. By letting him attend once Bouchardon had done his duty by the law; from now on he was quite within his rights to dispense with Clunet's presence.

Although denied further direct access to his client, little Maître Clunet threw himself into her defence with vigour and devotion. Now a second stream of letters, meticulously handwritten in a script worthy of a Dickensian clerk, poured into Bouchardon's office. Twice a week for four months Clunet addressed heartfelt appeals to Bouchardon's humanity, begging him not to inflict further suffering on a woman who, by her endeavours for Ladoux, had been of such service to France. He implored the Capitaine Rapporteur to arrange for her to be allowed bail. Every one of these letters received a polite but firm 'no'.

For the week following this interview Margarethe was left alone. Neither Clunet nor anyone else was allowed to visit her and Bouchardon himself did not contact her. He even refused her permission to contact the Dutch Legation in Paris on the grounds that her alleged crime was so heinous as to transcend normal procedure. He had commissioned a team of police investigators, led by an Inspector Carnier, to investigate her past activities and he was waiting for their report. He was still in no hurry. Although the delay could give her time to perfect her defence, he was gambling on it having the opposite effect; the longer she was kept waiting before being given an opportunity to explain, excuse or justify the behaviour that had led to her arrest, the less likely she would be to produce a coherent story. He knew from experience that waiting was bad for the nerves — particularly when those nerves were already shredded by prolonged isolation.

* * * * *

On the 20th February a final postcard arrived at the Elysée Palace Hotel. '*Ma chère* Marina, I am very astonished by your silence. What do you mean by this? I am still in hospital and await with impatience your news. I am expecting to be moved from here soon. Many kisses from your Vadime who loves you to distraction'.

But Vadime would wait in vain for a reply. His anxious, loving messages were neatly tidied away by Ladoux into an official file, where they have remained ever since. Over the years they have been perused by a motley assortment of inquisitive eyes — but the one person for whose eyes they had been intended would never even know they had been written.

* * * * *

Finally Bouchardon received Carnier's report. The Inspector had done his best. There were details of her date and place of birth, her marriage and divorce and her first trip to Paris. There were lists of her various addresses in Paris, her professional engagements as a dancer and the names of her more illustrious lovers. Mention was made of her extravagance and the extent of her debts; details were given of her travels to Berlin, Vienna, Holland, Vittel and Spain. But there was not a shred of proof that she had ever been a German spy.

Bouchardon resigned himself to further digging. First her lovers must be questioned.

> I certainly had enough to choose from. In addition to those listed in the report, there were many more whose visiting cards Mata Hari had left scattered about her room in the hotel. But, when I summoned those I could trace, I found myself facing a string of embarrassed gentlemen, married for the most part, all begging me not to identify them as they did not wish their indiscretions to be made public.

Although they would not have minded being associated with Mata Hari the dancer, they had no wish to be connected with Mata Hari the spy. Red-faced lover after red-faced lover denied that Margarethe had ever given them any cause to question her loyalty to France. No, they all assured him, she had never tried to make them talk about the war, she had never questioned them on military/diplomatic/political matters. They were very sorry, but it seemed they were unable to assist Monsieur le Capitaine in his enquiries.

His next step was to approach every bank in Paris in an

effort to track any secret accounts in which she might have hidden her ill-gotten gains. Bank after bank sent the same reply; no, they had no record of any account in the name of Zelle or MacLeod. They regretted they could not be of more assistance to the Troisième Conseil de Guerre.

More promising were the interviews with an assortment of chambermaids, dressmakers and shop assistants with whom Margarethe was known to have come in contact. The *femme de chambre* at the Elysée Palace Hotel was prepared to swear that 'the lady had a profound hatred for the English'. A housemaid who had once been employed by Margarethe remembered how 'she would frequently pour scorn on the Belgians and seemed to think it was quite funny that 200,000 people had died at Verdun'. A dressmaker who had made several outfits for Margarethe told a dramatic story of how 'Madame Zelle knew that my husband was a prisoner of war in Germany and offered to help me get a false passport in order that I might go there to visit him. I declared to Madame Zelle that I knew she was a spy, where-upon she drew herself up and threatened to have me done away with if I ever repeated that'.

But Bouchardon knew that none of these stories would stand up in court. From the moment that Margarethe had been arrested, rumours had started to fly around Paris. In the absence of any official statements about the charges to be brought against her, these rumours grew in absurdity and exaggeration with every telling. The press got hold of her request to Bouchardon that she be allowed a bath — within hours Paris was shrieking in horror about 'this vicious woman who insists on wallowing in a bath full of milk — while the children of Paris are unable to find a drop of fresh milk to drink'. Every person who had ever set eyes on the notorious dancer (with the notable exception of any who had been well acquainted with her) was now prepared to swear they had known all along that she was a traitor. He needed something more definite by way of proof than the excited gossip of servants.

On 21st February, his investigations having drawn a blank, Bouchardon surnmoned Margarethe from her cell. After a week in isolation in a freezing prison, maybe the unaccustomed warmth of his tiny office would loosen her tongue and lull her into carelessness. He started by asking her about her family and her marriage.

> She spoke in French and, if her grammar sometimes left a bit to be desired she always managed to find a picturesque phrase to express her meaning. She spoke elegantly and with the utmost propriety — never a coarse word. She told me of the solemn dramas that had unfolded in the Netherlands Indies, how her first-born child, a son, was poisoned, how her house was burned down, and her husband revealed himself as the devil incarnate. She spoke of her divorce and I had the impression that the suffering she had endured at the hands of her husband left her with a burning desire to avenge herself on all men.

He took her through her early career in Paris, questioned her about her days as the toast of the *Folies Bergère* and encouraged her to tell him about her many lovers. He listened patiently while she reminisced about her triumphs and her travels; and then he got down to business. He asked her to explain how she had come to be in Berlin at the start of the war, and in the presence of no less a person than Superintendent Griebel of the German Police. Margarethe was all bewildered innocence. 'I entered into relations with him in February or March 1914, when I wasn't even sure there was going to be a war. I am an international woman, and as a dancer and artiste it is only natural that I should have relations. He was my lover. But I swear to you that I have never seen him since.'

He asked her about Madrid — why did she go there? 'I was working for Captain Ladoux. I have been in his service, and in the service of France, since September 1916. It was chance that took me to Madrid. I was sent back there after I was arrested in England.'

Although Bouchardon still knew nothing about the radio messages, he knew of her association with von Kalle. How had she managed to make contact with the German Military Attaché so quickly if she wasn't working for the Germans?

> I swear to you that I did not know von Kalle. I did not know his address and I found his name from the Diplomatic book at the Hotel Ritz. As for contacting him — well after the delay in England I was trying to keep my word to Captain Ladoux and provide him with proof so that he would give me more serious jobs to do for him, and for which I would be well paid. Obviously there would have been no point in attaching myself to a doorman or a Maître d'Hotel. I had to introduce myself to the most interesting people I could find in order to make sure that I could learn something useful.

Argue as he might that these contacts were suspicious, that she was obviously lying and that they knew she was working for the Germans, Margarethe stood by her story.

Bouchardon learned nothing at that session and Margarethe was returned to her cell.

The interrogation continued at intervals for nearly two months. Going over and over the same ground Bouchardon questioned her about Berlin, Kiepert, and Griebel. Her answers were always the same: 'they were my lovers; the money they gave me was my fee; I am an international woman, of course I have travelled'. He asked her about von Kalle — her story was always the same. 'I was working for Captain Ladoux. I gave him my word and I did not betray him. I sent him valuable information from Madrid as proof of my sincerity. This information was correct — it deserves gratitude, not imprisonment. Why don't you ask Captain Ladoux? He will tell you.' Every inconsistency in her story — and there were several discrepancies in her mention of names, dates, places and so on — was pounced on by the frustrated magistrate. Not the least put out, Margarethe just shrugged them off with the explanation that her memory had never been very good.

Bouchardon was getting nowhere. He needed definite proof and he still had none. Neither in their conversations nor in any of her letters had she even come close to giving herself away. Her correspondence with Clunet had been carefully vetted and the only other letters she had written, to her maid Anna Lintjens in Holland, had been confiscated. None of them contained a single incriminating word.

At the end of March, however, Margarethe wrote a letter that was not so easy to withhold. It was addressed to the Chevalier de Stuers at the Dutch Legation in Paris. In an effort to enlist the assistance of her compatriots, Clunet had gone to the Chevalier and told him that she was being held in prison, that she was refused visitors and that his numerous requests for bail had been turned down. Although the Dutch had never been, and still are not, proud to claim Mata Hari as one of their own, the Chevalier had listened to Clunet's story and promised to look into the matter on her behalf. Prompted by her lawyer, Margarethe had added her own appeal to his.

Bouchardon was very tempted to confiscate this letter too. But Clunet had made a point of telling the magistrate that the Dutch Legation had been informed of Margarethe's arrest and continued detention. In these circumstances he would have to get permission from a higher authority if he was to continue to deprive her of the right to address an appeal for help to a representative of her own government. Ironically his request was passed to Margarethe's old friend Jules Cambon. As Minister for Foreign Affairs he had the ultimate say on matters that might affect France's international relations. But as Minister for Foreign Affairs Cambon was obviously in no position to go out on a limb for a suspected German spy. All he could do to help her was to recommend to Bouchardon that her letter to de Stuers be allowed to reach its destination. A recommendation from such an elevated source was tantamount to a command — and Bouchardon had no option but to comply.

But he could do his best to ensure that the letter did not bring an indignant posse of Dutchmen rushing to her rescue. So he enclosed a warning note to de Stuers to the effect that the charge of espionage brought against Madame Zelle was a very serious matter; de Stuers would be well advised to keep both himself and his countrymen at a safe distance. As a holding operation this seemed to be effective, for no official protest arrived from the Dutch Legation in response to Margarethe's appeal. But it did nothing to advance

Bouchardon's enquiries which remained at a standstill.

Then on 10th April a report from the Prefecture of Police arrived on Bouchardon's desk. It was an analysis of various chemical substances that had been found amongst Margarethe's possessions taken from the Elysée Palace Hotel. Most of these were straightforward, lipstick, powder, perfume and so on. But one item had caught the analyst's attention.

> A bottle labelled TOXIC made up of a solution of *by-lodure de mercure dans lyodure de potassium*. This mixture diluted 40 or 50 times with water constitutes an invisible ink of the first choice and the attached sample of writing demonstrates its efficiency. Possession of this substance could be justified on the grounds of its therapeutic value, but could also be used as an invisible ink. Otherwise nothing in her possessions was remotely suspicious.

Bouchardon was triumphant. He had his proof. But he had conveniently overlooked the bit about 'therapeutic value'. When he confronted Margarethe with this damning evidence, she calmly explained that she had ordered the substance to be made up by a chemist in Spain. When Bouchardon demanded to know what she used it for she unblushingly replied that it was an effective contraceptive douche.

In his memoirs Bouchardon makes no reference to Margarethe's explanation. It is possible that this omission was the result of nothing more sinister than a reluctance to mention such a delicate subject. But it is unlikely that he was too prudish to have it checked by a chemist. And in view of his next move it is reasonable to assume that her claim to have used the solution as a contraceptive was confirmed as plausible. For on 20th April Bouchardon told Ladoux that 'my investigations have ground to a standstill'. He was ready to give up.

He was not the only one. Indeed it seemed that the entire French Army was ready to give up. The two months that had passed since Margarethe's arrest had seen the greatest movement on the Western Front in three years of war. Under Ludendorff's astute command, the German armies had started a staged withdrawal from the so-called 'Noyon salient' — the huge bulge in the German lines that protruded at its closest point to within about sixty miles of Paris. When the bombastic General Nivelle launched his much vaunted 'blow of a gigantic fist' against what he had regarded as the most vulnerable point in the front line he found the enemy had gone. Employing a scorched earth policy Ludendorff had pulled his men out of the salient they had held for three years leaving behind poisoned wells, ruined villages, railway lines mangled beyond repair and trees blasted out of the ground. Instead of confronting an exhausted army cowering in the trenches Nivelle's forces met a wilderness.

But Nivelle was not dismayed. With cries of *'En avant, on les aura'*, he pushed his army after the retreating Germans. But by now Ludendorff had had time to establish a series of new defensive positions in a straighter, shorter and therefore much stronger line across the base of the bulge. This line, known to the Allies as the Hindenberg Line but to the Germans as the Siegfried Line, ran from Arras in the north-west to the Aisne river in the south-east. The only real success in the Allied attack on this line was when the Canadians took and held the notorious Vimy ridge in the middle of April. When Nivelle led fifty-four divisions of the French army against the southern end of the line in the Second Battle of the Aisne he was supremely confident of his ability to break through. And his confidence was infectious. Inspired by the news that the Americans had just come into the war, and urged on by the assurance that victory here would mean victory everywhere, his troops marched into battle with spirits higher than at any time since 1914.

Their attack ground to halt on the very first day. The Siegfried Line would not break. After the optimism and the promises, the disillusionment was too great to bear. The French Army mutinied. According to American historian Hanson Baldwin, it was:

> ... probably the largest mutiny in a great army in modern history. The futile bloodletting, the endless fighting, insufficient leave, poor recreational facilities, too great a gulf between officers and men, antiwar strikes, agitation and despair on the home front, German propaganda, and the virus of the Russian Revolution all played a part. Whole divisions refused duty.

Bouchardon's bombshell hit Ladoux's desk at the worst possible moment. The Military High Command, reeling under news from the Aisne, was under greater pressure than at any time since the beginning of the war. Morale had never been lower. Something had to be salvaged from the wreckage. If military success was out of reach then propaganda must compensate. Somehow the French people must be convinced that the government and the army were in control; and the Deuxième Bureau, along with every other government department, was under the strictest orders to prove its efficiency and demonstrate its achievements. This was most certainly not the moment to drop the case against a suspected German spy.

Under these circumstances Ladoux had no choice but to play every card in his hand — even the marked ones. As Bouchardon later recalled: 'On the 21st April the Ministry of War added copies of intercepted wireless messages between von Kalle and Berlin to the file of its charges [against Mata Hari]. At a stroke everything became clear'.

It was none of Bouchardon's business to question the sudden appearance of these transcripts. If Ladoux had chosen to withhold them until now then he must have had good reason for doing so. Neither did Bouchardon have any reason to suspect their authenticity — indeed it was logical to assume that the validity of any material passed to him by either Ladoux or the Ministry of War would already have been verified. If his natural inclination was to welcome any information that confirmed his own suspicions of Margarethe, this was only reinforced by the fact that he was under as much pressure as everyone else to deliver the goods.

From now on the tone of the interrogation sessions changed. With the text of von Kalle's radio messages to light his way Bouchardon was firmly in the driving seat.

Over and over again Mata Hari tried to wriggle out of it. But I always brought her back to the documents which would condemn her to death. She tried everything; she shouted, she wept, she smiled, she tried indignation and then she hurled abuse; she stamped her feet and accused me of being an unfeeling brute who was torturing a helpless woman with evil questions. I have a habit of walking up and down during interrogations — and now this was clearly starting to get on her nerves.

Up until then Margarethe had been able to meet every challenge Bouchardon had thrown at her confident in the knowledge that no evidence existed anywhere in the world to prove that she had ever been a German spy. Nothing had been put on paper by Kramer, she had thrown away his bottles of invisible ink, and she had never sent him so much as a postcard's worth of information. If she kept her head, and created sufficient trouble to make them long to be rid of her, the case would surely soon be dropped.

But when Bouchardon produced the transcripts her nerves did indeed threaten to give way. The more she struggled to extricate herself from her nightmare the deeper she seemed to sink into its viscous grasp. The more she cast about desperately for enlightenment the murkier it grew. Where had these radio messages come from? Who had sent them? Who had *invented* them? Was it von Kalle? Kramer? Ladoux? Why? Over and over and over again, why? There seemed to be no logic, no understanding, no answer. Now there was just misery and loneliness and terrible, haunting fear.

Her composure was in shreds, her pride in tatters. Her behaviour became irrational and unpredictable. When Bouchardon summoned her for further sessions of interrogation he never knew whether he would be confronted by a grovelling wretch or a haughty *grande dame*. He listened coldly to her belated attempt to tell the truth: 'I didn't tell you this before because I was ashamed, but now I have decided to confess that I did come into contact with the German Espionage Service'. But by now the true story of her dealings with Kramer, how she had intended to keep the money in return for her furs and how she had emptied the bottles of invisible ink into the Amsterdam canal, served only to incriminate her further. She had admitted receiving money from Kramer — the rest of the story could be discounted.

The same applied to her dealings with von Kalle. She confessed, 'it is true that he gave me three thousand five hundred pesetas, but he had shared some *grands intimités* with me in his room. Afterwards he offered me a ring, but I don't much like that sort of jewellery. So he gave me the three thousand pesetas instead'. Now she had also admitted receiving money from von Kalle — the rest of this story, too, was irrelevant.

At last she understood the extent to which Bouchardon was prepared to twist her words to suit his purpose. The enormity of what she could now see as a conspiracy against her was overwhelming. In the most pathetic of all her letters to Bouchardon she begged him for mercy. 'I cannot put up with this any longer. Mentally and physically you have given me so much pain that I now pray you to finish it. I beseech you to stop making me suffer.'

But Bouchardon was relentless. And the more he questioned her the less coherent she became. To the exclusion of all else she now focussed on the only two men who could prove, beyond question, her loyalty to France — Ladoux and Denvignes. Every meeting with Bouchardon was followed by a string of notes going over and over the same ground.

I can't understand what all the fuss is about. Colonel Denvignes and Captain Ladoux knew all about my contacts with the German Military Attaché in Madrid.

Why are they blowing it up into something big when I was working on behalf of the French?

I demand to be allowed to speak with Captain Ladoux. A meeting with him would sort out all the misunderstandings. If he was an honest man he would agree to see me. I have always been an honest woman — don't make me suffer any more in this appalling prison. I am losing my reason. I told you this last time and I am telling you again — a frank discussion with Captain Ladoux would suffice to sort it all out.

I demand that Lieutenant Hallaure and Colonel Denvignes should be summoned to give evidence on my behalf. Lieutenant Hallaure was the reason for my going in the first place to the boulevard St Germain. He sent me there to get a passport to Vittel. I didn't even know the name of Captain Ladoux and I certainly didn't know that the building contained the office of the French Counter-Intelligence Service. I tell you this because you state often that I *offered* my services to Ladoux. I never offered anything. I went there because of Lieutenant Hallaure and I went back to the German Military Attaché in Madrid because of Colonel Denvignes.

This is what I will say to Captain Ladoux when I see him. He had me sought to come to his office at the Ministry of War. He asked me to go into his service as a spy. He *gave* me the idea of being in the service of France. He *promised* me that if I succeeded in my mission I would be paid a million francs. He *knew* about the business in Madrid.

I am unhappy and I am ill. I am starting to go mad. With all my sincerity I swear that I haven't made the least attempt at espionage and I have always been sincere towards France. Captain Ladoux didn't understand me — he treated me like a complicated *Parisienne* but he was only dealing with a Hollander from the north, from Friesland where one deals with things in a straightforward manner without all these complicated detours. I repeat that I am not a traitor to France.

None of these desperate appeals made the slightest impression on Bouchardon. Indeed it is hard to avoid the suspicion that he was getting a perverse pleasure out of watching her struggle like a butterfly impaled on a pin. While there had remained a lingering doubt in his mind about her guilt he had behaved with the strictest propriety towards her. Now that he knew for certain that she was a spy he felt justified in making her suffer, just a little, while she was in his power.

But eventually he tired of his sport. She was beginning to disgust him. At the end of June, after Margarethe had been in prison for four months, Bouchardon declared himself satisfied. There was more than enough evidence to justify bringing her to trial — his dossier was now at the disposal of the Court.

THE FINAL ROLE

Once Bouchardon had made his decision the enquiry was out of his hands. His report on the interrogation was added to Ladoux's file and the whole dossier passed to Lieutenant Mornet, the lawyer charged with the prosecution. Unless he was called to testify at the trial, Bouchardon would have no more part to play in the matter. But he could not resist one more little dig. At their last meeting he told Margarethe that Vadime had been questioned about his relationship with her. Margarethe was horrified.

> I don't understand it. Captain Masloff has nothing to do with the Troisième Conseil de Guerre. He didn't even know I had been arrested because you wouldn't give me permission to write to him. Captain Masloff was my lover. He knows nothing about my life. He knows nothing at all about my visits to Captain Ladoux. I never mentioned any of this to him — we enjoyed being together, that's all. I certainly don't want him to come before the Conseil de Guerre — he is the bravest of officers with a great career in front of him — too great for him to risk it in any way.

She was right — Vadime had not been able to give

Bouchardon any useful information at all, even when the magistrate had pressed him as to whether she had ever quiz-zed him on military subjects. 'She only asked me in what area of the Front I was going to be so that she could send me some letters if the Russian troops with whom I was serving would permit it.'

The mystified Vadime had gone on to explain:

> She went to England in November 1916 to try and get back to Holland. But she returned to Paris because someone in London told her that if she entered Holland she would never be allowed to leave for France again. Having been in hospital in Epernay for treatment to my throat in February 1917, when I left hospital I obtained permission to go to Paris for three days and I went to the Elysée Palace Hotel. But I couldn't find Madame Zelle MacLeod who had left without leaving an address. On my return to the Front I found various letters from her, but I haven't seen her since.

The news that Margarethe had been arrested on charges of espionage had finally reached him by way of his commanding officer. 'The General had heard a rumour that I was going to marry this woman and he called me to him and told me to break off relations with her. I told him it wasn't true that I planned to marry her, but that I had gone to the Elysée Palace Hotel in Paris from Epernay to break with her.'

So not even her beloved Vadime was prepared to stand by her. His letters to the Elysée Palace Hotel give the lie to his story that he wanted to end their relationship, but since she had never received them Margarethe did not even have the comfort of that knowledge. Neither did Bouchardon see any reason to tell her that Vadime had added 'I am very surprised that Madame Zelle has been accused of espionage, because in the course of my relations with her she never gave me reason to suspect her on any point in any way'.

More than anything she had previously said, it was Margarethe's reaction to hearing that Vadime had been questioned about his association with her that convinced Bouchardon that she really did love the Russian. Her anxiety to protect her lover from any potentially damaging involvement with the Troisième Conseil de Guerre had been genuine and immediate. Far from wallowing in self-pity at being abandoned by him, or challenging his denial of their plans to marry, she had instantly sought to excuse his behaviour. 'It was all the fault of Colonel Denvignes. He must have sent a message to Captain Masloff's superior officer to warn him not to continue his relationship with me. Colonel Denvignes was still angry that 1 would not become his mistress.'

But she could not forgive Bouchardon the relish with which he had broken the news. It had revealed the depth of his contempt for her and demonstrated the futility of any further appeals to his sympathy. The following day, 29th June, she therefore made her final request to the magistrate through her lawyer, Maître Clunet, in the hopes that he would succeed where she herself would undoubtedly fail. '*Mon ami*, I have something to ask you, and I beg you to do it for me. Would you ask the Capitaine Rapporteur to let me have one picture of Vadime de Masloff? He took them all from me at the beginning. Would you have the goodness to ask him to send me one single picture?' But Bouchardon intercepted the letter. It was neatly filed away in the dossier alongside the letters from Vadime which had never been allowed to reach their destination.

* * * * *

Bouchardon's decision to send her for trial changed everything. Margarethe was now no longer 'suspected', she was 'accused' - the French, *'inculpée'* sounds even more ominous. There was a marked change in the attitudes of those around her - even the nuns responsible for looking after the prisoners in St Lazare seemed more reserved. They knew, as Margarethe herself must have known, that convicted spies, male or female, were sentenced to death. Already in that same year, 1917, two French women had paid the ultimate penalty for betraying their country: in January Marguerite Françillard had faced the firing squad for working as a courier for her German lover and in March Mademoiselle Dufays, a worker in a munitions factory, had been shot for selling secrets to Berlin.

Suddenly there were more important things to worry about than whether she had a hairbrush. Vadime's retreat meant that now it was just herself and Maître Clunet against the world. She must organise her defence, gather her witnesses and prepare to expose the conspiracy that threatened to kill her.

On 5th July she wrote to the Dutch Legation in Paris asking them to arrange for a minister from the Foreign Office in Holland to send her evidence of her altercation with the theatrical costumier in Berlin. It would be proof that she had no reason to be friendly with the Germans.

On 6th July she wrote to Anna Lintjens in The Hague,

asking her to send her various scrapbooks and accounts in order that she might prepare her defence. The letter also instructed her maid to explain to the Baron why she had not yet returned to Holland.

> Do not mention to him that I am in prison — he is not the sort of man to understand how accidents like that can happen. He would be very suspicious, not of my being engaged in espionage but of someone who could get themselves into such an undignified amount of trouble. Just tell him that at this stage it is getting more and more difficult for women to travel, but that as soon as possible I will come back to Holland to see him.

Not content merely with confiscating all her letters, the authorities seemed determined to isolate her completely. Since they obviously could not deny her access to her lawyer they had settled instead on the ploy of refusing her access to her money. If she had no money to pay his fees, maybe the devoted advocate would also abandon her to her fate and their clutches. But they underestimated her determination.

On 10th July she wrote three letters to Lieutenant Mornet, the prosecuting lawyer now in charge of her case. In the first one she was indignant.

> Why do you refuse me my money? I am a foreigner here but for the last fourteen years I have received and spent plenty of money in this country. If you wish to dispose of my cigarette case in solid gold that I have deposited here in the clerk's office I give you permission to sell it. From the weight in gold it must be worth 400f and that

way I will have some money for paying Maître Clunet — that way he will not have to abandon me. It is not just to refuse me my money and to prevent me from settling up with my advocate in the interests of justice.

When there was no immediate reply to this letter she sat down and wrote a second — this time she tried pleading.

You are pushing me to despair. I must resort, in the absence of my money from home, to a course of action which I never would have used. On 16th January 1917 I ordered some money to be sent to my friend Captain Vadime de Masloff. 1 sent him an order for 3000f and now, it is your fault that I have to do this, I have to ask you to get in touch with him with my regrets at having to ask him this, and request him to return the money to me.

When neither of these requests were granted she became defiant. In her third letter of the day she told Mornet:

My decision is made. If it is not going to be Maître Clunet who defends me before the court I refuse to have any other advocate to help me. I also refuse the help of a lawyer from the Bureau. I will defend myself. I have no need of a lawyer just to tell the truth and the facts about what happened between Captain Ladoux and myself at the Ministry of War here in Paris and in Spain. I will tell them myself. 1 have never committed or even attempted to commit any act of espionage, and that can easily be said without judicial researchers. I only hope that I shall have the strength not to cry.

In the space of one day she had run through the whole range of her emotions — the exercise left her drained and exhausted. But she emerged purged of all self-pity. Her treatment at the hands first of Ladoux and Denvignes, then of Bouchardon and now of Mornet had finally opened her eyes.

She had no illusions about her own morals. She knew, and admitted, that her life had been far from blameless, and that it was her own fault as much as anyone else's that she was now in such a terrible predicament. But she had never sunk to the depths of duplicity and distortion at which these men operated. She had been selfish, even grossly selfish, she had been greedy and inconsiderate. But she had never been cruel and she had never intentionally made another person suffer.

All her life she had craved the acceptance and admiration of those whose birth, fortune or ability had granted them a seat at life's high table. For more than twenty years her only ambition had been to join them. It had taken four months of imprisonment at St Lazare to make her realise that her demi-gods, the men of power and influence, those paragons of social, political and military excellence, were not only no better than she was, but infinitely, wickedly, unforgivably worse. Since the days of her marriage to Rudolph she had been grovelling before idols that now stood revealed as fiends — and as such they were worthy only of the utmost contempt.

Never again would she beg for their mercy. Never again would she give them the satisfaction of knowing that they had the power to hurt her. Never again would she play their games by their rules. The only concession she would make was the acknowledgement that it was to their ruthlessness she owed her newly discovered self-respect.

From that moment on she behaved with a calm dignity that earned her the admiration and affection of the only people she was allowed to see - the sisters of the Holy Order of Marie Joseph de Doret. While the threat of Clunet's desertion still hung over her she continued to prepare her own defence. The trial — or more properly, since it was to be conducted by the army, the court martial — had been set for 24th July. She had only two weeks in which to assemble her witnesses and collect the evidence to support her case.

Brisk and businesslike, she sent Mornet a list of the papers and letters she wanted to put before the court and of the people she wished to testify on her behalf: Captain Ladoux, Lieutenant Hallaure, Colonel Denvignes; the doctors who had looked after Vadime in Vittel; and a selection of her past lovers including the Belgian Marquis de Beaufort, and Colonel Messimy and Lieutenant Mege both of the Ministry of War. She was no longer surprised to find her requests ignored but the very business of writing helped to occupy her mind and her time. Not until the very last minute did she learn that one person, at least, had remained faithful to her. Frantic with worry at the thought that Margarethe might even for a moment have doubted his loyalty Maître Clunet swore to defend her with every shred of his energy whether she paid his fee or not.

Although she was touched by his devotion, Margarethe had by now taken a firm hold of her own destiny. Where once Clunet had been the guide and mentor to whom Margarethe had turned for help, now their roles were reversed. It would be her calm words that would comfort him and her strength that would support him through the ordeal of the trial. She had no wish to hurt his feelings by dispensing with his services as her lawyer, but she understood far better than he did what they were up against. Even the most hard-headed and articulate of advocates would have found it difficult to win this particular battle. And, as Bouchardon recalled, Edouard Clunet was neither.

> The old man Clunet was one of her most fervent admirers, more courtier than lawyer. Deaf and blind to all evidence to the contrary, he never doubted for a moment that she was innocent. He never asked to see her dossier. He didn't even want to know the exact charges she would face. To Clunet the very idea of suspecting *la reine du charme* was an abominable calumny. To accuse his heroine of criminal intentions against France was nothing less than sacrilege.

But when the 24th July finally arrived, Margarethe was very glad to have Clunet's hand to hold. For the duration of the trial she was moved from St Lazare to the Conciergerie, the prison adjacent to the Palais de Justice that had once housed Marie-Antoinette and Robespierre. The first session of the proceedings was to be open to the public and *tout Paris* joined an undignified scramble for seats. The excited babble in the court died suddenly as the accused made her entrance. Neither her composure nor her sense of theatre let her down. Wearing an elegant blue dress with a deep decolleté and a tricorn hat to match, and escorted by her lawyer, she walked calmly to her place in the dock.

The seven men who formed the Military Tribunal had already taken their seats. The president of the court martial was Lieutenant-Colonel Albert Somprou of the Republican Guard and the six judges belonged to different branches of the armed services: Adjutant Berthomé of the Artillery,

Police Captain Jean Chatin, Lieutenant Mercier de Malaval of the 7th Cavalry Regiment, Captain du Cayla of the Services Corps, Major Joubet of the 230th Infantry and Lieutenant Deguerseau of the 237th Infantry. But if the public had anticipated a spectacle they were disappointed. As soon as the court had been called to order and the various officials and lawyers had been identified, the Counsel for the Prosecution, Lieutenant Mornet, asked permission to address the Tribunal.

In view of the sensitive nature of much of the evidence that would have to be produced before the court, might he suggest that the rest of the trial be held behind closed doors? With grave looks and knowing nods, the Tribunal agreed. The court was cleared and guards were posted outside every door to discourage any inquisitive journalist who might be tempted to apply his ear to a keyhole. In addition the press were forbidden to publish any information whatever on the trial beyond that contained in a distributed statement: 'The dancer Mata Hari, appearing under her real name of Margarethe Zelle, appeared yesterday before the Troisième Conseil de Guerre on the grave charge of having supplied information to the enemy. The trial is continuing'.

Lieutenant Mornet then took the stage. With his Byronic profile and full biblical beard he had the appearance of an avenging angel and the voice to match. The courtroom reverberated to the exaggerated rolling of his 'r's' and the deliberate theatrical clarity of his every syllable. He started by apologising to the Tribunal. 'Messieurs, in all my career I have never felt quite so embarrassed. I am forced, in effect, to demonstrate to you that two and two makes four.' Then he proceeded to lay before them his evidence of the treachery of 'this sinister Salome who plays games with the heads of French soldiers'.

She was known to have been on good terms with many members of the German High Command and, in their company, had attended military manoeuvres of the Imperial Army in Silesia. She had been in Berlin, in the company of a Superintendent of Police, at the moment when war had been declared. She had been under surveillance from the Deuxième Bureau ever since they had been warned against her by the British. She had been paid 20,000 francs by the German spymaster Kramer in Holland. In Paris she had frequently entertained high-ranking foreign military officers; she had visited Vittel, in the Zone des Armées and only a few miles from the airfield at Contrexeville, where she had consorted with more highly placed officers; she had tried to infiltrate the Deuxième Bureau; and, most damning of all, she was known to have been in close contact with the chief of German Intelligence in Madrid, Hans von Kalle, who had given her the sum of three thousand five hundred pesetas in payment for her services. And here was his proof. Voice trembling with emotion Mornet read out to the court the text of the intercepted telegrams. 'Messieurs, need I say more?'

Now it was Clunet's turn. He made a pathetic contrast to Lieutenant Mornet. Pale, frail and clearly agitated, the old man did his best. He called first for Captain Ladoux to take the stand and testify on her behalf. The counter-espionage chief was not available. He called Colonel Denvignes. But the Colonel was suffering a bad attack of amnesia — he was afraid he had no recollection of having had any dealings with the lady beyond observing her close relationship with von Kalle in Madrid. He called Lieutenant Hallaure. Sadly the Lieutenant could not be spared from his military duties to attend the court martial. He called Colonel Messimy, ex-

Minister of War. A letter of apology was read out from the Colonel's wife. Her husband was suffering from a bad attack of rheumatism which prevented him from attending the proceedings; but, on his behalf, she could categorically deny that he had ever met Mata Hari. The doctors in Vittel had never been traced.

Almost in tears, Clunet asked for Margarethe herself to take the stand. As he escorted her from her seat his words of comfort were clearly heard in the expectant silence. 'Have faith in your old friend. Have faith in the judges. When they learn the kind of person you are they will be sure to acquit you. Here, lean on the arm of your old friend.'

Margarethe must have realised the significance of the fact that not one of the witnesses who might have been able to help her had been prepared to do so. But to have acknowledged the hopelessness of her situation would have been to surrender to it. As she faced her implacable judges she had to believe that beneath at least one of those splendid uniforms beat the heart of a man of integrity, a man who was immune to the rot that she had detected in the hearts of Ladoux, Denvignes, von Kalle and Bouchardon. For her life's sake she had to tell these men her story — for her sanity's sake she had to trust them to listen to it.

Patiently she repeated to them everything she had told Bouchardon. She had been in Berlin in her professional capacity as a dancer. She was 'an international woman' with friends and lovers in many countries. As for entertaining all those officers, where was the harm in that? Officers were wonderful men, worthy of her admiration, and who was she to deny them a night of happiness when they might so easily face death in the morning? She had accepted Kramer's money as fair compensation for the loss of her furs in Berlin. Her visit to Vittel had been for no other purpose than to join her friend Captain de Masloff. Ladoux had asked her to work for him — the idea would never have occurred to her. Von Kalle had paid her for their nights of love — if he chose to finance his passion out of Intelligence Service funds that only proved that he was cheating his masters, not that she was a spy. And, crucially, how could she be a traitor to France? She was not even French.

Her judges challenged her on every point of her defence. She remained calm. In Bouchardon's words: 'She played her final role — that of an innocent woman — with such artistry and self-control that, God forgive me, she ended up by believing it herself'.

But she could not make the judges believe her. Indeed that very self-control served only to convince them that they were confronted not merely by a spy but by a fiendishly clever one. On the afternoon of the second day of the trial they withdrew to consider their verdict. They had eight questions to answer:

1. Was she guilty of entering the entrenched camp of Paris in December 1915 with the intention of obtaining documents and information that would be of use to the enemy?
2. Was she guilty of delivering, during the first three months of 1916, documents and information to the enemy through their agent Kramer that could compromise military operations or threaten the safety of military establishments?
3. Was she guilty of maintaining contact, during May 1916 in Holland, with the German Intelligence Services with the object of furthering the interests of

the enemy?

4. Was she guilty of entering the entrenched camp of Paris for the second time in May or June 1916 with the same intention as (1) above?

5. Was she guilty of maintaining contact with those same German Intelligence Services during her stay in Paris from May or June 1916?

6. Was she guilty of making contact, in December 1916, with the German Intelligence Service in Madrid, through the person of the German Military Attaché von Kalle with the aim of furthering the interests of the enemy?

7. Was she guilty of passing to the enemy through their aforementioned Military Attaché material of such a nature as to compromise military operations or threaten the safety of military establishments?

8. Was she guilty of maintaining contact with those same German Intelligence Services since her return to Paris from Madrid in January 1917?

The wording of this list of charges enabled the judges to ignore all Margarethe's explanations and match every incident in her story to one or other of the questions. It took them very little time to come to their decision. They filed back into the courtroom in the early evening of 25th July and the President announced their decision.

Margarethe MacLeod, née Zelle, alias Mata Hari, is found guilty of all the charges against her. The Members of the Tribunal hereby pronounce upon the above mentioned Margarethe Zelle the sentence of death.

Clunet collapsed. Margarethe's face was blank. As she was led away from the court she was not heard to utter a single word.

*   *   *   *   *

Bouchardon, reluctant to miss the climax of his four month interrogation of Margarethe, had been present at the court martial. With the passing of the death sentence he had considered the matter closed. But, as he later recalled, Maître Clunet did not.

> Every day he came to the Troisième Conseil de Guerre, draped in his legal robes which, not being properly fastened, swept up clouds of dust from the corridors as he passed. With shaking head and sad expression he would say, 'No, no. It is not possible that Poincaré will allow that beautiful body, formed by the hands of the Graces themselves, to turn to dust and ashes'. Sometimes he tried to bargain with me. 'Let her return to Holland', he would beg, 'Germany would give us ten French officers in exchange. What do you say?' That poor old man was living in a world of make-believe.

But at least he was trying. On 14th August he lodged a formal appeal with the Military Tribunal against the death sentence. On 21st August it was turned down. On 26th September he took his appeal to the Supreme Court with a challenge to the right of the Troisième Conseil de Guerre to judge Margarethe's case. On 27th September this appeal too was rejected. He wrote to the Chevalier de Stuers at the Dutch Legation begging him to intercede on her behalf to get the sentence commuted to life imprisonment. Chevalier de Stuers regretted that he was not in a position to assist Madame MacLeod in this matter which must be left in the hands of the French authorities. When the date for the execution was set for 15th October Clunet was beside himself.

Margarethe, on the other hand, had withdrawn into a dreamworld. She smiled at him when he visited her in her old cell in St Lazare. She asked his opinion on her dress, reminisced about old acquaintances, discussed the weather and complained of being bored. She wrote occasionally to Anna Lintjens asking why she had received no reply to her previous letters, or sending her good wishes to the Baron. But any mention of the trial, her sentence or the appeals against it seemed to baffle her. Reality was no longer something she was unwilling to face — it was something she was utterly unable even to contemplate. Indeed, as far as she was concerned, it no longer existed.

EPILOGUE

So Margarethe Zelle MacLeod died and was almost immediately forgotten. Only Mata Hari lived on — partly in the memories but mostly in the imaginations of a public hungry, as ever, for scandal and excitement.

The myths and legends that have surrounded her story were born even before she died. Lieutenant Mornet's thunderous courtroom declamation of this 'sinister Salome who has been responsible for the deaths of more than 50,000 French soldiers' had opened the floodgates. Every person who had been present at her trial, and very soon even those who had not, had his own juicy snippet to add to the fiction; and every official who had been involved in the preparation of the case against her seized the chance to justify his actions and enhance his own reputation by painting her as the very incarnation of evil. Even today there are those who believe that she was responsible, among other things, for the death of Lord Kitchener, for the success of Ludendorff's submarine campanion against Allied shipping and even for the mutinies in the French army.

At the time even the wildest rumours were sanctioned by the French Military High Command. The more sensational they were the less chance there was that the truth would emerge. And their plan worked. For more than forty years no one was prepared to admit that her trial was a travesty of justice and that Mata Hari had been sacrificed to official expediency — and by then there were few who cared. Yet there has always been something fascinating about the combination of beauty and wickedness, and, black as the French Government tried to paint her, it was the glamour rather than the infamy of her story that caught the public eye.

The press, inevitably, found its own way to fill in the blanks created by the broad strokes of the censor's blue pencil. Among the more fantastic tales they produced were several claiming that she had not died at all; an impassioned lover had bribed the firing squad to load their rifles with blanks and had then swooped her into the saddle and galloped off with her into the morning mist; at the very moment of firing she had thrown open her fur coat and the sight of her naked body had caused every single member of the firing squad to miss his target. Rumoured sightings of the famous Mata Hari were still being reported more than ten years later. The *Daily Mail* of 3rd September 1929, under the headline 'Is Mata Hari Still Alive? — New Mystery of Beach Woman', reported that 'well informed sources declare that the mysterious woman found unconscious on the seashore at Montalivet near Bordeaux last week who gave her name as Gloria MacAlister and said that she had fallen from the British Steamer *Eagle* is in reality the Dutch woman spy Mata Hari who was condemned to death in the last years of the war'.

As is so often the way, the legends were much more entertaining than the truth, and Margarethe, mistress of make-believe herself, would not have begrudged the rumour-mongers their sport. But she would surely have been infinitely saddened by the final cruel stroke of fate. Her daughter Jeanne-Louise survived her by less than two years, dying suddenly of a cerebral haemorrhage at the age of twenty-one. So Margarethe was ultimately denied even the small triumph of leaving a descendent who might one day have been moved to seek the truth on her behalf.

SELECT BIBLIOGRAPHY

Papers relating to Mata Hari's trial, statements from witnesses, official correspondence, surveillance reports, etc, are contained in the 'Dossier Mata Hari' in the Archives of the Service Historique de l'Armée de Terre in the Château de Vincennes. The dossier also contains many of Mata Hari's own letters to her lawyer, the magistrates and her maid written during her imprisonment, together with the photographs and visiting cards that were found in her possession when she was arrested. Although this dossier is available to accredited researchers there were, in 1985, references in the dossier to other documents (apparently only a few) which were for the eyes of authorised members of the Service Historique only.

Documents and correspondence relating to Mata Hari's detention and interrogation by Scotland Yard are held in the Public Records Office in Kew.

Baldwin, Hanson. *World War I*, Hutchinson, 1962.
Bouchardon, Pierre. *Souvenirs*, Albin Michel, Paris, 1935.
Brittain, Vera. *Testament of Youth*, Gollancz, 1933.
Clarke, M.E. *Paris Waits*, Smith Elder, 1914.
Coulson, Major Thomas. *Mata Hari, Courtesan and Spy*, Harpers, 1920.

Fitzgibbon, Constantine. *Secret Intelligence in the Twentieth Century*, Hart-Davis MacGibbon, 1976.

Grigoriev, Serge. *The Diaghilev Ballet* (Trans: Vera Brown), Constable, 1953.

Holt, Claire. *Art in Indonesia*, Cornell University Press, 1967.

Hutton, Bernard. *Women Spies*, W. H. Allen, 1971.

Kahn, D. *The Codebreakers*, Weidenfeld, 1968.

Kupferman, F. *1917 Mata Hari*, Editions Complexe, Brussels, 1982.

Landheer, Ed. *The Netherlands*, University of California Press, 1943.

Lanoir, Paul. *The German Spy System in France*, Mills & Boon, 1910.

Newman, Bernard. *Inquest on Mata Hari*, Robert Hale, 1956.

Nicolai, Col. Walther. *The German Secret Service*, Stanley Paul, 1924.

Perreux, Gabriel. *La Vie Quotidienne des Civils en France, 1914-18*, Hachette, Paris, 1966.

Pougy, Liane de. *Mes Cahiers Bleu*, Editions Plon, Paris, 1977.

Reid, Anthony. *The Blood of the People, Revolution and the End of Traditional Rule in Northern Sumatra*, OUP, Kuala Lumpur, 1979.

Rowan, Richard W. (and Robert G. Deindorfer). *Secret Service*, William Kimber, 1969.

Schuchart, Max. *History of the Netherlands*, Thames & Hudson, 1972.

Seroff, Victor. *The Real Isadora*, Hutchinson, 1972.

Seth, Ronald. *Spies at Work*, Peter Owen, 1954.

Szekely, L. *Tropic Fever* (Trans: Marion Saunders), OUP, Kuala Lumpur, 1979.

Vandenbosch, Amry. *Neutrality of the Netherlands during the World War*, William Beardmans, Michigan, 1927.

Waagenaar S. *The Murder of Mata Hari*. Arthur Barker, 1964.

Wilhelmina, Queen. *Lonely But Not Alone* (Trans: J. Peereboom), Hutchinson, 1960.

Wit, Augusta de. *Java Facts and Fancies*, van Stockum, The Hague, 1912.

INDEX